THE
CREATIVITY
CATALOG

300 of the World's Most Creative Things
and How They Can Make You More Creative Too

THE CREATIVITY CATALOG

Donald Rattner
FOUNDER OF THECREATIVEHOME.COM

 THE CREATIVE HOME

HOUSE OF CARDS (1952) BY CHARLES AND RAY EAMES, REISSUED BY EAMES OFFICE

INTRODUCTION The Creativity of Things VI

THE PRODUCTS 1

300 of the world's finest products for nurturing and inspiring creative thinking at home, school and in the workplace

Housewares and Decor 6

Jewelry and Apparel 76

Shelving and Organization 82

Children 100

DESIGNERS AND BRANDS 146

Bibliography and Suggestions for Further Reading 180

Resources 182

Image Credits and Acknowledgments 183

About the Author 184

INTRODUCTION
THE CREATIVITY OF THINGS

WHY THIS BOOK • The subject of creativity is getting a great deal of attention these days. Educators and experts continue to publish books and papers offering their perspectives on creativity. Businesses large and small hire consultants to train staff in creative thinking as a way to spur innovation in their daily work. Parents scramble to learn about the latest techniques for advancing their children's mental development through creative activities. Add a hefty supply of blog posts, Web sites, conferences, and even degree programs in Creativity Studies, and it becomes evident that our enthusiasm for insights into this valued commodity shows no signs of diminishing.

Of course, we believe there's always room for one more book on any given subject, especially when it's our own. But *The Creativity Catalog* doesn't fall neatly into the usual categories of publication you'll find on the shelf. It's not an academic tome delving deeply into the latest theories about creativity. It's not a self-help guide to finding professional success by teaching you a particular skill set, like how to brainstorm effectively. And it's not an excursion into the psychology of self. What *The Catalog* is primarily intended to do is introduce you to some of the world's most creative things so that you can learn to be more creative by using and understanding them.

PURPOSE OF THE CATALOG • We've deliberately referenced the verbs "to use" and "to understand" in our statement of purpose because the products selected for *The Catalog* can be approached in two ways: as platforms for exercising individual creativity through direct use, and as models for devising things that provide users with the opportunity to be creative. Which approach you take in reading this book likely depends on your profile and objectives. If, for example, you're a parent or teacher looking for things that will encourage young people in your charge to develop their creative faculties, then you're probably going to evaluate the products for their potential effectiveness in achieving this goal. Individuals wanting to enhance their own capacity for creative thinking, whether for business or personal reasons, or to fit out a home or workplace with products that allow them to express their creativity, also will tend to view the contents of *The Catalog* from an applied viewpoint.

On the other hand, if you're an entrepreneur, manufacturer, or product designer wanting a deeper appreciation of how to make things incorporating a creative component, then you'll find *The Catalog* a rich source of inspiration and instruction offered up by an array of talented individuals, firms, and brands.

ALGUE BY RONAN AND ERWAN BOUROULLEC FOR VITRA (2004)

DEFINING CREATIVITY & RELATED TERMS

Creativity is a somewhat elusive concept. Its nuances defy simple and universal definition, a challenge made all the more difficult by our practice of applying it to a diverse field of human activities and disciplines. Not long ago creativity was primarily associated with the fine arts and applied design; today we also explore creativity in relation to the sciences, business management, innovation and entrepreneurship, psychological development and personal wellbeing in children and adults, philosophy, and technology. Crafting a succinct explanation of creativity that fits so many contexts is not an easy lift. Compounding the difficulty is our practice of variously describing a person, a process or activity, and a product, whether an idea in our mind or an observable performance or artifact, as creative. Nevertheless, from the voluminous literature that has appeared in recent decades there seems to be a general consensus that creativity encompasses two principal attributes: *newness* (or novelty) and *value* (sometimes called usefulness or appropriateness). Both conditions must be evident for something to be described as authentically creative; for example, you could compose some text by randomly writing one letter after another, but it would fail as a creative act since no one would understand its meaning.

Nonsense words might be an extreme case, but what if an object or idea you come up with is novel and of value to yourself and perhaps to a small group of other people—ought we deem it creative in the same general sense as a more widely known and accepted invention would be? The short answer in at least one school of thought is yes, but with qualifications that will be explained later on.

Innovation is a related term that is sometimes used interchangeably with creativity. According to its standard dictionary definition, to innovate is to change something that is established, typically by introducing new methods, ideas, or products. It is most commonly used in the context of business and especially entrepreneurship, and can be loosely considered a synonym for creativity when used in *The Catalog*. In effect, it means the implementation of creative ideas. A second related term is *imagination*, which is the process of bringing to mind things that don't physically exist or are not evident to the senses. Creativity demands imagination, yet not every act of imagination is necessarily creative—we can all mentally conjure up a unicorn without actually having invented or produced the beast.

Definitions of creativity are historically and culturally rooted. *The Catalog* is grounded in the Western tradition of equating creativity with originality and physical production, epitomized by the biblical story of Earth's creation. Eastern views of creativity, by contrast, commonly revolve around emotional and personal revelation. Neither tradition has been completely static through the centuries; for instance, the ancient Western belief that creativity was channeled from the divine was widely held until around the Renaissance, after which we gradually came around to the view that human beings are innately creative on their own. As time goes on, we can expect that our present definitions of creativity will undergo further transformation.

PRODUCT SELECTION • This book brings together a group of products that explore the relationship between a particular type of everyday object and human creativity. All the products share a common profile. They are well-designed, affordably priced by common standards, and reflect good to high production values. In terms of product type, they fall under the categories of consumer and home goods, and in subcategories ranging from accessories, lighting, furniture, and children's things to jewelry and apparel, storage and organization, wall and floor coverings, and decor. While any of these products would feel at home in a residential context, some would be equally comfortable in a workplace, commercial, or hospitality environment. Some are driven in their design by aesthetics, others are engineered primarily to serve a pragmatic purpose. Most were introduced within recent decades; a few are legacy products with longer histories. Whatever their context, typology, or background, they are united in their intent to enhance the quality of their surroundings and enrich the lives of their users. At the time *The Catalog* went to print every item was in production; we excluded one-off, handmade, and limited edition products to ensure that you, the reader, could obtain any item you wanted from *The Catalog*. We also omitted digital and tech products, both hardware and software, because they facilitate a different kind of creativity than the manually operated products in *The Catalog*, and would be better treated in a separate publication.

Of the many brands represented in the collection, a few can be considered large, international, or long-established companies, while the rest are small to medium-sized, regional, and more recently founded. The roster of designers is similarly diverse, mingling respected names and well-earned reputations with lesser known, emerging, and anonymous figures. Both brands and designers are global in origin and operation, aptly reflecting the state of international commerce today.

CREATORS AND USERS • *The Catalog* divides the world of consumer product design into two camps: conventional and creative. Our choice of labels is not to suggest that so-called conventional products lack creativity, of course, since just about any object with even modest design aspirations is invested with the imagination of the people or company that conceived it. Neither do we mean to imply that conventional products are uniformly commonplace or boring. Many of the world's most inspired and accomplished products, in fact, are conventional in the sense we're applying it here. Rather, we're trying to distinguish between a traditional and still dominant approach that confines creative design to a small circle of people working in a prescribed process and a less common one that turns us all into designers.

Let's have a look at conventional merchandise first. On the whole it's safe to say that most conventional products aimed at adults are designed so that we as consumers can use them as easily as possible (whether that goal is actually attained is another matter, but at least this is the stated intent among most design teams). Little is left to our imagination, because that is about the last thing we are thought to want to have to exert to enjoy a product. In fact, if we have to think deeply to discover what something does, how it operates, or what's required of it, then the design team could be criticized for failing in its professional responsibility to convey a clarity of function and purpose. In the traditional model for making things, creative responsibilities are strictly segregated by role: designers design, consumers consume. And since the designer leaves off from involvement with the product once it goes out into the market, creativity is also partitioned chronologically, occurring almost entirely in the product development phase.

A different philosophy underlies the products in *The Catalog*. Conceiving and fabricating a creative design product is only the first stage of a multiphase process of imaginative thinking involving both designer and user. The initial stage begins more or less the same way as it does with a conventional product—an individual or team of individuals set out to carry a project from idea to realization. Where it starts to deviate from the traditional model is in the conception of the product with regard to our role as users. Instead of devising an object that is nominally ready to fulfill its function out of the box, the designer of a creative product makes something that empowers and even requires us to physically and imaginatively manipulate it in order for it to serve its purpose. Because we're called on to exercise our creative skills, the nature of our engagement with the object is qualitatively distinct from the routine effort of assembling a piece of merchandise according to its instructions, or mechanically operating a product by turning it on and off.

Unlike the conventional object, whose design has been completely worked out by the time it appears in stores, a creative product invites us to be a protagonist in the latter stages of its evolution. No more are we passive consumers of goods but collaborative, co-creative members of the team of people that originally launched the product. As has happened with so many facets of contemporary culture, the rigid boundaries separating the experts from the "crowd" in the discipline of product design have fallen away and a new, more reciprocal relationship between the two formed in its place. The circumstances giving rise to this transformation are the same as elsewhere: the emergence of the creative class, the shift from an industrial to a knowledge economy, and of course, the advent of the Internet. Devised in the era of mass production and the expectation of mechanical efficiency on the part of the workforce, the traditional authoritative, top-down model of product delivery was right for its time—just as the more democratic paradigm of creative design is right for ours.

CONVENTIONAL VERSUS CREATIVE: A CASE STUDY • Creative design can affect our entire experience of a product, from the search stage to the moment we start using it, as the following case study will show.

Imagine you need to buy a large rug for one of the rooms where you entertain in your home. You visit a number of stores and showrooms and surf the Internet to see what's out there. Chances are the majority of the rugs you come across will be rectangular in shape, are available in up to a half-dozen standard sizes, and have their patterns already imprinted in the weave *(p. XII, top)*. You eventually select a particular rug to buy at one of the stores you toured during your search and have it trucked to your home because it's too big to lift it yourself or fit into the trunk of your car. The two burly individuals with advanced muscular development who deliver the rug are kind enough to lay it down on your floor for you before concluding the transaction and departing. Other than placing any furniture on top of the rug that needs to go there, you'll likely have little to do with your rug in the future except look at it and clean it.

Now let's see what happens when you opt for a creative floor covering instead, using the Stitch Interlocking Rug as a case study *(p. XII, bottom)*.

Finding nothing like it in stores, you discover Stitch on the Internet and order it online. When it arrives at your door it comes packaged in triangular boxes, each weighing just a couple of pounds and containing ten pieces. The pieces are shaped to fit together in the fashion of a jigsaw puzzle, except that there is no single, right answer to how the pieces are to be joined. Instead, you're free to place the pieces in any configuration you want, in any quantity you want, and in any assortment of colors you want. You can even change your mind as you go and modify the rug by adding and taking away pieces, or swapping out colors. If you ever tire of your arrangement in the future you can do the same then.

If you need to move or put the rug in another space at a later date, you could pack it up yourself and reassemble it with little trepidation as to whether it will fit. What happens if your new space turns out to be irregular or nonrectangular in plan? Such a situation is a real dilemma for conventionally shaped rugs, which look awkward when thrust into environments they were not intended for; unfortunately, there's little you can do about a single-piece floor covering when confronted with this conflict except try to sell or store it. A flexible carpet, meanwhile, can be easily manipulated to have its perimeter harmonize with the contours of just about any surrounding space.

Creative design even affords a degree of financial flexibility when it comes to buying things. Should budget be an issue for you, you can choose to limit the number of pieces you purchase initially until you're prepared to cover the cost of the remainder. Perhaps you're able to utilize a smaller area rug in the meanwhile. You might eventually decide that the more modest covering meets your needs perfectly well. Conventional products, by contrast, are sold as monolithic, indivisible units at an equally fixed price—you can't chop a pair of blue jeans in half so as to reduce your outlay before taking them home. Sure, rug dealers are known to haggle a bit, but at the end of the day either you purchase the whole rug for a stipulated sum or you leave empty handed. An inflexibility of design sometimes correlates to an inflexibility of financial commitment.

THE NEW CREATIVITY • The tale of the Stitch Rug illustrates how far the traditional definition of creativity has been stretched beyond its historical boundaries in how we think about the concept today. For a long time creativity has been popularly viewed as an attribute of people working

THE CREATIVITY CATALOG

XII

A CONVENTIONAL RUG.

STITCH INTERLOCKING RUG BY NAURIS KALINAUSKAS (2005).

in the artistic and design fields—painting, sculpture, literature, industrial design, music, architecture, dance, and the like. Among their talents is said to be a knack for composition, the act of identifying, joining, and arranging parts to form a larger, aesthetically cohesive whole. This aspect of creativity is captured in our description of the Stitch user who, guided by personal taste in form and shape, assembles an entire rug out of loose pieces. In the past, observers might have hesitated to attach the label of creativity to efforts of this sort by nonartists, but in today's more inclusive environment it would be assigned to one of four tiers of creative behavior defined by academics studying innovation. Some have called their framework The Four C's; we prefer the catchier moniker of The New Creativity, in recognition of the shift in historical thinking it represents. Whatever you name it, it's commonly agreed that the novel achievements of acknowledged geniuses and trained professionals working in a broad range of fields, from sports to science, social work to sculpture, belong in the upper echelons of the graduated creativity scale. More modest acts of imagination and inventiveness executed by regular people in the course of daily life get assigned to the tiers below.

Since most products are designed by trained professionals, their creative contribution to a product like Stitch normally gets classified at a higher level than user input. Users apply their inventive talents to a creative product in the act of manipulating it; designers utilize their creative expertise to conceive and manufacture the product in the first place. Common to both parties, however, is problem-solving. Granted, the scope of problems addressed by the user is relatively modest: they need only to figure out how many pieces they will need, the colors they want, and how best to arrange the pieces they acquire. The originating designer, it must be said, went through a more extensive problem-solving phase in developing the Stitch Rug concept.

To appreciate the designer's role as problem-solver, think about the Stitch Rug from the user's point of view, and identify the numerous practical problems associated with a conventional rug the designer has resolved in devising a creative version. Feel constrained by having to choose from a handful of standard sizes that don't really suit your situation? Stitch's piece-by-piece assembly frees you from the rigidity of standard dimensions and lets you modulate size to within a few inches. Oddly shaped space? Position the tiles to nestle into almost any conceivable area. Not seeing a color palette that quite works for you? Devise your own by deciding which color options to use. Change your mind about a layout? Add, subtract, or exchange tiles at will. Constricted budget? Buy some now, more later. Expect to move location in a few years? Stitch can be reconfigured to suit a new environment with ease. Suggest a potential problem, and in almost every instance the designer has come up with a workable solution.

Now, to solve a problem you first have to figure out what the problem is. In some respects problem-finding is even more fundamental than problem-solving, since without the right problem a designer might travel down the wrong path in a wasted effort to create the wrong product. Finding the correct problem starts by questioning what we believe to be true or necessary. In the evolution of the Stitch Rug an early line of questioning might have gone something like this:

- Why do rugs have to be rectangular?
- Why do rugs have to be made in one piece?
- Why do rugs have to leave the factory or workroom completely finished?
- Why should rugs be designed only by rug designers?
- How can we make finding the right rug easier?

By thinking critically about what is currently true, the designer begins to ponder what could also be true, or true instead, in the future. Calling truth into question lies at the root of innovation, which we defined earlier as a form of creativity in which an established condition is changed, often by devising new methods, ideas, or products. Whether you're a product designer, a service provider, a government official working on behalf of your constituents, or a teacher with a lesson plan matters little; the takeaway is that innovative thinking is a teachable skill that starts with framing the right problem by recognizing there exists a problem to be framed. The risk in being complacent with the status quo is that opportunities for new ways of doing, making, and understanding things could be lost. Little wonder that businesses, educators, governmental officials, and parents alike promote innovative thinking as a vital skill: in a period characterized by highly competitive markets and rapid technological and social change, innovation just might be one of the keys to a successful future.

PLAY • You're never too late to learn how to think innovatively, but common sense and modern science suggest an optimal time to start is during childhood. That is the period when we are most free to exercise our penchant to experiment, invent, imagine, and create through the medium of play. When we age, our willingness to explore, go out on a limb (figuratively or literally), take chances, question authority, and simply play for the sake of play has a habit of weakening. Some have argued that the creative impulse actually begins to be suppressed as early as our grade school years, where traditional rote memorization, standardized testing, top-down delivery of information from teacher to student, overly structured play, and the suppression of certain types of behavior inhibit the free thinking necessary for an innovative society. Regardless of whether this assessment is justified, just ask yourself this: when was the last time you answered the question "What did you do today?" with "I played"?

We'll hazard a guess it's been a very long time indeed. One reason is that pure, self-directed play among adults is regarded by some as frivolous at worst, a merely entertaining diversion at best. In point of fact, play constitutes a vital means for nurturing our creative faculties both as children and adults. To play is to leave a rationally grounded, comfortable world and enter a fanciful domain where almost anything is possible. Through play, a hoard of discarded cardboard and paper scraps is transformed into a robotic humanoid *(opposite, right)*, a piece of slate and a stick of chalk into artistry *(opposite, bottom left)*, assorted pieces of cut wood into fanciful creatures and faces *(opposite, top left)*. Play is the

INTRODUCTION

freedom to improvise, to break out of the expected, practical, and rationalist way of doing things to test new ideas. Its path is circuitous and meandering rather than linear, zigzag and sinuous rather than sequential. Pure play has no end, no particular goal at the outset; serendipity necessarily must reign if the imagination is to run its course.

Unlike conventional things, creative products integrate the principle and mechanics of pure play into their design. Compare a standard jigsaw puzzle to the Stitch Rug or any one of the other puzzle products in *The Catalog (pp. 61, 115, 122)*. To correctly complete the jigsaw puzzle you have to fit the pieces together exactly, and there is only one solution. The

PLAYSHAPES BY MILLER GOODMAN.

MAKEDO CONNECTOR KITS (2009).

WOODY CHALKBOARD TABLE AND CHAIR BY ERIC PFEIFFER FOR OFFI (1996).

process of discovering that solution has a beginning, middle, and an end: the beginning is when the pieces are lying scattered on the table, the middle happens after some of them have been connected, and the end is reached when they have all snapped together. The pieces comprising the creative puzzle products, in contrast, will join in nearly limitless combinations, none of which could be considered mistaken or incomplete. There is no real endgame insofar as there is no predetermined and predictable outcome. There is no impetus to rush to judgment by settling on any one constellation of parts too early in the session. Freed from the physical and conceptual boundaries that constrain our imagination, we are encouraged instead to explore alternative arrangements of pieces wherever they might lead us, and to do so interminably—in other words, to play, to be flexible and intuitive.

Psychologists have identified two types of thinking correlating to the jigsaw puzzle and the creative product. To solve the jigsaw puzzle we employ what they call *convergent thinking*. Convergent thinking is employed when a problem calls for a single solution or action. It entails a process of narrowing down the range of possible answers until the correct or preferred one is selected. It is normally the proper approach when solving a jigsaw puzzle or a standard mathematical equation. In the context of the creative product and creative problem-solving in general, however, it is frequently ineffective because it limits possibilities at precisely the moment when we are looking to expand them. *Divergent thinking* works the opposite. Instead of constricting our path of investigation, divergent thinking opens our mind up in all directions. It propels us to look for more options, not fewer, and to consider possibilities that might not otherwise be apparent.

The challenge for adults looking to be creative is that we are often weighed down by the custom of convergent thinking, whereas children innately default to divergent thinking. A charming story told by a department store detective poignantly illustrates these contrasting tendencies. The detective recounts how he occasionally looks down from a balcony inside the store to survey the normal goings-on of the business day. Often a parent and child will enter the store and begin to make their way across the floor. Invariably, the adult is looking straight ahead and never notices the person in view on the balcony. Meanwhile, the child routinely intuits the detective's presence, looks up, smiles, and waves hello. Why? Because children are more attuned to the world and its possibilities. Their cone of vision is wider than grown-ups', in part to learn by taking in as much as they can through their senses. Adults tend to suffer from tunnel vision, a contrary condition that blinds us to things other than what we see directly in front of us. Creativity thrives when the breadth of vision is sweeping, and suffers when it is narrowed.

One suggestion for expanding your own cone of vision is to recall a childhood lesson on seeing stars at night. To make out the faintest of the stars, the ones least obvious to the eye, we were told to avoid staring straight at the dim light of the distant star because it would largely disappear from view when we did. Instead, we learned to avert our vision from where we thought we saw the star in order to see it better.

Sure enough, when we shifted our eyes away, these previously dim stars suddenly became brighter and more visible. The creative process is not unlike looking at faint stars. To find the most innovative and fresh ideas, don't just look straight ahead where you expect the answers to lie. Look to where you think they aren't. Play with the possibilities.

Sometimes it's best to play at things with little direct connection to the problem you're trying to creatively address. Albert Einstein famously played piano and violin to remove himself from the task of solving difficult scientific problems when he encountered mental blocks, activities which often helped him eventually arrive at the answers he was looking for. Others might choose to jog, cook, or, like Archimedes, play in the bath.

The relationship between play and creative thinking runs deep. As the Swiss psychologist and child-development expert Jean Piaget said, "Play is the answer to how anything new comes about." He could just as well have been speaking about the evolution of the Stitch Rug or the genesis of countless other innovative products and services as he was about child behavior.

FRIEDRICH FROEBEL AND THE OBJECT OF PLAY

We all know that children love to play with toys. The best examples provide children—and adults smart enough to use them—with a mechanism for learning about the world through the senses. Creatively designed toys elevate the value of play by stimulating the imagination to levels other teaching methods are unable to achieve. Scientific studies, for instance, have shown that children who have an opportunity to play with one creative toy and then are given another will go on to produce more creative output with the second toy than a will a control group that initially performed only rote blackboard exercises.

Yet, as integral to fostering creativity as toys have come to be, it was not until a German educator named Friedrich Froebel introduced a teaching system for young people revolving around a specially designed suite of products in the 1830s that they emerged as essential tools for childhood development *(pp. XVIII-XIX)*. Organized into what he called "gifts" and "occupations," the twenty or so sequentially numbered products Froebel and his successors devised incorporated a diverse palette of materials and formats, including balls of yarn, wood blocks, colored papers and threads, sticks, hinged slats, steel rings, drawing and pricking tools, modeling clay, and a construction kit not dissimilar to latter-day Tinkertoys. Accompanying each gift and occupation was a thoughtfully composed curriculum of activities and exercises intended to teach children their lessons while bringing them into harmony with the material and spiritual world.

Today only a handful of the original gifts and occupations remains in production, but the effects of Froebel's pedagogic program on global culture can hardly be underestimated. Among other things, we owe no less than the institution of kindergarten to him; it was Froebel who coined the term *kindergarten* in the progressive belief that a child could grow intellectually and emotionally if cultivated properly, much like a natural garden can flourish with proper care. Until then there was little acceptance of the

A SAMPLING OF THE WOOD KINDERGARTEN GIFTS DEVELOPED FOR THE FROEBEL CURRICULUM. CLOCKWISE FROM UPPER LEFT: FIFTH GIFT, J. W. SCHERMERHORN & COMPANY; SIXTH GIFT, MILTON BRADLEY COMPANY; FOURTH GIFT, E. STEIGER & COMPANY; THIRD GIFT, MILTON BRADLEY COMPANY. ALL WERE PROBABLY MANUFACTURED BETWEEN 1880 AND 1900.

idea that human beings could develop cognitively at an early age and, therefore, no curriculum to teach them how. Though most of the spiritual philosophy underpinning Froebel's teaching methods has since withered away, his conviction in the educational value of products designed for hands-on interactivity has endured to this day. Almost every elementary school classroom has its supply of blocks, drawing supplies, and creative toys, while some programs, such as Montessori and Waldorf, make them a centerpiece of their curriculum. A similar scene can be witnessed in homes occupied by children, with parents taking the place of school officials in stocking bedrooms, family rooms, yards, and other play-oriented spaces with the appurtenances of creativity.

Though Froebel operated without the benefit of modern scientific discoveries in neurological development, he turns out to have been remarkably prescient in his promotion of object play. Findings over the last fifty years corroborate his implicit premise that a kind of top-level "hotline" exists between hand and brain, and that this interdependent channel of communication expedites the emergence of cognitive faculties, motor coordination, and even the capacity for language in the child. What's more, the hand turns out to be much more of an equal partner in this relationship than our popular perception of the brain as the mastermind of all things suggests. It seems the hand teaches the brain as much as the brain guides the hand. So the widespread notion that ideas originate in the brain initially as immaterial abstractions and are only then realized in two- or three-dimensional form through action gets it partly backwards. We are actually more

IN CONTRAST TO THE THREE-DIMENSIONAL QUALITIES OF FROEBEL'S WOOD BLOCKS, THESE GIFTS AND OCCUPATIONS EMPHASIZED TWO-DIMENSIONAL AND LINEAR COMPOSITION. CLOCKWISE FROM UPPER LEFT: EIGHTH GIFT (STICKS), MILTON BRADLEY COMPANY, SPRINGFIELD, MASSACHUSETTS, C. 1900, COLLECTION YVONNE SIMONS AND MAX SPOERRI; SEVENTEENTH GIFT (PAPER INTERLACING), ALBUM OF EXERCISES, ST. LOUIS, MISSOURI, 1878; FIFTEENTH GIFT (SLAT WORK), E. STEIGER & COMPANY, NEW YORK, C. 1900; SIXTEENTH GIFT (JOINTED SLATS), MILTON BRADLEY COMPANY, C. 1880; NINTH GIFT (RINGS), MILTON BRADLEY COMPANY, C. 1880.

UNIDENTIFIED NEW YORK KINDERGARTEN CLASSROOM, 1899. NOTE THE VARIETY OF COMPOSITIONS EACH CHILD HAS ASSEMBLED AT THEIR DESKS AND ON THE FLOOR USING THEIR FROEBEL GIFTS. THE CLASSROOM'S SQUARE TABLE ARRANGEMENT IS EQUALLY TELLING; THE FROEBEL SYSTEM GENERALLY ESCHEWED THE TEACHER-CENTRIC VERTICAL HIERARCHY AND STUDENT INDIVIDUALISM IMPLIED BY FRONT-FACING DESKS SET IN ROWS IN FAVOR OF ARRANGEMENTS MORE CONDUCIVE TO GROUP COLLABORATION.

prone to generate innovative ideas in the course of physically interacting with material things than we are by pure reflection. That is why younger children are often better equipped to learn from doing than gazing at a chalkboard containing symbolic representations of knowledge, such as mathematical equations, while seated motionless at their desks. This applies to adults too. Even simple movements, like jotting down notes in a journal or doodling on a Post-it, or more complex ones, such as mocking up a cardboard prototype of a proposed new product, can help catalyze creative breakthroughs and insights.

Many years after Froebel's revolutionary development of the gifts, Michael Ondaatje, author of *The English Patient*, dubbed the close interrelationship of thinking and doing *thinkering*. The history of human creativity is dotted with Ondaatje's thinkerer types. Uber-creative Thomas Edison was a serial thinkerer. So was Henry Ford. Toss in painter Diego Rivera, Leo Tolstoy, and Marie Curie, and you begin to get the idea—or could, if you became a thinkerer yourself. Besides enjoying a boost in your personal creativity, you might also find yourself rewarded for thinking with your hands for another reason: by rendering your ideas visible—externalizing them, as it were—you enable others to experience them as well. And when others can experience your ideas, they are better equipped to collaborative effectively with you and in a group, which in turn will lead to still more innovation.

We've come up with a name for that genre of products linking hand and mind in fruitful union: we call it The Creativity of Things.

CREATIVE CONNECTIVITY •

Froebel designed several of his gifts and occupations to function as a system of parts. A child instructed to play with one of gifts 2 through 6, for example, was handed a set of finely finished wood blocks fit snugly inside a wooden box enclosed with a sliding lid. The child was directed to first open the box, remove and separate the parts, assemble the parts in different three-dimensional groupings as guided by a teacher or lesson book, and then return them to their box the same way they were found. When using other designs, such as those containing sticks, slats, and pieces of parquetry, a child might lay the pieces on a table in a variety of patterns before placing them back in their container, or play with the pieces until arriving at an arrangement pleasing enough to glue together in a model or paste into an album for taking home or displaying in class. Regardless of the final disposition of the pieces, among Froebel's goals was to sensitize the mind of the child to nature's way of creating infinitely diverse arrangements by combining a multiplicity of parts, a technique evident in such natural phenomena as snowflakes, crystals, and as we now know, molecular particles and genetics.

The opportunity for continuous creation through the combination and recombination of interconnected parts and standardized units likewise drives many of the products in *The Catalog (opposite)*. Like their natural models, these products enable one part to unite with another in order to form larger clusters. Clusters can be modified by adding, removing, or reconfiguring parts. Some products are composed of identical parts, others come with

INTRODUCTION

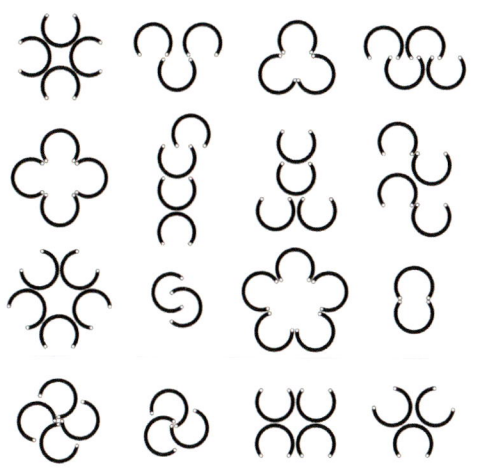 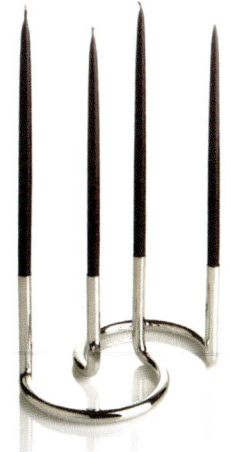 

(LEFT) PLAN DIAGRAM FOR COMBINING MULTIPLE UNITS OF THE ARCHITECTMADE GEMINI CANDLE HOLDER, DESIGNED BY PETER KARPF IN 1965. (CENTER) THE GEMINI CANDLE HOLDER IN PRACTICE. (RIGHT): PLATE XXXIV, THE PARADISE OF CHILDHOOD BY EDWARD WIEBÉ, PUBLISHED IN SPRINGFIELD, MASSACHUSETTS, IN 1869, SHOWING SUGGESTED LAYOUTS FOR THE METAL RINGS CONTAINED IN THE FROEBEL SYSTEM'S NINTH GIFT.

an assortment of shapes. Either approach is viable provided the pieces are interchangeable with each other. In nearly all cases, multiple sets of any given product can be mixed together to build still larger assemblies. Since the parts of a creative product retain their original shape and ability to connect after use, the products theoretically remain open to play indefinitely.

There is nearly universal consensus among the people who think about these things that creativity itself is by its very nature *combinatorial*. As human beings we are constantly amassing new information in the form of knowledge, memories, experience, bits of inspiration, and pre-existing ideas, which we then amalgamate into novel concepts of our own, largely on an unconscious basis. From this vast and heterogeneous trove we draw out ideas we believe to be original during conscious acts of creativity. Essentially, we synthesize disassociated thoughts and concepts embedded in our minds to produce new ones. Those that are new only to ourselves have limited value, whereas those new to the world have potentially tremendous value. Gutenberg, for example, revolutionized the delivery of information by judiciously combining the idea of a bound book, a wine press, and advances in metallurgy, chemistry, and labor relations to produce the printing press. Creatives are among the first to acknowledge the synthetic method they draw on for their work. No less an authority than Steve Jobs—a person not prone to award credit for an idea to anyone other than himself—tacitly acknowledged as much when he said:

> "Creativity is just connecting things. When you ask creative people how they did something, they feel a little guilty because they didn't really do it, they just saw something. It seemed obvious to them after a while. That's because they were able to connect experiences they've had and synthesize new things. And

XXI

the reason they were able to do that was that they've had more experiences than other people."

Almost a century earlier, auto tycoon Henry Ford had put his own accomplishments in a similar perspective:

"I invented nothing new. I simply assembled into a car the discoveries of other men behind whom were centuries of work. . . . Had I worked fifty or ten or even five years before, I would have failed. So it is with every new thing. Progress happens when all the factors that make for it are ready, and then it is inevitable."

And then we have the case of Albert Einstein, no stranger to creative discovery himself. In a letter written to a colleague in 1945, Einstein declared that "combinatory play seems to be the essential feature in productive thought." There is no more elegant representation of his observation than the spare equation Einstein is most widely associated with: $e = mc^2$. In a narrow sense Einstein invented nothing: the values of energy, mass, and the speed of light were already known by the time he arrived at his formula. Einstein merely fused them into an elegantly simple set of relationships—and changed the world by doing so.

THE VALUE OF CREATIVITY • Einstein's accomplishments, of course, constitute extreme creativity, the likes of which we mortals can only dream of. Yet we place enormous value on individual creativity, for good reason. On a fundamental level, creativity is what makes us human and elevates us above the rest of the animal kingdom. Most of what we have and think as human beings stems from human ingenuity. And while we are personally engaged in creative activity we experience an emotional lift and sense of self-fulfillment that gives us pleasure.

A few years ago a team of business educators and academics discovered one of the reasons personal creativity and, in particular, the interactive experience underlying creative design, affords us such positive feelings. They termed their finding the IKEA Effect, after the iconic Swedish purveyor of inexpensive modern furniture (and meatballs) whose products frequently require assembly (or ingestion) on the part of the customer. The team ran several experiments in which they asked one group of people to assign a monetary value to things they put together themselves, and another group to put a price on similar pre-assembled products. Data showed very clearly that participants who had a hand in constructing an object assessed it at a higher price point than those presented with a finished product. Stripping away external and variable factors, the IKEA Effect highlights the critical role interactivity plays in determining our relationship to our material surroundings. Simply put, when we personally give shape to something we experience a deeper sense of ownership, pride, and self-worth than when we acquire the object in a fully formed state. Creatively designed products and the environments they occupy capitalize on this human trait by providing the opportunity to invest ourselves in their making.

Creativity skills yield practical as well as emotional rewards. Businesses of all kinds value creative skills now more than ever as a pipeline to the innovative products and services vital to survival. In the case of start-ups, creativity fuels their birth, launch, and growth trajectory. At home and in our personal life, creativity empowers us to solve pragmatic problems and improve the quality of our lives, whether by maximizing shelf space for storage, figuring out how to open a jammed desk drawer, or coming up with a new recipe to make brussels sprouts taste good.

There exists a political and social dimension to creativity as well. Froebel made this connection apparent in his educational scheme for kindergarten. For Froebel, kindergarten was more than just a training program for advancing a child's individual creative and thinking skills; it also aspired to be a model community that would lead people to live in harmony with nature and each other. Froebel's gifts embodied this message in microcosm. Just as children under his tutelage were motivated to find positive relationships among the parts of a gift, so too would they be encouraged to forge similarly fruitful relationships among family, community, and even nations in later life *(below)*.

The notion that creativity can have implications on a national scale has enjoyed a fairly lengthy run since Froebel's day. In the second half of the 20th century there was a concerted push in the United States to inject creativity studies into elementary school education as a weapon to fight the perceived threat of authoritarian communism. More recently, we've seen innovative thinking rise to the level of a national business plan for resuscitating or maintaining an edge in a country's

COLOREM CHALK CUBES BY MIRJAM HÜTTNER FOR NAEF (2010).

economic competitiveness. Approving comments we made earlier about the democratization of the user-designer relationship in the current model for product delivery associate creativity with a particular political outlook. These and other connections made between the political and creative stem from the essential character of creativity itself. For if creativity is born from questioning conventional wisdom, that is, by challenging the authority of received truths, then it stands to reason that the political environment in which creative acts take place must be of the kind that will tolerate this sort of free and progressive thinking. Similarly, the right to choose implied by the creative act—even if it's as individualized and politically inconsequential as deciding between colors in a puzzle rug, or where to mount some hooks on a wall—hints at the possibility of personal choice in more elevated spheres of daily life, including the right to decide what type of government we want to live under.

In their own small way, the designs contained in *The Creativity Catalog* celebrate freedom: the freedom to choose, to marry disparate ideas and things in novel combinations, to make the world our own while finding our place in it. They furnish evidence of our humanity, our unique talents for imagination, invention, and innovation. As tools for learning and exercising creative skills, they bring value to us individually and collectively. Yet, despite these rewards, some might ask whether the genre of hands-on creative products will remain relevant in coming years as our daily routines become increasingly digitized and dematerialized under the influence of onscreen interaction. To which we would respond: more than ever. The reason? Recent scientific evidence indicates our brains react differently to three-dimensional objects than to their two-dimensional representation on computer screens, such that we risk stymieing our neurological development if we diminish meaningful contact with the material world. In other words, much that we have written about here with regard to acquiring knowledge through touch does not necessarily apply to the touch screen. Yet it's equally true that

ARTIST PATRICK MARTINEZ CONSTRUCTING AN INSTALLATION OUT OF HIS JIX STRAW CONNECTORS (2012).

information technology has greatly advanced the quality of our lives and is integral to our future. Our joint mission as people therefore must be to arrive at a growth strategy that synthesizes the best of what the digital and material domains have to offer. One thing seems patently clear: we ought to keep a hand in both. •

INTRODUCTION

THE SIX ATTRIBUTES OF CREATIVE DESIGN

We've developed a checklist of six attributes that you can use to test whether a product or concept qualifies as a work of creative design as defined in *The Catalog*. An object or concept under consideration must demonstrate all six characteristics to qualify; partial scores don't cut it! We also compare a conventional and creative product in the context of each attribute to show in concrete terms how the presence or absence of that attribute determines whether a product is creatively designed or not.

1: FLEXIBLE, CHANGEABLE, TRANSFORMABLE, CUSTOMIZABLE

These four related terms characterize a fundamental property of creative objects, namely, that they are mutable in appearance. Precisely how a product is made to be flexible depends on its design.

For things constructed out of interconnected parts, change comes about by changing parts *(top)*. Products composed of soft materials, like modeling clay, textiles, or metal meshes, are inherently pliant and molded into different shapes by hand *(middle)*. Some designers cause their products to be altered by enabling users to contribute their own content to the product after it leaves the box, such as a mobile that lets you clip pictures or artwork of your choice to the hanging wires *(bottom)*, or a stem vase that requires you to furnish a container for holding water (p. 72). User-generated content, as it's sometimes drily called in contemporary jargon, also pertains to multifunctional creative products incorporating surfaces you can draw, render, or paint on, then erase and reutilize (pp. 19, 20, 144).

Regardless of how an object is customized, two conditions have to be respected in the course of its transformation. First, the means by which the object is altered must be consistent with the designer's intention, and second, the product must remain open

TECTUS BY JO NIEMEYER FOR NAEF (1996).

GARLAND LIGHT BY TORD BOONTJE FOR ARTECNICA (2004).

DIY 419 MOBILE BY RYUSAKU KAWASHIMA FOR FLENSTED.

to further change. These stipulations explain why grabbing an object and smashing it to pieces does not demonstrate creativity in either the person who thought this would be a good idea, or in the object that was shattered (though it might well have been before its destruction).

Incidentally, *customization* is a keyword in the field of creative design, one whose definition is worth parsing here. Our dictionary informs us that *to customize* is to "modify (something) to suit a particular individual or task." The term *modify*, of course, is a synonym for change. Being a transitive verb, it requires an object, a function served in the context of creative design by the product. The definition goes on to refer to an individual and a task. The former points to a personal preference or value, the latter a pragmatic need or job. Explaining customization by referring to both individual and task reminds us that personal creativity and practical utility are not so much mutually exclusive terms as they are complementary and intertwined.

A COMPARISON OF FLEXIBLE AND NON-FLEXIBLE PRODUCT DESIGNS

NON-FLEXIBLE

This backpack represents a non-flexible approach to design since little changes about it during normal use other than slight variations in outward shape as things are put in or removed *(right)*. If you use this backpack to carry the same size and type of load day in and day out it would probably be perfectly adequate. If your needs vary, then perhaps less so. For example, there may well be times the bag won't be big enough to hold everything you want to transport, or have the right-sized compartments to fit some of your belongings. At other times it's going to be too large for what's inside and will feel like you're carrying around an empty sack. You could solve this problem by buying additional bags in more sizes and configurations, but that incurs expense, consumes space, and adds clutter.

FLEXIBLE

The Arkiv Mission Knapsack utilizes a modular design that lets you attach or detach supplementary storage compartments so you can adjust the size and shape of the pack to meet your needs each time you use it *(opposite)*. Compartments attach to the knapsack's sides and back, and to each other, by means of slide-through rails and Velcro clasps. The bag's flexible system reduces the likelihood of either excess weight or insufficient capacity. It could well do away with the need to acquire other bags altogether. And unlike the generic, non-flexible version of the backpack, Arkiv allows you to configure your bag to serve specialized activities, like photography or bird-watching, while still satisfying routine use.

A CONVENTIONAL KNAPSACK.

INTRODUCTION

ARKIV MODULAR KNAPSACK BY MISSION WORKSHOP.

2: INTERACTIVE

Interactivity has been elevated to something of a buzzword in the digital age. Take another trip to the dictionary and you'll even discover that a standard definition of *interactive* is cast entirely in the context of computers:

> Allowing a two-way flow of information between a computer and a computer-user; responding to a user's input: a fully interactive map of the area.

It's gratifying to know that one of our six attributes of creative design is so well attuned to the current zeitgeist, especially since we're trafficking in goods that are unflinchingly analog. But in truth the word was coined well before there were computers, first appearing sometime around 1830. Does that date ring a bell? It should: this is just around the time that Friedrich Froebel was conceiving his first kindergarten gifts, marking the emergence of the interactive educational toy.

The timing was hardly a coincidence. Before it acquired its digital connotations, the term *interactive* meant to "act in such a way as to have an effect on another; act reciprocally." This perfectly describes the relationship between a child and a Froebel gift. The child brings about a change of state in the gift by acting to reconstitute its parts; observing the effects of his or her changes, the child then manipulates the gift further, repeating the succession of action and reaction until the assignment or session is completed. The same back-and-forth cycle characterizes the relationship between users and the creative design products in *The Catalog*, with the implication that the cycle could continue indefinitely as open-ended play.

Flexibility and interactivity clearly go hand in hand; however, they are not synonymous. In the first place, flexibility precedes interactivity; a product has to be designed from the start to be amenable to transformation if the user is to interact with it. Conversely, not all changeable things automatically deserve to be called interactive. Certain brands of sunglasses feature a type of lens that will darken or lighten depending on lighting conditions, but that does not make them interactive, since they perform this feat without human prompting.

Interactivity connotes another, more subtle meaning in the context of creative design. As a user you tangibly engage the object, of course, but you also indirectly interact with the product's originating designers by interpreting their design concept through actual use. While you might choose to keep that interaction an entirely private experience, the results of your engagement and those of other users nonetheless offer designers potentially valuable feedback, which they could draw from in further developing or expanding a line of related products.

A COMPARISON OF INTERACTIVE AND NONINTERACTIVE PRODUCT DESIGNS

NONINTERACTIVE

Despite their often palpable beauty and charm, the great majority of candleholders can be safely described as conventionally conceived products with no opportunity for users to modify their appearance or inject their personality into them, save for the minor choice of candle color *(top)*.

INTERACTIVE

Unlike the static, monolithic body of its noninteractive counterpart, the center section of the Morpheo Crystal Candlestick consists of nine separate movable pieces aligned on a center stem *(bottom)*. To alter the silhouette of the candleholder, slide the pieces off the stem and then restack them in a different order. With 362,880 possible sequences to choose from, you should be able to produce a new configuration for every occasion for the rest of your life, the lives of your offspring, and everyone else you know or have ever known.

A CONVENTIONAL CANDLEHOLDER.

MORPHEO CRYSTAL CANDLESTICK BY SELAB FOR SELETTI (2008–2009).

3: TACTILE

The principal agent for interacting with creative products is the human hand. It is through the motion of the hand that we physically manipulate the parts, transform the shape, or modify the content of a creative object. All creative products therefore incorporate the element of touch and by extension the movement of the body. There are many benefits to tactile experiences not only with creatively designed products, but with our surroundings generally. For children, hands-on interaction with the natural and material world has been shown to enhance neurological development. Among adults, building ideas in three-dimensional form can be a powerful stimulus for eliciting innovative concepts and products to share with others.

A COMPARISON OF TACTILE AND NON-TACTILE PRODUCT DESIGNS

NON-TACTILE

Once you set this conventional clock to the correct time, you probably won't have to touch it often again except to slam on the snooze button every now and then *(top)*. A simple glance in its direction will tell you all you need to know.

TACTILE

Jonah Dimon's Numbers Cube Clock for Areaware consists of four loosely connected LED cubes programmed to display the time *(bottom)*. You can array the blocks in their conventional sequence of hour and minute, or lose track of time altogether by moving the cubes into unexpected relationships with each other. Totally confuse your roommate, family member, or coworker by surreptitiously shuffling the cubes around when they're not looking.

A CONVENTIONAL DIGITAL CLOCK.

NUMBERS CUBE CLOCK BY JONAS DAMON FOR AREAWARE (2006).

4: OPEN-ENDED

We previously stated that genuinely creative products accommodate repeated modification and are without a preset path to a solitary solution. How do we evaluate designs that fall into a middle zone between conventional and creative, such as toys that morph into three or four different configurations, or household goods that contain just enough interchangeable parts to qualify as changeable and transformable? Strictly speaking, these products do yield more than one possible result, and can in truth be modified recurrently by repeating the same series of modifications over and over again.

Still, we prefer to clear up any prospective murkiness in our concept of creative design by stipulating that a creative product must put forward the opportunity for open-ended play, meaning that the number of potential permutations it presents to the user is inexhaustible, or at least nearly so. After all, who among us is going to stand on semantic technicalities when asked whether the Morpheo candleholder, with its staggering 362,880 possible arrangements, should be deemed an authentically creative product, assuming it meets the other five criteria on our list? What's important in judging the effectiveness of a creative product is whether the user is given the room to exercise the free play of the imagination without quickly bumping up against the constraints of limited choice, not whether such constraints exist in the abstract.

A COMPARISON OF OPEN AND CLOSED PRODUCT DESIGNS

CLOSED DESIGN

A closed design product is an object that cannot be systematically added to, diminished, or otherwise altered in shape, size, or appearance. The operative term in this definition is *systematic*; while this bookcase *(top)* could certainly be altered using normal carpentry techniques, such alterations are not anticipated in the design of the bookcase and will necessarily be ad hoc, that is, unique to the individual who made them.

OPEN DESIGN

Muuto's Stacked Shelving System is a reconfigurable storage product comprising three variously sized and finished units as well as an optional podium, all of which can be stacked and clamped together in diverse arrangements to satisfy aesthetic and practical requirements *(bottom)*. An unlimited number of units can be joined together to expand assemblies boundlessly. An exceptional example of open design by architect and designer Julien De Smedt of JDS Architects.

A CONVENTIONAL STORAGE CABINET.

STACKED SHELVING SYSTEM BY JULIEN DE SMEDT FOR MUUTO (2007).

5: SELECTIVE

All creative acts involve choice. A writer selects which words from the dictionary to use in a sentence. A mathematician plucks terms from the lexicon of mathematics to formulate an equation. A coder chooses what commands to put in a string of code, a chef chooses ingredients for a dish, a fashionista selects an assortment of clothing and accessories to wear. Creative designs compel us to think by making choices in order to use the product. Conventional products might prompt us to make choices too, but they are generally mechanical rather than thoughtful in nature.

People who are adept in making fruitful choices from the options available to them have the skills to be creative; people who consistently come up with *compelling combinations of choices* have the potential to be the most creative of all.

A COMPARISON OF SELECTIVE AND NONSELECTIVE PRODUCT DESIGNS

NONSELECTIVE

You walk into a clothing shop and buy a t-shirt with a drawing of a scary monster on it *(top)*. You wear it. It looks the same. You keep wearing it until you either tire of it, it disintegrates, or it gets lost in the laundry.

SELECTIVE

Dr. Lakra's Mutant Monsters *(bottom)* is a game created by a Mexican artist and tattooist of the same name (actually, we think he made it up). It consists of eighty-four recycled cardboard triangles combined in sets of four to illustrate monstrously charming creatures dreamed up by Dr. Lakra, whose work is in the collection of New York's Museum of Modern Art and is shown in international galleries. Shuffle the cards and select your own choice of triangular pieces to generate one of 190,000 other freaky characters. With so many options you're unlikely to ever run out of creative juice.

A CONVENTIONALLY PRINTED T-SHIRT.

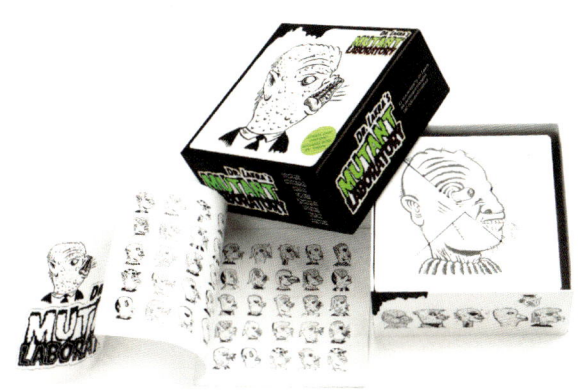

DR. LAKRA'S MUTANT LABORATORY FOR GENERAL MONSTERS (2012).

6 SYSTEMS-BASED

Creative products are built on systems. A system is an interconnected set of parts organized to achieve a particular purpose. A product constitutes a system if all three factors—parts, a mechanism for networking the parts into a complex whole, and an ultimate function or purpose—are evident in its design.

How do you know when the parts of a system are being successfully networked to form a complex whole? To answer, ask yourself three questions about the design: First, do the parts impact each other in the process of using it? Second, do the parts produce a different effect when acting in concert than when they stand on their own? And third, is the interconnectedness of the parts resilient, that is, does it persist over time? If the answers to these questions are all in the affirmative, then you have a system.

By the way, systems are as prevalent in nature as they are among things of human invention. Our bodies, for example, are elaborate systems of interconnected parts working together to form a complex whole. Snowflakes and crystals are self-organizing systems of recurring and additive geometric shapes. On the other hand, a pile of sand sitting on the ground is little more than a jumble of similar yet physically detached particles, lacking the means of interconnecting for a recognizable purpose. Ditto for an assortment of objects you randomly take off your shelf and drop on a tabletop. When it comes to systems, mere adjacencies among parts do not a connection or purpose make.

A COMPARISON OF SYSTEMIC AND NONSYSTEMIC DESIGNS

To reinforce our initial point that a creative product must incorporate all six attributes for creative design as we've enumerated them here, you can practice assessing whether a product is a systemic or nonsystemic design by using any of the product comparisons in this section. (Spoiler alert: our creative examples fall consistently into the first camp, the conventional ones in the second!) •

NOTES

XVI. "…otherwise be apparent." Simonton, *Origins of Genius*, 85–87.

XVI. "…these contrasting tendencies." Dubner, *Think Like A Child*. You might know Stephen Dubner and his economist accomplice, Steven D. Levitt, as the duo behind the successful book and media series *Freakonomics*.

XVII. "…rote blackboard exercises." Howard-Jones, *The Effects of Play*.

XVIII. "…to teach them how." Brosterman, *Inventing Kindergarten*. Not only does Brosterman write insightfully about Froebel's educational philosophy and its historical context, he makes a compelling case for it having laid the groundwork for artistic modernism.

XVIII. "…appurtenances of creativity." Ogata, *Designing the Creative Child*. This is an excellent book for those interested in the intersection of child creativity and product design, valuable if nothing else than for the sheer amount of information and reference material it provides on the subject. Unfortunately, its strengths are somewhat marred by the author's ambivalence about the validity of creative playthings.

XX. "…on a Post-it." The bane of every librarian's existence, the Post-it nonetheless figures prominently in discussions of creativity, both for its historical origins and its adaptability to brainstorming and other creative endeavors, including illustration art. Check out post-it.com/wps/portal/3M/en_US/PostItNA/Home/Ideas/Articles/Wall-art-Creator.

XX. "…breakthroughs and insights." Brown, *Play*; Sawyer, *Zig Zag*; Wilson, *The Hand*. Worried that you've never been much for doodling for fear of having your artistic skills (or lack thereof) mocked? Fret not! Consult Roam's *The Back of the Napkin* to build some easy-to-learn skills and get your confidence back.

XX. "…thinking and doing *thinkering*." Sawyer, *Zig Zag*, 198–200.

XXII. "…*than other people.*" ibid, 153–172.

XXII. "…**then it is inevitable.**" Burkus, *The Myths of Creativity*, 55–56.

XXIII. "…**in their making.**" Norton, *The IKEA Effect*.

XXIII. "…**of authoritarian communism.**" Ogata, *Designing the Creative Child*.

XXIV. "…**the material world.**" Brown, *Play*, 184–189.

XXVIII. "…**have ever known.**" To arrive at this figure we used the factorial function $n! = n \times (n-1)!$, where n is the number of parts to be placed in a specific order and ! the symbol for successively diminishing integers. The total $n!$ is the number of different sequences the set of parts can be placed in. Since the Morpheo candleholder has nine parts, the value of n is 9, and $n! = 9 \times (8 \times 7 \times 6 \times 5 \times 4 \times 3 \times 2 \times 1)$, which equals 362,880.

PlayPlax, a creative crossover toy for children and adults, offers an even more intensive foray into combinatorial mathematics. A set of PlayPlax contains forty-eight square acrylic pieces in five colors, each with four slots in which other pieces can be inserted. Since the number of pieces and their slots are finite, it should be possible to determine how many different sculptural assemblies can be formed from one set if all the pieces of the set are used.

To make a long story short, the number of possible permutations of a single PlayPlax set is about 1.75×10 to the 75th power. Which is a lot. And that is not even taking into account the factor of colors, only the position of the pieces themselves. Nor does it account for combinations formed from fewer than the forty-eight pieces in the box.

The formula used to arrive at the above figure, for those who like to ruminate on these matters, is: $b_n = 2^{(n-1)} * n!$.

XXXII. "…**or purpose make.**" Donella, *Thinking in Systems*.

ASSEMBLAGE MODULAR STORAGE BY SELAB FOR SELETTI (2010).

Housewares and Decor 6
Jewelry and Apparel 76
Shelving and Organization 82
Children 100

THE PRODUCTS

HOUSEWARES AND DECOR

10-Unit Modular Furniture System by Shigeru Ban for Artek (2009) 6

Abyss Reconfigurable Table Lamp by Osko+Deichmann for Kundalini (2007) 8

Adaptation Vase by Brandon Perhacs (2009) 8

Alexander Girard Alphabet Blocks by House Industries for Uncle Goose (2006) 9

Algue by Ronan and Erwan Bouroullec for Vitra (2004) 9

All of a Piece Tableware by Dana Cannam Design and Earnest Studio (2013) 10

Alphabet Blocks by Pat Kim for Areaware (2013) 11

Alto Modular Stair Carpets by Liza Phillips Design (2006) 11

Appo Cork Tray by Carlo Trevisani for Seletti (2011–2012) 12

Architect's Cubes by John Bennett and Gustavo Bonevardi for MoMA (2010) 12

Arkiv Modular Knapsack by Mission Workshop 13

Assemblage Modular Storage by Selab for Seletti (2010) 14

BIRDs by Kristian Vedel (1959), reissued by ArchitectMade 15

Blank Wall Clock by Martí Guixé for Alessi (2010) 16

BrickCase for iPhone 5 by SmallWorks 16

CandlestickMaker by Ron Gilad for Designfenzider 17

Cella by Peer Clahsen for Naef (1979) 17

The Chairs Game by Pico Pao for MoMA (2010) 18

Chalkboard Clocks by Enrico Azzimonti for Diamantini & Domeniconi 19

Chalkboard Vase by Ricardo Saint-Clair for MoMA (2005) 20

Corniches by Ronan and Erwan Bouroullec for Vitra (2012) 20

Crystal LED Light by QisDesign (2009) 21

Cubebots by David Weeks for Areaware (2010) 22

Cubicus by Peer Clahsen for Naef (1968) 23

Desktructure Desktop Organizer by Héctor Serrano for Seletti (2012) 23

Diamant by Peer Clahsen for Naef (1981) 24

DIY 419 Mobile by Ryusaku Kawashima for Flensted 24

DIY Art Wallpaper by Tempaper 25

The Dots Coat Hooks by Tveit & Tornøe for Muuto 26

Dovetail Wood Animals by Karl Zahn for Areaware (2012) 26

Eliot Modular Planters by Andrew and Richard Erdle for Good Erdle 27

Equilique Acrobats by John Perry 28

Flare Table by Marcel Wanders and Javier Mariscal for Magis (2003) 28

Flexus Menorah by Herbert and Jeanne Atkin (1995) 30

Flower Loop by Black+Blum (2009) 30

Garland Light by Tord Boontje for Artecnica (2004) 30

Gemini Candleholder by Peter Karpf (1965), reissued by ArchitectMade 32

Grape Wine Rack by Robert Bronwasser for Goods (2007) 32

Hanging Screens by René Barba and Werksdesign for Koziol (2005-2006) 33

Hanno the Gorilla by David Weeks for Areaware (2009) 33

Hex Table by Incorporated for Lerival 34

Honey Lights by Dante Donegani and Giovanni Lauda for Rotaliana (2004) 35

Ikamo by Heiko Hillig for Naef 38

Imago by Heiko Hillig for Naef 38

Infinite Tree by Johannes Molin for Areaware (2013) 39

Infinity Wine Rack by Ron Arad for Kartell (1999) 39

Interchangeable Earrings and Watches by Hubert Verstraeten for Tamawa (2010-2011) 40

Kaleido Trays by Clara von Zweigbergk for HAY (2012) 41

The Ladders Game by Pico Pao for MoMA (2011) 41

Les Perles Candlesticks by F. X. Balléry for Y'A PAS LE FEU AU LAC (2010) 42

Loop Candleholder by Black+Blum (2006) 42

Magnetic Vases by Peleg Design for Decor Craft (2005) 43

Menorahs by Agayof Art & Judaica 43

Menorahs by Laura Cowan (2009–2012) 45

Modular Magnetic Matzo Plate by Laura Cowan (2012) 46

Modular Screen by Moorhead & Moorhead for Lerival 46

Modulon by Jo Niemeyer for Naef (1984) 48

Molecule Building Set by ferm LIVING 48

Mondri 3-in-1 Vase by Frank Kerdil for PO 49

Morpheo Crystal Candlestick by Selab for Seletti (2008–2009) 49

Mosaik by Kathrin Kiener for Naef (2002) 50

My Bricks by Selab for Seletti (2008–2009) 50

My House of Cards by Selab for Seletti (2008–2009) 51

Nordic Light Candleholder by Jonas Grundell for Design House Stockholm 53

Numbers Cube Clock by Jonas Damon for Areaware (2006) 53

Numero Clock by Roost 54

Opaline Glass Modular Vase by Selab for Seletti (2009) 54

Pantone Food Trays by ROOM Copenhagen 55

PaperForms Wall Paneling by Jaime Salm for MIO (2004–2013) 56

PolyHex by Incorporated for Lerival 57

Presepe Nativity Set by Massimo Giacon and Laura Polinoro for Alessi (2007–2010) 58

Programma 8 Tableware by Franco Sargiani and Eija Helander for Alessi (1975–2009) 58

Puzzle Wine Rack by Gideon Dagan (2005) 61

Rhombins Desktop Storage and Play by Eric Pfeiffer and Scot Herbst for AMAC (2011) 61

Scrabble Pearl Edition by Winning Solutions for Hasbro 62

STACT Wine Wall by Eric Pfeiffer (2012) 63

Stitch Interlocking Rug by Nauris Kalinauskas (2005) 66

Table Table by MOS Architects for Lerival (2010) 67

TableTalk Trivet by Nel Linssen for Goods (2000) 67

Tectus by Jo Niemeyer for Naef (1996) 68

Terrain Vase by Stephan Jaklitsch for MoMA (2010) 68

Tetris Mirror by Julia Dozsa for FIAM (2010) 69

Trask Lamp by Jaime Salm and Roger C. Allen for MIO (2009) 69

Try It Trivet by Dror Benshetrit for Alessi (2009) 70

Ty DIY Shower Curtain by Grain (2008) 71

Urbio Modular Garden and Wall Organizer by Enlisted Design 71

Ursa the Bear by David Weeks for Areaware (2009) 71

VaseMaker by Ron Gilad for Designfenzider 72

Wall Frames by Wexel Art (2010) 73

Yuki Screen by Nendo for Cappellini (2006) 74

JEWELRY AND APPAREL

Kishut Modular Jewelry by Hila Rawet Karni (2009) 76

Sportivo Linkable Jewelry by Italianissimo 78

Stix+Stones Necklace by Brandon Perhacs (2007) 78

Switch Gear Interchangeable Jewelry by Lisa Monahan (2008) 79

Thewrap by Roxi Suger for Angelrox (2006) 79

UNO Magnetic Jewelry by Luis Pons 80

SHELVING AND ORGANIZATION

Boogie Woogie Shelving by Stefano Giovannoni for Magis (2004) 82

Bookworm by Ron Arad for Kartell (1999) 84

Cloud Modular Shelving by Ronan and Erwan Bouroullec for Cappellini (2004) 84

Componibili Storage System by Anna Castelli Ferrieri for Kartell (1969) 85

Cubit and Cubitec Shelving by Doron Lachisch for DLP Plastics 86

DrawerDecor Liner System by KMN Home (2010) 88

Ivy Modular Coatrack by MOS Architects for Lerival 88

Joint Venture Shelving by Matt Gagnon for RS Barcelona (2011) 89

Key Modular Storage by Housefish (2008) 90

Loopits Stretch and Store by Heather O'Donahoe for Quirky (2013) 90

Mix Boxes by The Utility Collective (2010) 91

Modular Bookshelf System and Bins by Giulio Polvara for Kartell (1974) 91

Optic Storage Cubes by Patrick Jouin for Kartell (2006) 92

OTO 100 Storage System by Pil Bredahl for Muuto (2000) 92

Stacked Shelving System by Julien De Smedt for Muuto (2007) 93

Tetrad Shelving by Brave Space Design 94

USM Modular Furniture by Fritz Haller (1963) 95

Way Basics Storage Cubes (2008) 98

Yube Cube Modular Storage (2010) 99

CHILDREN

3Doodler Printing Pen by Maxwell Bogue and Peter Dilworth (2013) 100

Alphabet Factory Blocks by House Industries for Uncle Goose (2012) 102

Architectural Standard Unit Building Blocks by Melissa & Doug 103

Automoblox by Patrick Calello (2004) 104

Balancing Blocks by Fort Standard for Areaware (2012) 105

Ball of Whacks by Roger von Oech for Creative Whack Company (2006) 105

Bauhaus Optical Top by Ludwig Hirschfeld-Mack (1923), reissued by Naef 106

BiModal Blocks by Tim Boyle for Brinca Dada (2012) 106

Building Block Menorah by Decor Craft 107

Changeable Lunchboxes by Whipsaw for Yubo (2007) 107

Child's Chair by Kristian Vedel (1957), reissued by ArchitectMade 108

Colorem Chalk Cubes by Mirjam Hüttner for Naef (2010) 109

Dado Construction Toys by Fat Brain Toys (2007-2010) 109

Dr. Lakra's Mutant Laboratory for General Monsters (2012) 111

Eames House Blocks by House Industries for Uncle Goose (2010) 111

Eco-Dough by Eco-Kids (2008) 112

Extreme Stunt Kit by Wall Coaster (2009) 112

Fractiles Magnetic Tiling Toy (1998) 113

Free Universal Construction Kit by F.A.T. Lab and Sy-Lab for Adapterz LLC (2012) 113

Froebel Gifts, reissued by Red Hen Books and Toys 114

Grimm's Spiel und Holz Design Creative Toys 115

Imaginets by MindWare 118

Jix Straw Connectors by Patrick Martinez (2012) 118

Kaleidograph Pattern Design Toy by Kaleidograph Design (2011) 120

Kidz Paintable Placemats by Modern-Twist 121

KidzPuzzle Cushion by BuzziSpace (2009) 122

Ladrillos Shelving by Javier Mariscal for Magis (2005) 122

LEGO Storage Bricks and Heads by ROOM Copenhagen (2012) 123

Little Flare Customizable Table by Marcel Wanders for Magis (2005) 123

Magna-Tiles Construction Toys by Valtech (1997) 124

Makedo Connector Kits (2009) 124

Marble Track System by Matthias Etter for Cuboro (1985) 125

Miller Goodman Wood Toys by Zoe Miller and David Goodman 126

My Space Divider by Björn Dahlström for Magis (2005) 128

Organeco Building Blocks by Hape 128

Paolo Creative Toy by Remember 129

Playable Metal by Metal ART 129

PlayableArt Creative Toys by Bernd Liebert 130

PlayPlax by Patrick Rylands (1966) 131

Plus-Plus Building Toy by Geared for Imagination (2012) 132

Q-BA-MAZE Marble Runs by Andrew Comfort for MindWare (2011) 132

QuaDror Building Blocks by Dror Benshetrit for Decor Craft (2013) 133

Snap Circuits Electronic Toys by Elenco 134

Spiel Building Blocks by Kurt Naef for Naef (1954) 135

Strawz Connectible Drinking Straws by NuOp Design (2007) 135

Suspend by Melissa & Doug (2012) 136

Tegu Magnetic Blocks (2009) 136

Toobalink by Metre Ideas and Design (2012) 138

WallCandy Arts Wallpapers and Stickers 138

Wood Blocks by Uncle Goose 141

Woodmobiel by Ben Fritz for OOTS! 141

Woody Chalkboard Table and Chair by Eric Pfeiffer for Offi (1996) 144

XYZ Alphabet Blocks by Christian Northeast for Fred and Friends 144

ZOOB Construction Toy by Michael Joaquin Grey for Infinitoy (1993–1996) 145

HOUSEWARES AND DECOR

10-UNIT MODULAR FURNITURE SYSTEM
BY SHIGERU BAN FOR ARTEK (2009)

Noted Japanese architect and 2014 Pritzker Prize—winner Shigeru Ban based this modular design on L-shaped units that can be combined to make different kinds of seating, from individual chairs to multi-seat configurations. As an extra bonus the pieces can also be used as table bases for tops of varying sizes. Assembling one package of ten modules takes under ten minutes thanks to a simple system of connecting rods.

The highly ecological and ethical 10-Unit System is made from UPM ProFi, an environmentally innovative composite. Its principal raw materials are recycled paper and plastic. The composite has proved to be tough, and humidity resistant. It is an environmentally sustainable material that can be disposed of by incineration, or recycled back into the production process. All materials in the composite are nontoxic.

One pack of ten pieces makes a stool, chair, or table base. Benches, settees, and coffee tables require two packs. Pews and soccer stadium seating require three or more packs. Be the first on your block to make a hundred seats in a row!

Available in White, which has a mottled finish similar to travertine, and Black.

Discover these items at thecreativehome.com

7

THE CREATIVITY CATALOG

ABYSS RECONFIGURABLE TABLE LAMP BY OSKO+DEICHMANN FOR KUNDALINI (2007)

This design by Osko+Deichmann fundamentally rethinks the conventional idea of a table lamp. Instead of a fixed form with a weighted, stable base surmounted by a focused light source, we have a linear, repositionable 43-inch-long (109 cm) loop with no visible beginning, middle, or end. Its vertebrate-like casing allows for infinite combinations of self-supporting forms that seem to float freely in space.

The lamp, if we might call it that, is lighted by a 10-watt, high-voltage LED strip and encased in a modular, injection-molded opal polycarbonate.

Made by Italy-based Kundalini, a source of innovative illumination since 1996. The fixture is CE listed, which is the European equivalent of the UL listing common in the U.S. Works with standard U.S. wall outlets.

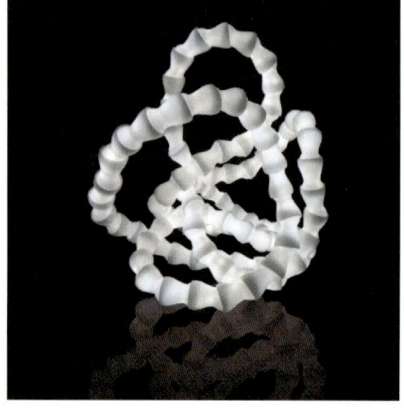

ADAPTATION VASE BY BRANDON PERHACS (2009)

Adaptation Vase is a finely crafted interactive vase that invites a unique approach to flower arranging. It's designed with four magnets set in a wood base, plus four glass tubes and four stainless steel spheres. Simply insert the stainless steel spheres into the tubes and place them on the magnets in the base. The tube vases may then be tilted, swayed, and turned into any desired configuration. Add water and flowers to create a unique centerpiece that can change like the seasons—or even more often.

The base is made from wood sustainably harvested locally from Bainbridge Island, Washington where designer Brandon Perhacs is based. It measures 9 by 2½ by ¾ inches (22.8 by 6.3 by 1.9 cm).

Made in America. Flowers not included.

Discover these items at thecreativehome.com

HOUSEWARES AND DECOR

ALEXANDER GIRARD ALPHABET BLOCKS BY HOUSE INDUSTRIES FOR UNCLE GOOSE (2006)

Alexander Girard (1903–1993) is widely known for his contributions to the field of American textile design, particularly through his work for Herman Miller from 1952 to 1975, where he created fabrics for design greats George Nelson and Charles and Ray Eames.

This set of contemporary alphabet blocks is an homage to Girard's playful mid-century style and his long-held admiration for folk art. Created by the design company House Industries to coordinate with the San Francisco MOMA's exhibit on Girard, the twenty-eight wood blocks feature a cleverly adapted factory logo puzzle. Can you spell F-U-N?

Made in America and printed with child-safe nontoxic inks, although you definitely don't have to be a child to appreciate them. Blocks are 1¾ inches (4.5 cm) square. In their box the set measures 14 by 9 by 1¾ inches (35.5 by 22.8 by 4.4 cm).

ALGUE BY RONAN AND ERWAN BOUROULLEC FOR VITRA (2004)

Algue are modular, connectible ornaments created by the world-famous fraternal design team of Ronan and Erwan Bouroullec. Reminiscent of plants, the pieces can be joined together to form web-like meshes of indefinite size and complexity. By varying their density, you can achieve a range of effect, from a light, diaphanous curtain to a nearly opaque space divider.

Made of injection-molded plastic, Algue come in packs of twenty-five and will cover approximately ten square feet (1 m^2) in area for each pack, depending on assembly.

Each piece measures approximately 11¾ by 21¾ by 16 (29.9 by 55.2 by 40.7 cm). Available in Green, Red, Transparent, and White. Colors can be mixed or remain monochromatic.

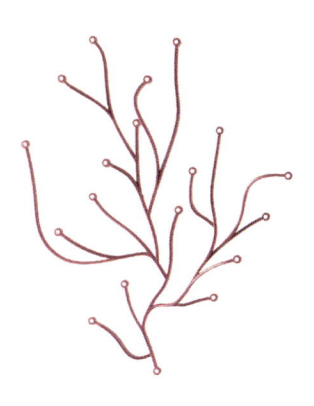

THE CREATIVITY CATALOG

ALL OF A PIECE TABLEWARE BY DANA CANNAM
DESIGN AND EARNEST STUDIO (2013)

All of a Piece Tableware is a collection of interchangeable modular elements that connect to form various serving, display, and organizing pieces for the table. The elements forming the collection are few in number, consisting of no more than a tray, shallow bowl, candleholder, and an end cap, made of marble, granite, or wood. Yet out of this limited palette comes a rich assortment of beautiful housewares, from trivets to centerpieces, key holders to cheese servers. The secret ingredient? Hidden magnetic connections buried inside the modules make assembling every piece a snap. For an even more intensely atmospheric effect, insert an LED light source between the modules and really watch the table light up.

All of a Piece is a genuinely collaborative effort of Dana Cannam Design and Earnest Studio, two Netherlands-based design firms that clearly make a pretty good combination of their own.

Discover these items at thecreativehome.com

HOUSEWARES AND DECOR

ALPHABET BLOCKS BY PAT KIM FOR AREAWARE (2013)

Most alphabet blocks are . . . well, blocks. This beautifully designed letter set is exceptional in having each letter cut out of a block of wood to reveal itself in the round.

Designed by Brooklyn-based Pat Kim, the blocks are made from mahogany and pine woods. The dark, tight grain of the mahogany makes for a pleasing contrast with the lighter, heavily grained pine.

Stack the blocks, write out words with them, teach a young child the letters of the alphabet—these stylized Alphabet Blocks are an heirloom toy and desktop accessory for young and not so young alike.

Each block is approximately 2 inches (5.0 cm) in each direction. Comes in a presentation-quality wood box.

ALTO MODULAR STAIR CARPETS
BY LIZA PHILLIPS DESIGN (2006)

Alto Steps are modular carpet pieces that provide a fun, attractive and functional enhancement of one of the most important architectural features in any multi-level space. Their benefits are many: they prevent slipping, muffle noise, soften the staircase's hard materials, and are customizable in their layout.

All the components in Alto are made to order from the finest Himalayan wool hand-spun by Tibetans in the Kathmandu Valley of Nepal. The wool is rich in lanolin oil, which is important both for the absorption of the dyes as well as the plush texture for which Tibetan rugs are famous. Traditional vegetable dyes or eco-friendly Swiss Ciba colors are used exclusively.

Design a stair treatment using any combination of the standard components of treads, deep steps and landings. The components come in several color schemes, each of which contains a range of complementary hues and decorative patterns.

THE CREATIVITY CATALOG

APPO CORK TRAY BY CARLO TREVISANI FOR SELETTI (2011-2012)

Next time someone asks you to put a cork in it, make it a cork tray instead. Appo Cork Trays are a great way to repurpose some of those empty wine and beverage bottles you're forever throwing out. Slide an Appo into the neck to transform the vessel into an eye-catching centerpiece or serving tray for hors d'oeuvres (also known as appetizers and finger food). They also work well for creating nifty tabletop or shelf displays.

The small tray is made from sustainable and durable cork, and measures 7 inches (17.7 cm) in diameter and 3 inches (7.6 cm) in overall height.

ARCHITECT'S CUBES BY JOHN BENNETT AND GUSTAVO BONEVARDI FOR MOMA (2010)

The eight Architect's Cubes in this collection, each made of a different natural, synthetic, or composite material, can be combined to create a large cube or arranged individually as sculptural building blocks. Architects John Bennett and Gustavo Bonevardi designed this emphatically tactile tabletop piece to encourage the creative exploration of cubic forms and materials.

The size of the cubes varies slightly due to the unique nature of each material used. An Architect's Cube nominally measures 1¼ inches square (3.1 cm^2). The tray is 10 by 1½ by 1½ inches (25.4 by 3.8 by 3.8 cm).

Discover these items at thecreativehome.com

ARKIV MODULAR KNAPSACK
BY MISSION WORKSHOP

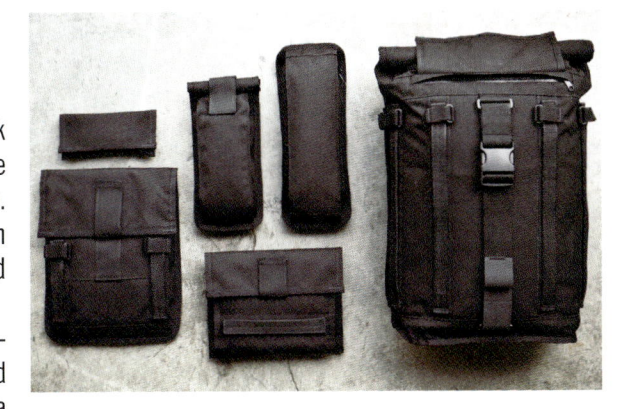

The ultimate in modular transport, the Arkiv Modular Knapsack gives you an arsenal of removable accessories to customize your backpack. Add and subtract components as needs dictate. No more running out of room one day, then carrying around an empty sack of potatoes because of one or two things you had to handle the next!

All Arkiv bags and accessories feature waterproof materials, multiple weatherproof compartments, urethane-coated YKK zippers, and an internal frame sheet. Made in America and backed by a lifetime warranty. Available in Black Cordura, Dark Gray Cordura, and Waxed Canvas.

COMPONENTS INCLUDE:

Small or Large Pack and Folio: Packs can be used in either roll-up mode, or in a traditional flap-down configuration, and come with a Folio case. The two front-mounted Arkiv rails allow for the additional attachment of accessories. A U-lock slot in the back can double as a handle when the Folio is used as a stand-alone bag.

Laptop Case: This weatherproof roll-top Laptop Case combines dense foam and two layers of waterproof fabric to create a protective and versatile laptop case. Two extra front-mounted rails allow for the addition of the Folio, Tool Pocket, or Utility/Cell accessories. A U-lock slot in the back can double as a handle when the Laptop Case is used as a stand-alone bag. Fits on the front panel.

Tool Pocket: A medium-sized weatherproof pouch for carrying the tools of your trade. It features one urethane-coated zipper pocket and one annex rail for the addition of the cell pouch. Belt loops and a U-lock strap enable you to use this accessory as a hip tool pack. Fits on the front panel, laptop case, and folio.

Utility/Cell Pocket: Weatherproof zippered Utility Pocket, sized to hold smartphones and compact point-and-shoot cameras. Compatible anywhere on pack.

Vertical Roll Up Pocket: Weatherproof top loader. Sized for cylindrical objects, such as water bottles. Fits side panel.

Vertical Zippered Pocket: This versatile side compartment has a two-way zipper that works well for storing long items. Fits on the side panels.

Shoulder Strap: Converts all accessories into a quick and easy shoulder bag. Constructed from heavy-duty nylon webbing.

THE CREATIVITY CATALOG

ASSEMBLAGE MODULAR STORAGE BY SELAB FOR SELETTI (2010)

Together we nest, divided we stack! Assemblage is a set of ten modules that fit snugly inside each other, and then slide out so they can be stacked for use as shelving and storage. Twelve metal clamps with a striking red tightener hold the units together, and also make it possible to configure the units to your liking or change them when the need arises.

Assemblage was a 2011 winner of the prestigious European Consumer Award for design.

Made of lacquered MDF; available in Black and in White. Module sizes measure from 23⅝ square inches down to 9½ with a consistent depth of 15¾ inches (from 60 cm down to 20 cm, with a depth of 40 cm).

Discover these items at thecreativehome.com

BIRDS BY KRISTIAN VEDEL (1959), REISSUED BY ARCHITECTMADE

Kristian Vedel (1923–2003) designed his charming and timeless family of BIRDs back in 1959. Though only the small child BIRD was originally produced, it quickly became one of the most successful Danish wooden products from the 1950s. Today, the entire expressive BIRD family has been reintroduced by ArchitectMade, including the originally designed parent and grandparent BIRDs. (The grandparents are distinguished from the parents by their rounder, more squashed torsos—I guess the effects of gravity work on wooden animals the same way it does on us humans.)

By swiveling their heads in virtually any direction, a BIRD can be made to express almost any conceivable frame of mind, be it happy or sad, curious or nonchalant, alert or asleep. Turning the bodies upward or downward makes them either male or female, lending still more variety to these deceptively simple creations.

Each BIRD is handmade by a small wood-turning company in Denmark using only high quality smoked and natural oak wood. Collect a gaggle all at once or build a collection one at a time.

A child stands about 3 inches high (7.5 cm), a parent 4¾ (12 cm) and a grandparent 4⅜ inches (10.5 cm). All are available in a light Natural Oak and a darker Smoked Oak.

THE CREATIVITY CATALOG

BLANK WALL CLOCK BY MARTÍ GUIXÉ FOR ALESSI
(2010)

It's time to read the writing on the wall. Actually, it's not the wall where you'd be reading the aforementioned writing, it's the face of the Blank Clock by Alessi, which happens to be designed to hang on a wall.

You see, the face of Blank Clock is coated so it can be used as a whiteboard to jot down time-sensitive notes, make doodles, or serve as an empty canvas on which to express your inner artist. When it's time to move on, simply erase your handiwork and do something else. You'll never feel guilty for writing on the furniture again.

Blank Clock comes with a black marker; you can also use colored markers if it's polychrome you're after.

The diameter of the battery-powered clock is 15¾ inches (40 cm). And by the way, it also tells time.

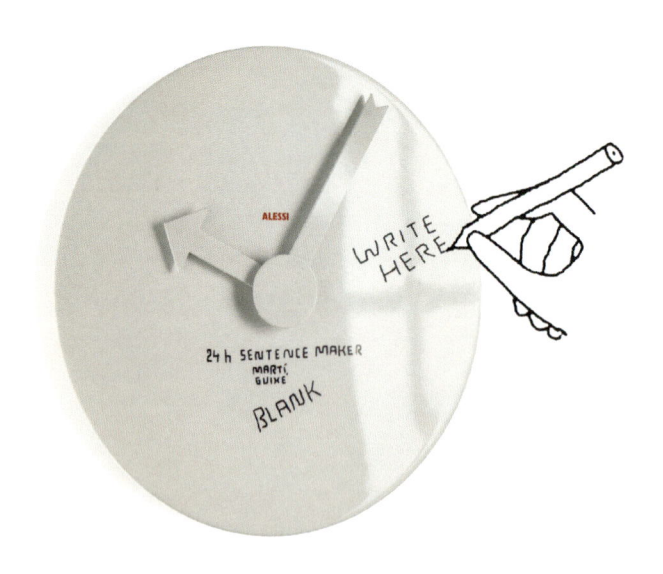

BRICKCASE FOR IPHONE 5 BY SMALLWORKS

Marry the most successful modular design concept of the 20th century with one of the seminal products of the 21st: yes, we're talking about LEGOs and the iPhone (good guess). BrickCase is an iPhone 5 case that turns your phone into a platform for building anything you want out of LEGOs or similar brick systems.

Make a stand for viewing, a handle for grasping, a sculpture for showing off your artistic skills. Create a tabletop adornment, then pull it all apart and build something else. Because you can.

While you're having all this fun, the tough, high impact ABS BrickCase is providing added protection for your phone against bumps, scratches, chips, and dirt. You still have access to all your needed buttons and features, including camera and flash. BrickCase can even improve your cellular antenna reception and reduce dropped calls. Yes, it's that's cool—and functional too.

Single-piece construction. Available in lots of colors.

Discover these items at thecreativehome.com

HOUSEWARES AND DECOR

CANDLESTICKMAKER BY RON GILAD FOR DESIGNFENZIDER

Designer Ron Gilad likes to do only half his job. He wants you to do the other half.

Take his CandlestickMaker. He's designed a lovely porcelain base on which to set a nicely sized candle. Only thing is, the base is purposefully designed so it can't sit on a flat surface. That's where you come in.

You place the porcelain element on some kind of vessel, be it a glass, or vase, or other object that you select, on which the CandlestickMaker can rest.

That makes you a partner of the designer, a collaborator in the creative process. Co-creative, interactive, reconfigurable, customizable, unpredictable design—it's why we admire Ron Gilad.

The base measures 4 inches (10 cm) in diameter and 3 inches (7.5 cm) high. Candles not included.

CELLA BY PEER CLAHSEN FOR NAEF (1979)

Play cubic hide-and-seek with this approximately 4 inch (10 cm) maple wood cube designed by Peer Clahsen. Nestled inside the outer cube is . . . another cube, then another cube . . . then another—well, you get the idea. Cella can be said to symbolize the journey from the material to the spiritual world, just as people in ancient cultures could only reach the divinity by penetrating the innermost sacred chamber of the temple. Nine half-cube shells in Cella create a mind-bending game of spatial exploration with endless permutations.
Available in Blue, Gray, Maple, and Red.

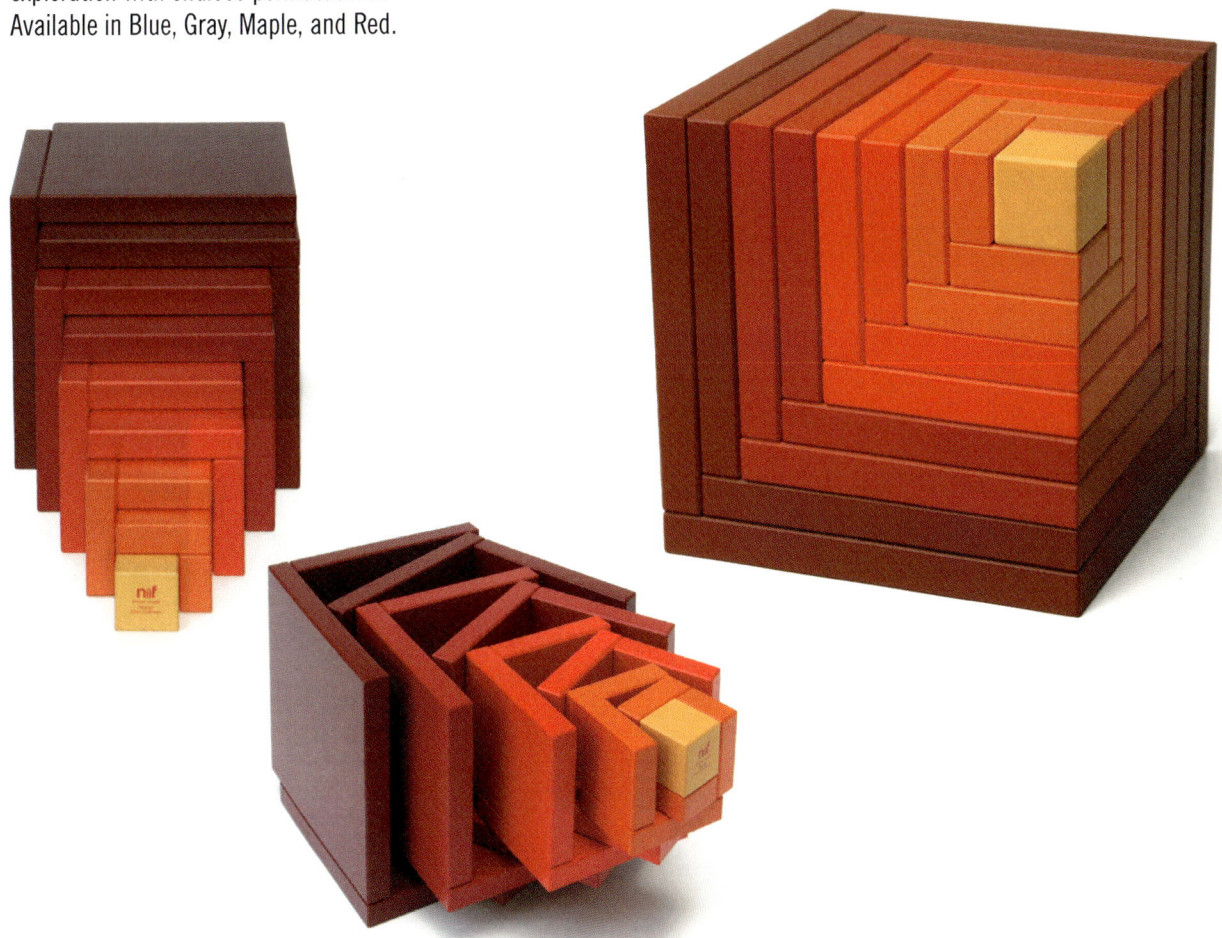

17

THE CREATIVITY CATALOG

THE CHAIRS GAME BY PICO PAO FOR MOMA (2010)

Designing a chair is no game, but stacking a bunch of miniature ones to make a sculpture out of them can be! The Las Sillas Stacking Chairs Game challenges your sense of equilibrium and visual acumen as you pile one cardboard chair on another. Put them up, take them down, start again. Those stacking chairs in the auditorium were never nearly as much fun.

Each set comes with one assembled chair and pieces to assemble fourteen more, plus a sheet showing sample configurations. Combine sets for even more grandiose constructions. Up to ninety-nine people can play with The Chairs Game at once. The box measures 9¼ by 7 by 17¾ inches (23.5 by 17.5 by 45 cm).

Discover these items at thecreativehome.com

HOUSEWARES AND DECOR

CHALKBOARD CLOCKS BY ENRICO AZZIMONTI FOR DIAMANTINI & DOMENICONI

Tabla is a wall or shelf clock that brings you something old and something new. What's new is its modern design qualities—a sleek clock face, rounded corners, and exposed birch ply construction. What's old is the chalkboard surface for doodling away on with the real chalk pieces and eraser that come with the clock.

A neat hidden drawer slides out from the sides to store supplies when not in use.

In case Tabla is a little larger than what you were looking for, take a gander at its smaller cousin, Tablita. Tablita is a charmingly cute chalkboard clock that can be mounted on a wall with a hook, or attached to a fridge or other metal surface by means of magnets. The clock has a recessed shelf to store a piece of chalk and comes with a magnetic felt pad for erasing.

Time to get a chalkboard clock.

Tablita measures about 7 by 13 by 1 inches (18 by 33 by 2.5 cm). Tabla stands a proud 18½ inches square (47 cm^2) and is about 4 inches deep (10 cm).

Designed in Italy by Enrico Azzimonti for Diamantini & Domeniconi, a specialized manufacturer of classically modern clocks.

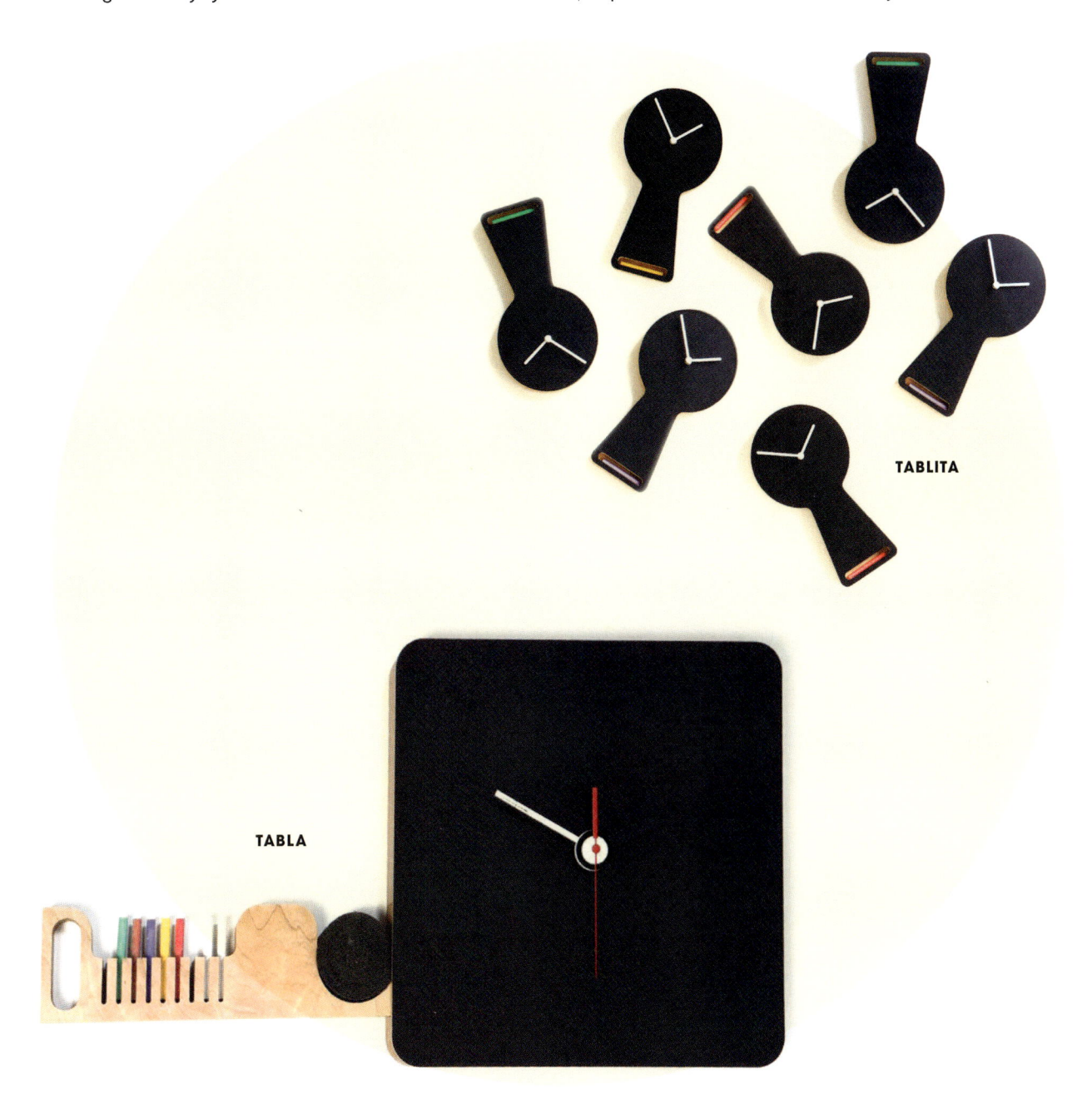

TABLITA

TABLA

THE CREATIVITY CATALOG

CHALKBOARD VASE BY RICARDO SAINT-CLAIR FOR MOMA (2005)

Designer Ricardo Saint-Clair likes to create pieces that foster communication and interaction (bingo!). His playful Chalkboard Vase features a chalkboard front that can be used for drawings, messages, and doodles of all kinds.

But wait! That's not all. The top of the bud vase houses a removable glass tube designed to hold water and flowers. A small hole on the side of the vase holds the chalk that comes with the vase.

Chalkboard Vase was included in the 2012 show *Destination: Brazil*, a MoMA exhibit highlighting lifestyle products from Brazil.

Measures 8 by 8 by 1½ inches (20.3 by 20.3 by 3.8 cm). Optional mounting hardware included.

CORNICHES BY RONAN AND ERWAN BOUROULLEC FOR VITRA (2012)

Not only is Vitra's Corniche Shelving System a unique design, it also has a unique inspiration. Says designer Ronan Bouroullec: "The same way that we hang our belongings on a rock jutting from a cliff before diving into the sea, we need small, informal storage in everyday life too." Now, we don't know about you, but we're not diving off of cliffs on a routine basis, yet we can certainly relate to the need for places we can quickly drop items on, as well as a shelf display that's not the usual straight slab.

And this is the reason that Corniches were shaped by the famed Bouroullec Brothers as individual, isolated protrusions in space. Whether as a key rack beside the front door, a spot to put everything we need to have at our fingertips in the bathroom, a pedestal for a small collection of objects, or a broad wall display, Corniches are a new way to enhance the walls we live within.

Corniches hang by a hidden support system that can hold any size shelf, which means you can effortlessly swap them around when the mood strikes without remounting. Holds up to 44 lbs per shelf (20 kg). Hardware included.

Dimensions from 8¼ to 18 inches long (21 to 45.7 cm) by 5¾ to 8½ inches deep (14.6 to 21.6 cm).

Sold individually. Available in Black, Japanese Red, and White.

Discover these items at thecreativehome.com

HOUSEWARES AND DECOR

CRYSTAL LED LIGHT BY QISDESIGN (2009)

The hexagon assumes three-dimensional and luminous form in this unique reconfigurable LED lighting element by QisDesign. Thanks to the low-heat qualities of LED lighting, you can arrange the eight hex crystals by hand in a nearly infinite array of configurations using their magnetic points of connection. Then add still another layer of variability by altering the color and lighting effects of the crystals with the included remote control. Light, form, and imagination intertwine in a pure play of creativity. Perfect for tabletop, shelf, and niche display—anywhere you want the eye to be engaged.

Combine multiple light sets and you can make an even larger crystal palace. Winner of a Red Dot Design Award.

Unit dimensions are 2⅞ inches across each direction (7.3 cm). Made of polycarbonate with RGB LEDs.

THE CREATIVITY CATALOG

CUBEBOTS BY DAVID WEEKS FOR AREAWARE (2010)

Robot toys are usually made of plastic and require batteries—but not the Cubebot family! Inspired by the Japanese Shinto Kumi-ki puzzles, the Cubebot is a nontraditional take on the toy robot achieved by fusing ancient Japanese traditions with contemporary toy culture.

Cubebot's powerful hardwood frame can hold many poses, and his elastic-band muscles and durable wood limbs make him impervious to breakage. When it's time for him to rest, he folds into a perfect cube. Cubebot combines problem-solving and spatial-reasoning tasks (returning him to cubic form) with action and pretend play (altering his poses and imagining him as an animate figure).

The original Cubebot is marked by his purely cubic head and classic proportions. His sibling, Cubebot Guthrie, has a trapezoidal head and more faceted limbs. Third mate Cubebot Julien is the one with the peaked top and extra-long legs. These bots measure 6¾ inches high (17.1 cm) in a small version, and up to 9½ inches high (24.1 cm) in a medium one.

Bracketing Brothers Bot are the Micro Cubebots, comfortably lilliputian at 4¼ (10.7 cm) high, and XL Cubebot, topping off at a gargantuan 23 inches tall (58.4 cm), with a fully extended wingspan of 31 inches (78.7 cm). XL is so special, each version of this limited edition item is hand-signed by Brooklyn-based designer David Weeks.

Made from sustainably harvested cherrywood. Some sizes are available in colors, all come in Natural. Recommended for children and grown-up humans ages three and up—and up and up. An enduring classic that will withstand generations of play.

GUTHRIE (BACK), JULIEN (MIDDLE), ORIGINAL (FRONT).

XL: SIGNED LIMITED EDITION

FAMILY PORTRAITS

MICRO

Discover these items at thecreativehome.com

HOUSEWARES AND DECOR

CUBICUS BY PEER CLAHSEN FOR NAEF (1968)

An infinite number of cubic constructions can be generated from the approximately 4-inch-square cube (10 cm^2) that subdivides into ten equally sized cube components. The parts fit exactly on and into each other, making an unlimited number of imaginative combinations possible. Suitable for adults and children who may one day grow up to be adults.

Available in Blue, Gray, Maple, and Red.

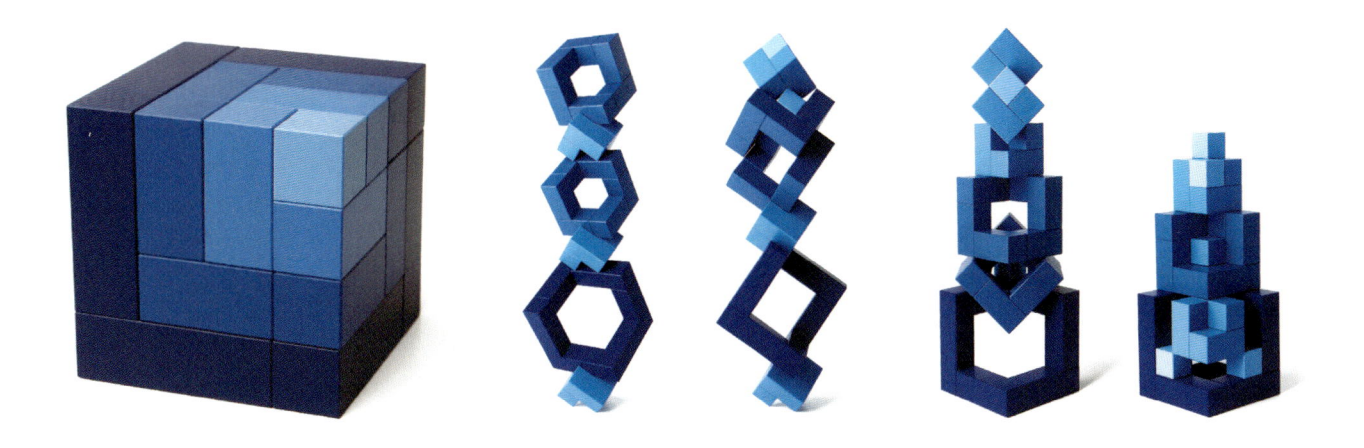

DESKTRUCTURE DESKTOP ORGANIZER BY HÉCTOR SERRANO FOR SELETTI (2012)

Raise your hand if you've ever stored your desk stuff in a coffee mug you got for free. Okay, how about if you use a mishmash of mixed up containers on your desk, or know someone who does? Enough said. Now's the time to turn your desk from mess to best in show with the Desktructure desktop organizer.

This charming collection of porcelain containers is shaped to look like a postindustrial urban neighborhood of warehouses and factories, along with a high-rise condo or two. Line them up for a neat streetscape, or scatter them around as need dictates. Either way you've got a great way to organize your stuff in a classy and durable accessory. It's architecture for the desk!

Aligned Deskstructure measures 13 by 2⅝ by 4⅜ inches (33 by 6.5 by 11 cm).

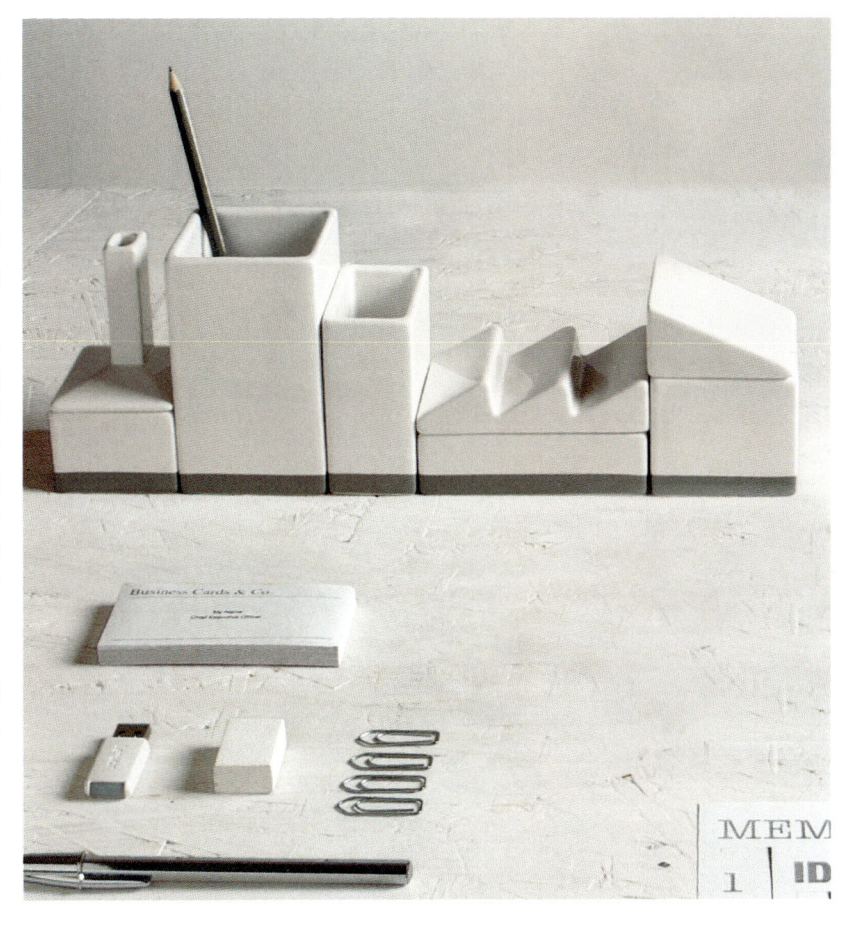

THE CREATIVITY CATALOG

DIAMANT BY PEER CLAHSEN FOR NAEF (1981)

This design by Peer Clahsen is a veritable diamond among play objects. An octahedron which can be disassembled into fifteen pieces that fit perfectly together, the pieces can then be recombined to form ever new geometric variations and fascinating constructions. A shape-making game which appeals to every age group and is as varied as the cut facets of the precious stone for which it is named.

Available in Blue, Gray, Maple, and Walnut.

The dimensions of the piece when assembled in its pure diamond form are approximately 5 by 5 inches by 7 inches (12.5 by 12.5 by 18 cm).

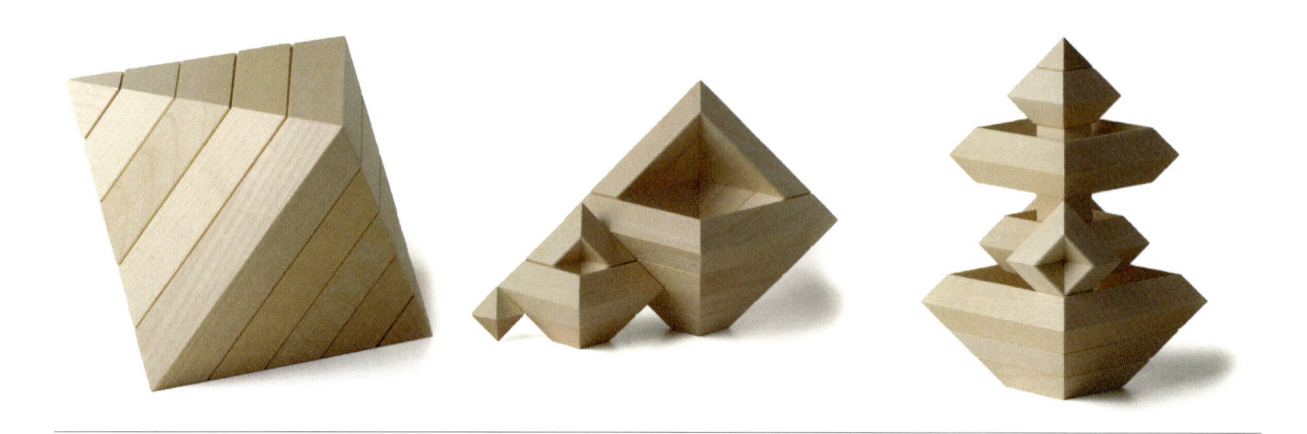

DIY 419 MOBILE BY RYUSAKU KAWASHIMA FOR FLENSTED

Designer Ryusaku Kawashima had a brilliant idea: transform the concept of the mobile into a DIY exercise by letting the user determine the content. Result: the DIY 419 Mobile. Using the brightly colored clips at the ends of the stainless steel suspension wires, you can attach all sorts of things, from fine art cards to family photographs to crafts. Then watch them turn in never ending combinations. Suitable for kids and grown-ups alike.

Available in a 4-piece and 7-piece design.

Discover these items at thecreativehome.com

HOUSEWARES AND DECOR

DIY ART WALLPAPER BY TEMPAPER

Did you or your kids ever think of being a modern Michelangelo by creating artwork on a wall? Of course not, because your spouse would do harm to you (and you'd scold your kids) if anyone tried. Well, put down the battle-axe, because help has arrived in the form of Tempaper DIY Art Wallpaper. It's a peel-and-stick wall covering that comes blank and ready to take paint, crayon, pencil, marker, pastel, and just about anything else you can throw at it.

Tempaper is as easy to install as it is to uninstall. Just remove the backing along the top edge and roll it down your wall, pressing with your hands to smooth it out as it sticks. No glues, pastes, water, or brushes are needed, and yet it will stay put until you're ready to move on. To take it off just pull from a corner and let 'er rip.

Since it's self-adhesive, you can use the paper not only on walls, but on any smooth surfaces in good condition, such as doors, cabinet faces, ceilings, and paneling. For best results, surfaces should be primed or painted with an eggshell or satin finish; the paper is not recommended for applying to matte or flat finishes.

Tempaper is made in America and sold in a roll 20½ inches wide by 33 feet long (52.1 by 1006 cm) for a total of 56.37 square feet (5.2 m^2).

THE DOTS COAT HOOKS BY TVEIT & TORNØE FOR MUUTO

Muuto's The Dots are hooks with looks. Actually, they're a family of circular hooks that come in several colors and Small, Medium and Large sizes to give you maximum flexibility in form and function. Place the hooks wherever and in whatever assortment of sizes and colors you like. Their attractive hues and visible wood grain make them aesthetically appealing as well as useful, and their composition an opportunity for creative composition.

Design firm Tveit & Tornøe had this to say about their creation: "This characterful little family of hooks is a friendly addition to any wall. The Dots are proud of their round edges and will treat your clothes with the greatest care. They will also let you arrange them on your wall in the pattern you like. Being a very social set of hooks, The Dots love to welcome other Dots to join them on the wall. The only thing The Dots demand from you is that you uncover them every now and then and admire their shape and material."

Each size dot is about 2½ inches (6.2 cm) deep. Diameter of the Small Dot is 3½ inches (8.8 cm), Medium is 5 inches (12.7 cm), and Large is 6¾ inches (17.1 cm).

THE CREATIVITY CATALOG

DOVETAIL WOOD ANIMALS BY KARL ZAHN FOR AREAWARE (2012)

Imagine a fantasy zoo of wooden animal toys whose body parts were designed to be freely detached and exchanged with each other. Wouldn't that be fun? Well, thank you, Karl Zahn and Areaware for making this dream a reality!

The Dovetail Collection of reconfigurable animal figures comes in alligator, alpaca, and horse. Oh, and a pile of crocodile parts. Choose a favorite animal, or for even more creative delight collect two or three or more to mix and match. Kids and fun-loving adults will get a kick out of assembling new creatures such as an ele-gator, alli-hor-paca, or other funny fantasy concoctions made by putting the movable parts together in different and unexpected ways.

Dovetail's bestiary is made from solid beech wood, and finished with natural tung oil. So no major tummy ache if you or your child happens to teethe on it a bit.

Animals run from about 5 to 7½ inches long (12.7 to 19 cm). Not for children under six.

CROC PILE

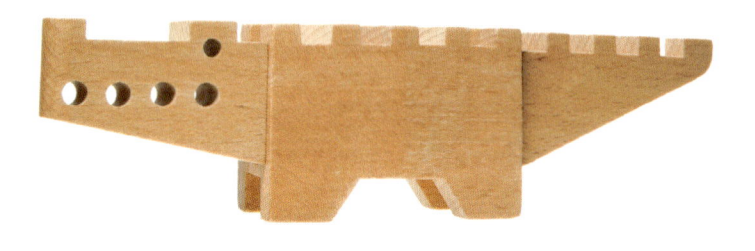

ALLIGATOR

ALPACA

HORSE

Discover these items at thecreativehome.com

HOUSEWARES AND DECOR

ELIOT MODULAR PLANTERS BY ANDREW AND RICHARD ERDLE FOR GOOD ERDLE

Andrew and Richard Erdle, a father-and-son duo, teamed up to create a modular planter system that's perfect for the urban and interior gardener. Being gardeners ourselves, we find the Eliot's rounded triangular shape, protruding feet, and matte white stoneware clay to be more at home, so to speak, in the context of a built environment than the traditional terra-cotta pots we commonly use outdoors.

We also like that we can use the planters individually as accent pieces or, better yet, grouped in clusters to form a sinuous line or figure of greenery.

Modular means mobility. Move your Eliots around to track the sun or season, place them on sills or counters as space becomes available, or shift them whenever you feel like refreshing your decor. And as your garden grows just add more units to grow with it.

There are no drainage holes, so you never have to worry about water leaking out or rings forming on the furniture. Fill the bottom with sand, stones, or charcoal to absorb moisture. Ideal for succulents and other plants that don't require regular watering.

Handmade in America. Dimensions are 5 by 6 by 7½ inches (12.7 by 15.2 by 19 cm).

EQUILIQUE ACROBATS BY JOHN PERRY

Sculptor John Perry was playing around with some rare-earth magnets one day and, experiencing one of those creative sparks that creative people sometimes get, suddenly had an idea about how to apply them to figures of people. He soon began to sculpt a series of acrobatic figures in which he embedded the magnets and, lo and behold, discovered that they could be stood one upon the other in amazing ways.

Thus was born Equilique, a unique interactive art piece for adults that's equally appealing to young people with a penchant for creative play. Each set includes three performers, a base plate, a ball, prop, and hoop. The pieces can be configured in a nearly infinite array of different positions and still retain their balance, much the way real circus acts can do. Except these never have to come down for lunch!

Combine acrobats from multiple sets to form even bigger sculptures. Figures are made from durable ABS, the spiral and hoop from super-strong polycarbonate. Figures are approximately 5 inches tall (12.7 cm).

FLARE TABLE BY MARCEL WANDERS AND JAVIER MARISCAL FOR MAGIS (2003)

Get a leg up on your neighbors by being the first to have a table that can be continually customized. It's all thanks to designer Marcel Wanders, who came up with the idea of making detachable table legs out of injection-molded polycarbonate so they can be both transparent and hollow, and still hold up the table. Marcel then teamed up with co-designer Javier Mariscal to create eight patterns which they had printed on plastic-coated art paper that could slip easily into the hollow legs with the print side facing out.

That gives you the choice of what you want your table to look like. But the opportunity for creativity doesn't stop there: for those of you who can wield a crayon or brush they provided blank sheets of paper on which to exercise your talents—or the talents of people you can cajole into service.

But why stop there? In truth you can fill the legs with pretty much anything that doesn't require feeding. Coins? Confetti? "Popcorn" packing material? Old campaign buttons? The possibilities are intriguing.

The tabletop is made of MDF with a white polymeric cover, and is available in square and rectangular shapes. Each Flare table comes with a set of Stripe design inserts for the legs; other inserts are purchased separately.

The sides of the Square top are 31½ inches long (80 cm), while the Rectangular top measures 31½ by 63 inches (80 by 160 cm). Legs stand 27¾ inches high (70.5 cm).

Discover these items at thecreativehome.com

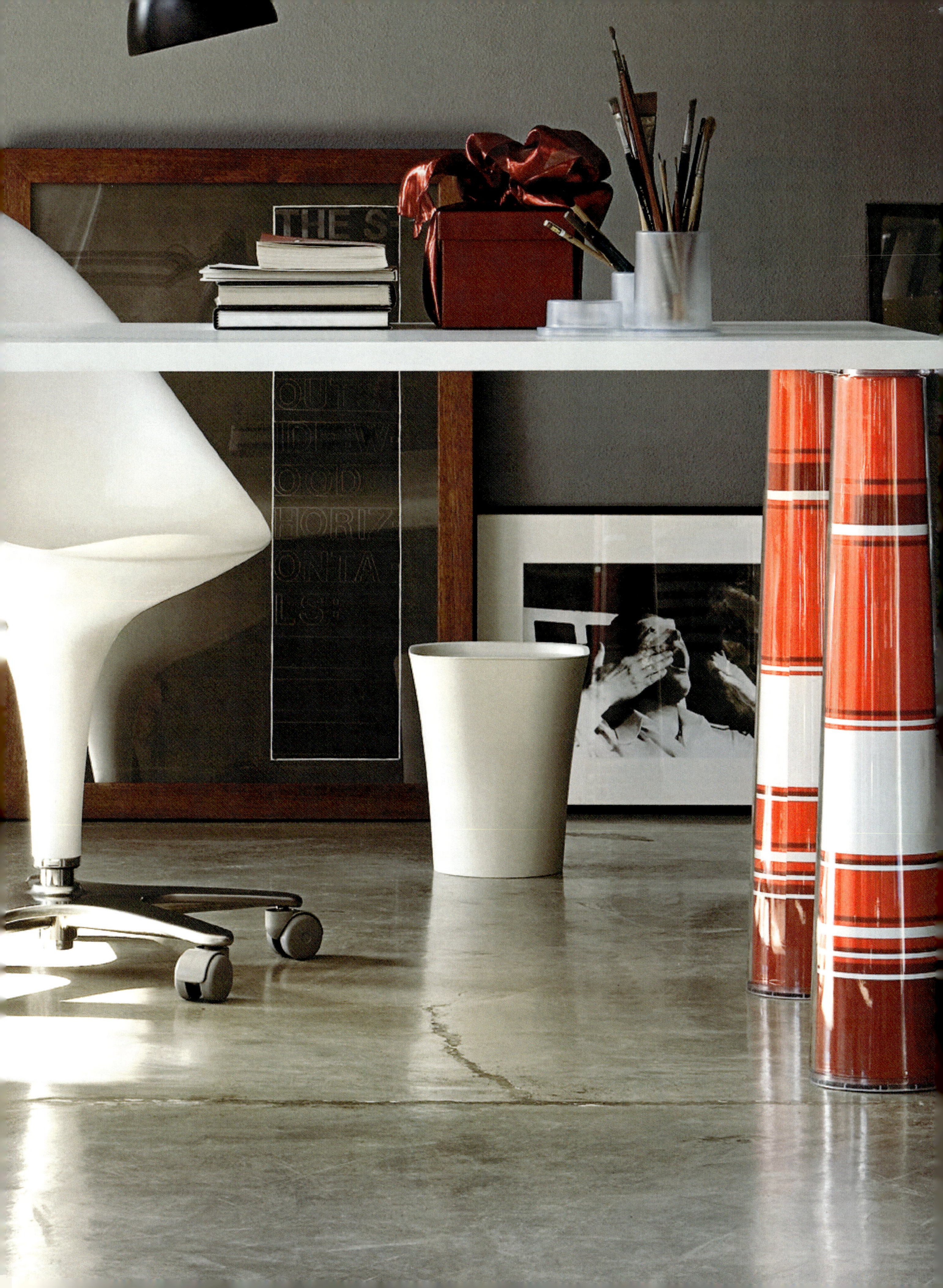
THE S

FLEXUS MENORAH BY HERBERT AND JEANNE ATKIN (1995)

The Jewish holiday of Hanukkah can be traced to 164 BCE, when Jews recaptured and reconsecrated the Temple in Jerusalem after years of occupation by Syrian forces. Today the holiday is commonly celebrated by the lighting of candles on eight successive nights. The candles are placed in a specially designed candle holder, called a menorah. In bringing forth light and warmth during the darkest times of year, the candles can be said to represent for Jews everywhere the triumph of freedom over oppression. The theme of freedom is subtly evoked in the Flexus Menorah, designed by Herbert and Jeanne Atkin. Unlike traditional menorahs, Flexus lets you or your children determine where to position the candles, each held in its own glass pedestal.

With its clean lines and elegant transparency, you can use Flexus as a reconfigurable candelabra troughout the year.

The *shamash*, or principal candleholder, measures 1 by 1 by 3 inches (2.5 by 2.5 by 7.6 cm). Standard candleholders are 1½ inches high (3.75 cm). Candles not included.

FLOWER LOOP BY BLACK+BLUM (2009)

An elegant yet minimal flower vase made from free-flowing steel with a polished chrome finish. The form looks appealingly simple and unique from every angle. Loop can be used individually or looped in with other vases to create a vine-like interwoven cluster. Like its cousin, the Loop Candleholder, Flower Loop's sinuous interconnecting base design was inspired by a very special spiral found inside the Golden Rectangle, which is a shape many believe to be at the root of well-proportioned design in nature as well as man-made objects.

A removable water tube makes refilling easy. To start things off, each package includes one holder and a high quality artificial calla lily, whose slender proportions work beautifully with London-based Black+Blum's design. Dimensions are 5½ by 5½ by 11½ inches (14 by 14 by 29 cm).

GARLAND LIGHT BY TORD BOONTJE FOR ARTECNICA (2004)

Made from a continuous metal strand designed to wrap around a lightbulb, the configurable Garland Light mesmerizes with its delicately etched floral patterns, shimmering surfaces, and complex silhouette. With a simple clip, the Garland shade secures to the base of a hanging bulb and is ready for you to mold. Intertwine multiple Garlands to create larger shades.

You can hang the shade on a pendant bulb, or purchase it with a plug-in light cord for a ready-to-hang configurable fixture.

Garland is included in the permanent collection of MoMA and the Victoria and Albert Museum in London. Available in Silver and Brass.

Discover these items at thecreativehome.com

HOUSEWARES AND DECOR

31

THE CREATIVITY CATALOG

GEMINI CANDLEHOLDER BY PETER KARPF (1965), REISSUED BY ARCHITECTMADE

Designer Peter Karpf has been exploring reconfigurable design since he first emerged as a creative force in the 1960s. Shaped in polished stainless steel in the form of a half circle, the Gemini candleholder is deliberately shaped to encourage the user to explore different arrangements when used with other Geminis. The result is an open-ended and versatile design system that yields enormous visual variety with just a single module. The piece is also very beautiful when used alone, as the strong curve of the base creates a lovely visual path from one flame to the other.

The Gemini comes one to a package. Each holder is 4¼ inches wide by 4½ high (11 by 11.5 cm).

ArchitectMade produces elegant Black and White Birgitta candles to fit the Gemini. The candles are ½ inch in diameter by 8⅝ high (1.3 by 22 cm), made of 100% stearin, a natural by-product, and have a burning time of about three hours.

GRAPE WINE RACK BY ROBERT BRONWASSER FOR GOODS (2007)

What better inspiration for a wine rack than a bunch of grapes? Grape is a modular wine rack that can be mounted on a wall, placed on a table top, or sat upon a floor. Interlock multiple units for a growing wine collection in all sorts of appealing configurations.

The rack is made of expanded polypropylene, a 100% nontoxic, recyclable closed-cell foam. Because it's both lightweight and strong, the material is used as a packing material for high-end electronic goods which need maximum protection with minimal added weight during shipping. Reducing shipping weight has the added benefit of lowering the carbon footprint, adding to its environmentally friendly qualifications.

One unit holds twelve bottles and measures 23⅝ by 15¾ by 7 inches (60 by 40 by 17.7 cm). Grape is sized to accommodate Champagne-sized bottles too.

Discover these items at thecreativehome.com

HOUSEWARES AND DECOR

HANGING SCREENS BY RENÉ BARBA AND WERKSDESIGN FOR KOZIOL (2005-2006)

Koziol hanging modular screens let you create customized space dividers to your own specifications. Simply connect the panels using the steel hooks provided, then place them wherever you want in your space. They work equally well as subtle room dividers, decorative wall hangings, or light diffusers in front of windows. Great for presentations, shows, and traveling installations too.

Designs include Silk, which suggests the swirling forms of hanging drapery; Stixx, cut to reveal faceted surfaces that reflect light in multiple directions; and Alice, whose swirling, floral motifs bring a touch of the outdoors inside, all year round. Each pattern comes in a variety of translucent and solid colors. Being modular, the panels are interchangeable, so you can combine multiple hues and styles or work within a more constrained palette.

Made in Germany from injection-molded plastic. Approximate size of each panel is 10½ inches square (26.6 cm^2). Hanging rod not included.

Stixx was designed by René Barba in 2005, while Silk and Alice were developed by Koziol's in-house design team Werksdesign in 2006.

ALICE **SILK** **STIXX**

HANNO THE GORILLA BY DAVID WEEKS FOR AREAWARE (2009)

Hanno was an ancient Greek voyager who is said to have discovered gorillas 2500 years ago. Lucky for us he did, because Brooklyn-based designer David Weeks was able to model this award-winning reconfigurable wooden animal figure after them. Much like its quick and powerful real-life counterpart, the aptly named Hanno the Gorilla can flex into all sorts of poses thanks to its ingenious construction of hardwood blocks and elastic bands.

Made from durable and sustainably harvested new-growth beech, Hanno is built to last for generations, not months like so many disposable objects of play today. An investment in a toy of this nature will return itself many times over, not least because it's suitable for both children and adults as long, as they're three years old and up.

Dimensions of the big gorilla is 12 by 6½ by 3½ inches (30.5 by 16.5 by 8.9 cm), while the smaller though still plenty tough Hanno Jr. stands 8½ by 4½ by 2½ inches (21.6 by 11.4 by 6.4 cm).

THE CREATIVITY CATALOG

HEX TABLE BY INCORPORATED FOR LERIVAL

Hex Table is nearly a textbook example of what makes modularity such a compelling design approach for the modern environment. It's flexible in arrangement and variable in size, sleekly minimal in shape yet lively in the play of light across its reflective surfaces, practical in function, and engagingly interactive.

Use it as a side table, coffee table, seating, pedestal, or sculptural accent—or all of them.

Made of stainless steel in a brushed finish; powder coating is available on request for an additional charge. Height is 16 inches (40.6 cm) and width 13 inches (33 cm).

Discover these items at thecreativehome.com

HOUSEWARES AND DECOR

HONEY LIGHTS BY DANTE DONEGANI AND GIOVANNI LAUDA FOR ROTALIANA (2004)

In the 1930s, the world-famous sculptor Brancusi created a piece called Endless Column, a name which pretty much tells the story behind the work. A series of repetitive and interlocking forms stacked one on top of the other, the sculpture could, theoretically at least, keep rising as high as one had units to stack.

The Rotaliana Honey Light builds on this tradition, but with a twist: rather than use solid modules for stacking units as Brancusi did, the designers Dante Donegani and Giovanni Lauda employed triangular, translucent components to form a honeycomb envelope that's open on the interior. A light fixture is mounted at one end and sends its luminous glow through the casing for a unique faceted visual effect.

Lamps come in three models: H, a fixture that hangs from a ceiling; F, a floor lamp; and T1, a lamp that can be placed on either the floor or a table. Choose from one of the packaged sets for the model and size you want. The nice thing is, as with most modular pieces, it's expandable. Order extra shades if you find yourself in a space with a higher ceiling or just feel like changing proportions. Separate bases are available, too, if you ever want to break up your fixture into multiples.

The piece is literally a snap to put together and requires no tools. Shades are made from injected polycarbonate and are available in Translucent and Black. Fixtures use a standard 150-watt incandescent bulb. The F Floor and T1 Floor/Table Lamps plug into standard U.S. outlets, and the F Lamp comes with a foot dimmer. Shades measure 7¾ inches (19.6 cm) at their narrowest and 6¾ inches (17.1 cm) high.

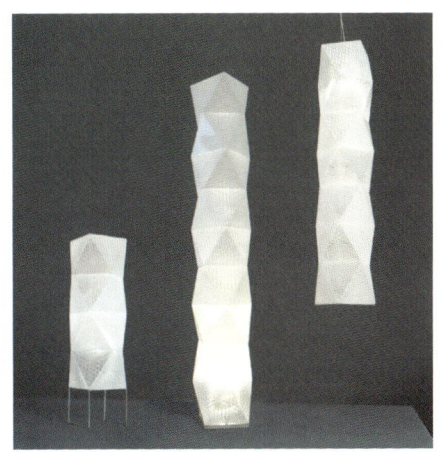

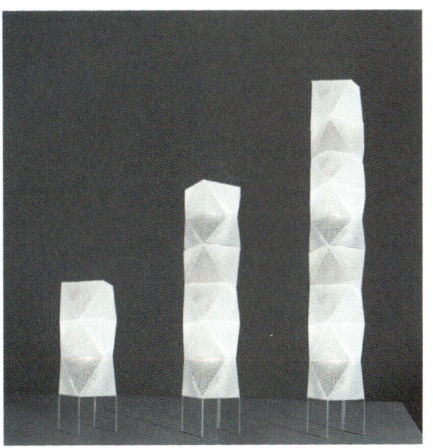

HOUDINI WINE RACK BY ED KILDUFF FOR METROKANE (2003)

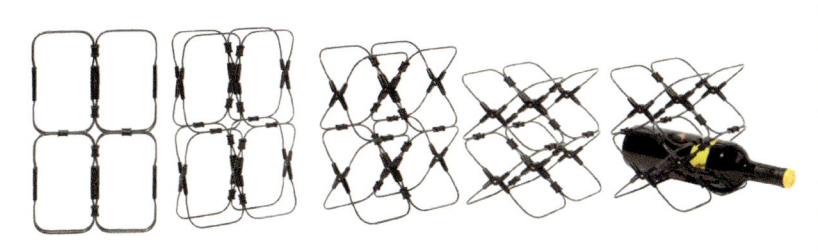

Rack up a wine collection with style! The Houdini modular wine rack is an expandable bottle storage system that can be tailored to fit the size of your space and the size of your collection. Simply connect additional racks horizontally and vertically to expand your holdings. You can just as easily disconnect them when you've been drinking faster than you've been buying.

Thanks to its lightweight, wire-frame design, Houdini will fit almost anywhere. Tabletop, shelf unit, floor—you can even place racks in the fridge for chilling. When not in use, fold them flat for compact storage.

THE CREATIVITY CATALOG

HOUSE OF CARDS BY CHARLES AND RAY EAMES (1952), REISSUED BY EAMES OFFICE

Here's a chance to build a house with one of the greatest American design teams ever: Charles (1907–1978) and Ray (1912–1988) Eames. A house of cards, that is.

Starting in 1952, the celebrated creatives began producing what would eventually be five different sets of cards, each card slotted to interconnect it to the others in the deck. This newly reissued set is the first since 1974, and combines images from the earlier Pattern and Picture decks.

The Eameses described the images on the cards as being of "good stuff," chosen to celebrate "familiar and nostalgic objects from the animal, vegetable, and mineral kingdoms." There are also some vibrant patterns and fabrics from different cultures among them.

Cards come in two sizes. Medium measures a hefty 4½ by 6⅞ inches (11.4 by 2.2 cm); Small is similar to a standard deck of cards, being 2⅝ by 3⅝ inches (6.6 by 9.2 cm).

IDEAPAINT ERASABLE SURFACE COVERING (2008)

It's time to heed the writing on the wall. Or on doors. Or panels. You see, IdeaPaint is a dry-erase paintable covering that can transform just about any smooth surface into an erasable canvas. Use your dry-erase markers to jot down your creative ideas before they disappear forever, communicate with family members or co-workers, teach lessons to students, or give your child a way to scribble and produce artwork on a grand scale without giving you apoplexy.

IdeaPaint is a cost-effective, high-performing, and environmentally responsible alternative to traditional whiteboards. It will suit almost every type of surrounding, from homes and schools to offices and restaurants.

Available in White and in a Clear finish that goes over colored backgrounds. Suitable for most sealed, nonporous surfaces, including stained wood, painted drywall, plastic, metal, aluminum—even chalkboards that have lost their tooth. Comes in a Pro and DIY version.

Go ahead, put some IdeaPaint on, then leave your mark!

Discover these items at thecreativehome.com

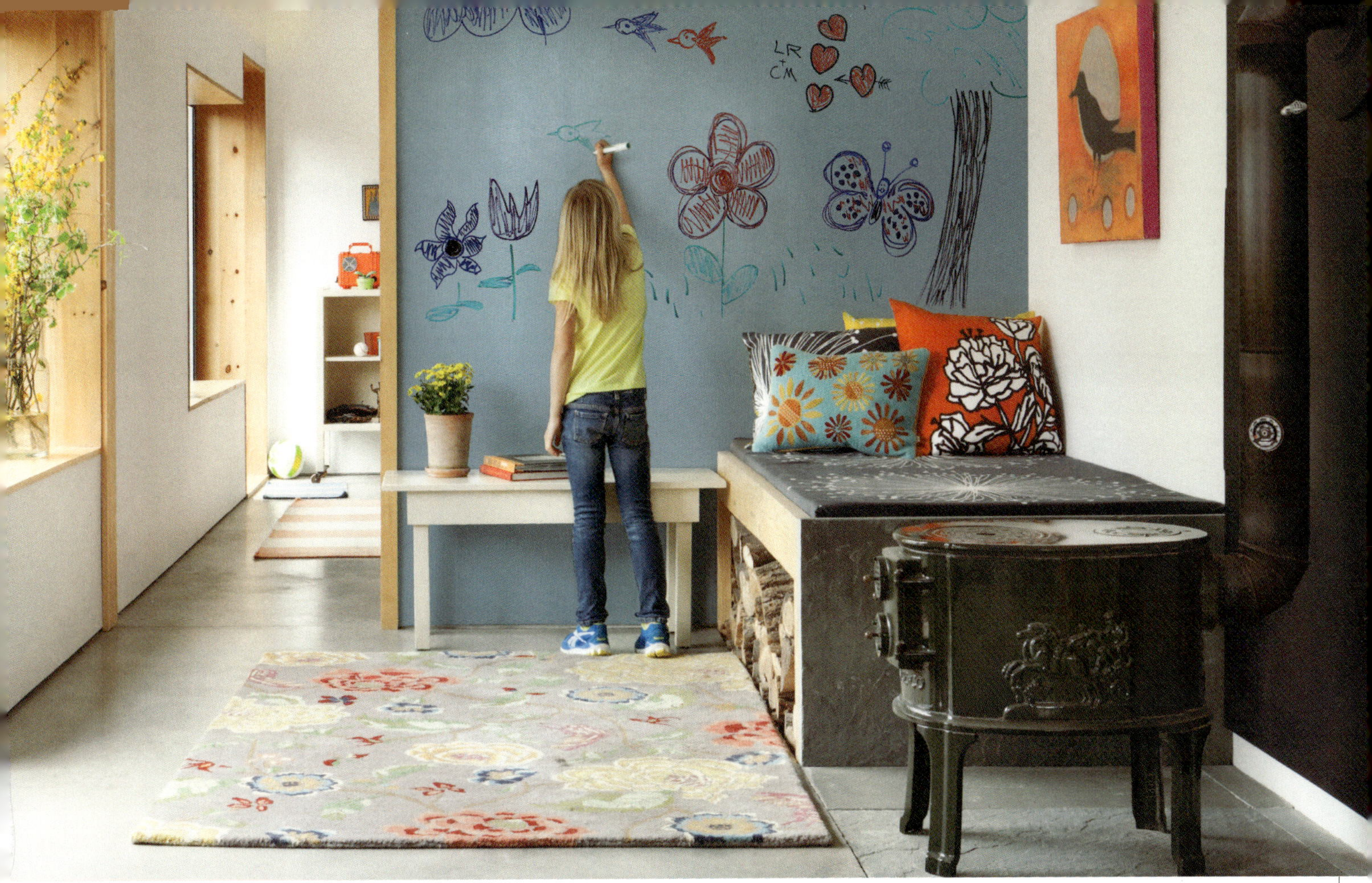

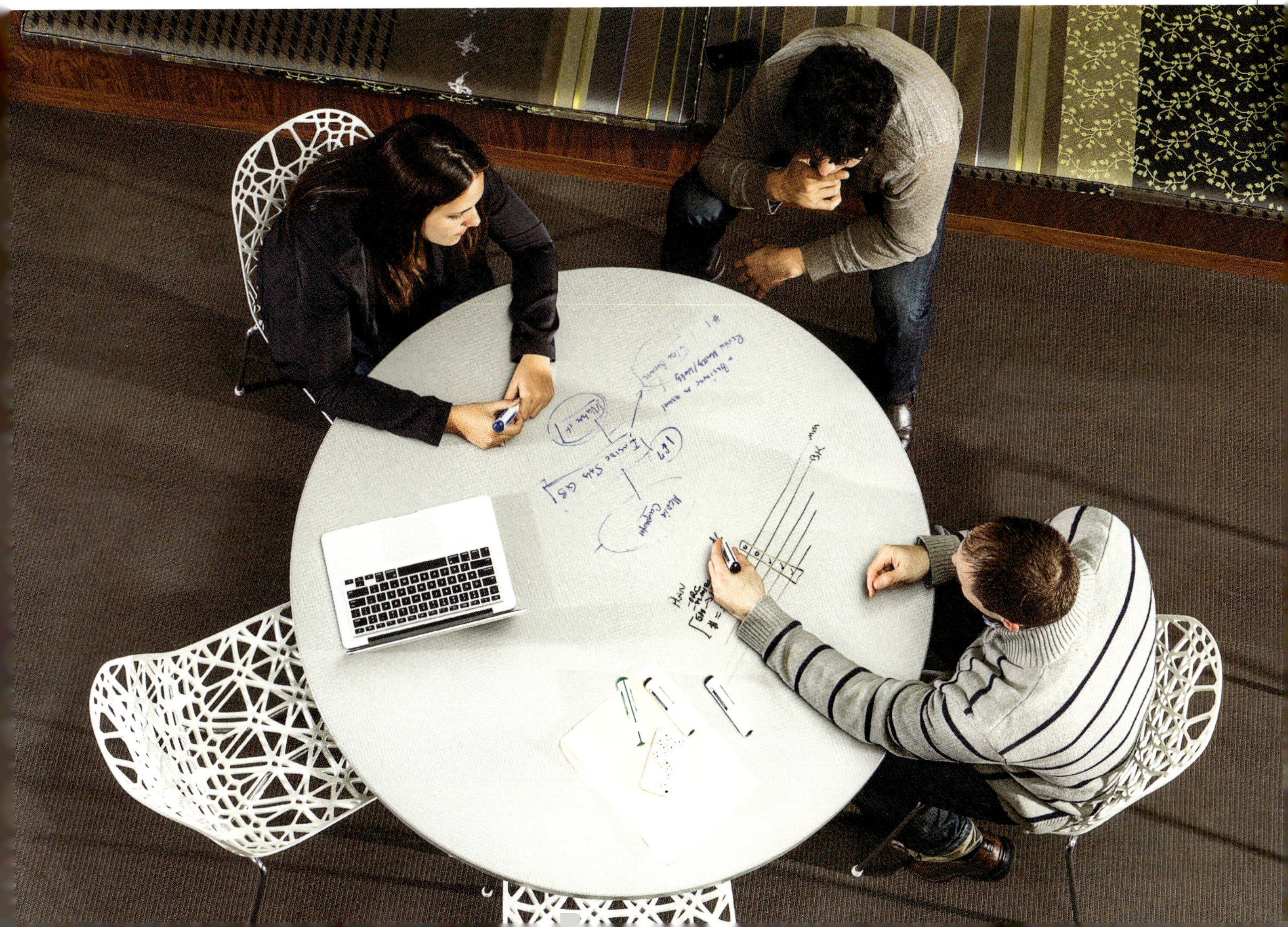

THE CREATIVITY CATALOG

IKAMO BY HEIKO HILLIG FOR NAEF

In an instant, the six balanced and contrasting color motifs animate every single maple wood cube—an incentive to discover one's own creativity. How many patterns can possibly be arranged? Ikamo is a wonderful new variation on the traditional mosaic principle with a unique three-dimensional character.

The dimensions of the cube are approximately 1 inch (2.5 cm) in each direction. A container frame for laying Ikamo on a tabletop surface or displaying it on an easel is included and measures 6¾ inches square by 1¼ inches (17 cm^2 by 3 cm) for a 36-piece set.

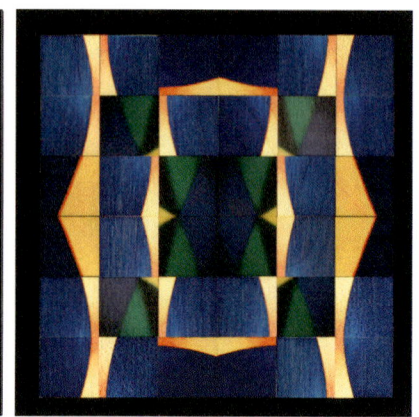

IMAGO BY HEIKO HILLIG FOR NAEF

Be your own Vasarely—or Sol LeWitt or Ellsworth Kelly (in gray tones)—by manipulating thirty-six beautifully finished cubes set in an attractive display frame. Call it the Mosaic Principle: six different graphic patterns on each maple cube allow you to create billions of pictures simply by rotating them—more if you have the urge! The resulting piece is so emphatically a work of art (well, billions of works) that the Imago comes with an attractive black frame for hanging your piece on a wall or laying it on a tabletop for display.

The dimensions of the cube are approximately 1 inch (2.5 cm) in each direction and the display frame measures 10⅝ inches square by 1 inch (27 cm^2 by 2.5 cm). The frame can be mounted on a wall, placed on an easel or laid flat on a tabletop for display.

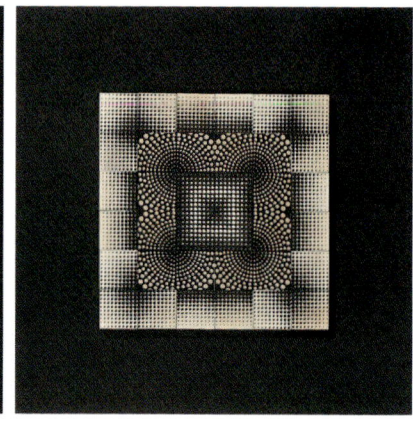

Discover these items at thecreativehome.com

HOUSEWARES AND DECOR

INFINITE TREE BY JOHANNES MOLIN FOR AREAWARE (2013)

Scandinavian designer Johannes Molin merges math, nature, and personal genealogy in his interactive tabletop accessory Infinite Tree. The math? Each wood "leaf" has the proportions of the Golden Ratio, a measure thought to drive our ideas of classic beauty. Nature? That refers to the piece's tapered silhouette and center pole suggestive of an evergreen tree. Genealogy? Evergreen trees are ubiquitous among the forests of his native Scandinavia.

Mix these ingredients together and you get a delightful tabletop accessory formed from wood slabs that can be rotated 360 degrees around the pole. Swivel them one way and you get a twisted helix shape; push them another way and you get a pure pyramid. Push them again and you get . . . anything you want!

Great for the holidays, but versatile enough to look good on display all year round.

Infinite Tree is made from sustainable beech wood (it's only natural). Measures 17 by 9¼ by 4¼ inches (43.1 by 23.4 by 10.7 cm).

INFINITY WINE RACK BY RON ARAD FOR KARTELL (1999)

Infinity is a colorful, curvilinear, modular bottle-holder designed by Ron Arad, a world-famous creative master who works in a wide range of artistic media. The modules easily fasten together to form a collection of rings which hold the bottles; the overall shape of the rack is up to you. It comes in a practical 16-piece package; as you grow your bottle collection you can also extend the rack by the addition of more modules.

Available in opaline colors Blue, Orange, White, and Yellow.

Individual modules measure 1¼ by 3½ by 5¾ inches (3.2 by 8.9 by 14.6 cm). Made in Italy.

THE CREATIVITY CATALOG

INTERCHANGEABLE EARRINGS AND WATCHES BY HUBERT VERSTRAETEN FOR TAMAWA (2010-2011)

EARRING SET

In 1907, a Belgian chemist named Leo Baekeland came up with one of the earliest forms of plastic, which he dubbed Bakelite. By the 1920s this incredibly hard yet initially malleable material had become a favorite in radios, housewares, jewelry and . . . snooker balls.

Fast forward to 2008, when fellow countryman Hubert Verstraeten met with a Belgian snooker ball manufacturer and struck a deal to be supplied with Bakelite spheres he could use to create a line of high quality design products.

Among the first pieces to come out of Hubert's studio was a beautiful collection of earrings, each composed of two Bakelite spheres. Hubert had the brilliant idea of devising the earrings so that one of the spheres was fixed, while the other could be slid off its post and exchanged with a sphere of an alternate color. Thanks to the suite of eight colored spheres in each set, you can customize your earrings every day of the week (and twice on Sunday).

Inspired by his beautiful Bakelite bauble, Hubert went on to design an interchangeable watch made of stainless steel and set into a Bakelite three-quarter sphere, with a classic leather band. Hubert could have left the design at that, but fortunately he implemented one more idea: make the Bakelite ball casing interchangeable, so the wearer can slip it out of one color shell and insert it into another. That means you get to enjoy not one, not two, but eight luscious Bakelite colors for adorning your wrist.

The sets come in beautiful cases suitable for gifting.

WATCH SET

Discover these items at thecreativehome.com

HOUSEWARES AND DECOR

KALEIDO TRAYS BY CLARA VON ZWEIGBERGK FOR HAY (2012)

The hexagon comes home to roost. And nest. And stack. And adjoin in an infinite number of attractive patterns—all in the form of the Kaleido Tray collection, created by Danish designer Clara von Zweigbergk for Danish design house HAY.

These boldly colored, powder coated steel trays come in five different sizes, so you can tailor your tray collection exactly to your needs and tastes. Beyond their functionality, they're also a fun way to exercise your creative powers effortlessly as you arrange them in different ways to suit the moment. Happily, thanks to their interlocking hexagonal design, they will always look good!

Dimensions range from 7½ to 17¾ by 4½ to 15½ inches (19 to 19.7 by 11.4 to 39.3 cm). Purchase trays individually or in a set of seven. Not for use with food.

THE LADDERS GAME BY PICO PAO FOR MOMA (2011)

Be a social climber by playing with ladders. Miniature ladders, we mean. These charming cardboard forms interconnect in surprisingly arresting arrangements, so you can build tabletop sculptures on your own or as a game with friends. See who can build the tallest, the baddest, the handsomest concoction. Then take them down and start again.

The striking box measures 5 by 5½ by 9¾ inches (13 by 14 by 25 cm) and comes with sixteen ladders. Combine sets for even grander installations.

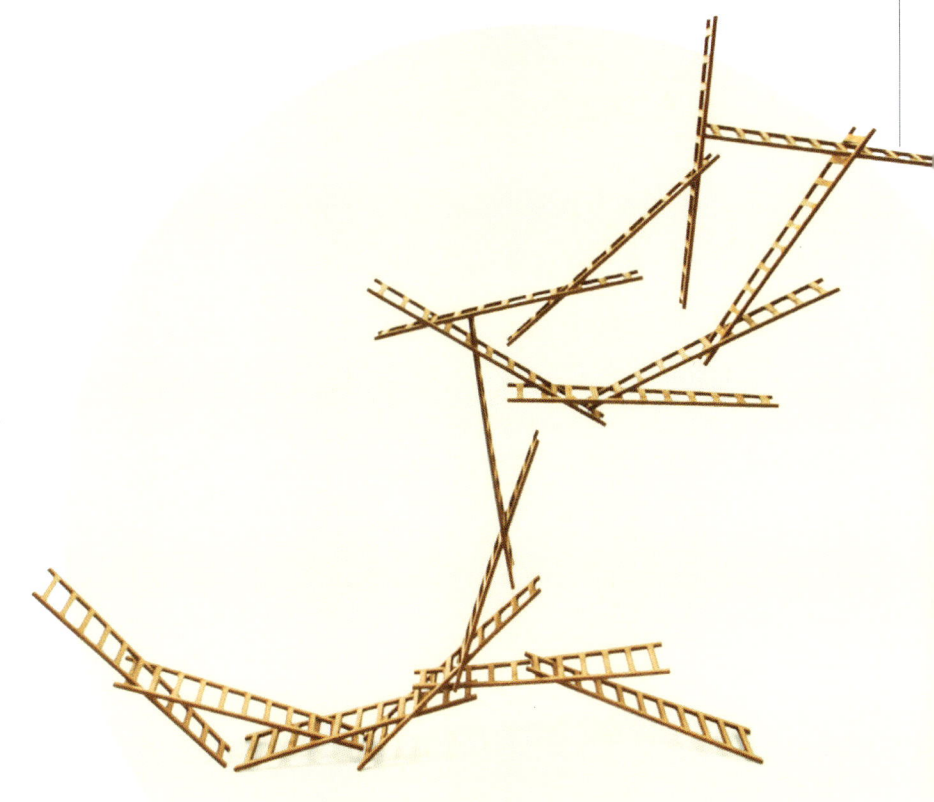

LES PERLES CANDLESTICKS BY F. X. BALLÉRY FOR Y'A PAS LE FEU AU LAC (2010)

It's no coincidence that Les Perles candlesticks are handmade in the Jura Mountain region of France, an area known for its traditional wood toys. Not only are Les Perles candlesticks made from horn wood, but they also incorporate an element of play in being formed by sliding differently shaped wood pieces down a metal stem resting on a lacquered steel base.

Interactive, reconfigurable, fun: Vive Les Perles! Vive la France!

Available in Black, Natural, and Red. Bases are steel. Small sets rise to 10¼ inches high (26 cm), Large to 13 inches (33 cm). The "Extra" in Extra Large refers to the number of candlesticks (three), of which the tallest is a Large.

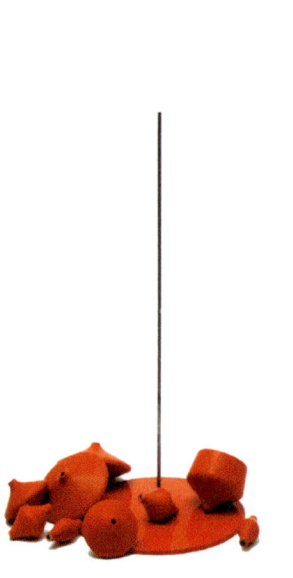

LOOP CANDLEOLDER BY BLACK+BLUM (2006)

A simple yet beautiful candelabra, Loop can be used individually or clustered together by means of its distinctive curvilinear base. The curves of the base were inspired by a very special spiral found inside the Golden Rectangle, which is a shape many believe to be at the root of well-proportioned design in nature as well as man-made objects.

Loop is available in a Black, Satin Chrome, or Polished Chrome finish over steel. One candleholder per box. Dimensions are 8 by 5 by 11 inches (20.3 by 12.7 by 27.9 cm). Candles not included.

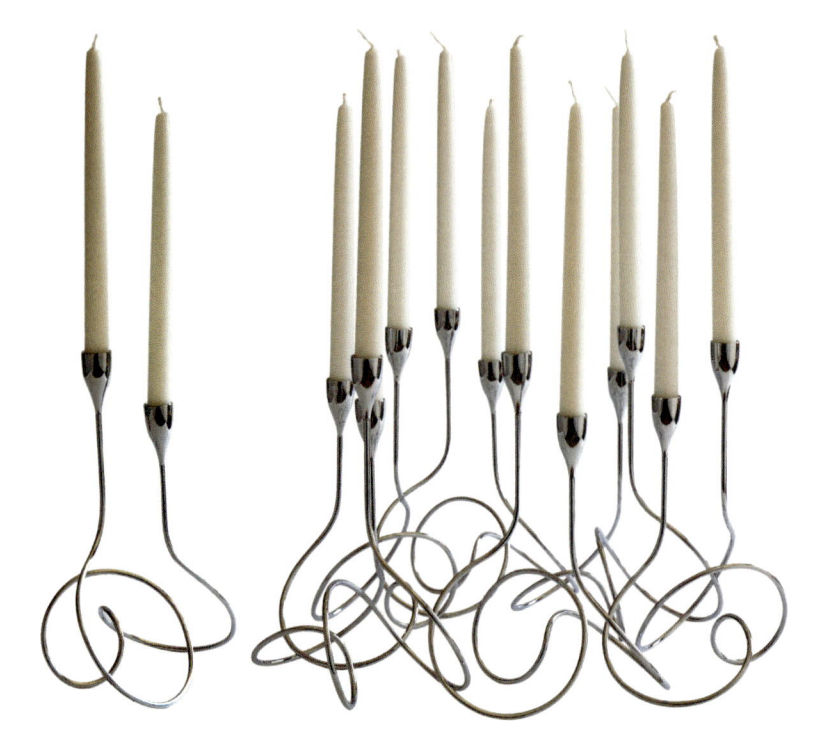

Discover these items at thecreativehome.com

HOUSEWARES AND DECOR

MAGNETIC VASES BY PELEG DESIGN FOR DECOR CRAFT (2005)

This set of slender, stylish brushed aluminum stem vases is the perfect complement for your dinner table. The innovative design, concealing a small magnetic plate beneath a tablecloth, runner, or place mat, provides a magical and playful effect. Configure the vases to suit each table setting. Amaze your guests with your balancing dexterity by making these seemingly precariously perched vases refuse to tip over.

The vases hold water and are suitable for real and artificial flowers.

Five vases and magnetic bases to a package. The dimensions of each vase are ⅝ by ⅝ by 9⅝ inches (1.5 by 1.5 by 24 cm).

MENORAHS BY AGAYOF ART & JUDAICA

Hanukkah is a Jewish holiday celebrating the recapture of the Second Temple after it had been desecrated by foreign invaders. Sometimes called the Festival of Lights, it is commonly observed by lighting eight candles successively over an eight-day period. The candles are placed in a specially designated candelabra called a menorah, which has nine arms. The extra candle—normally positioned just above or below the adjacent candles—is called the *shamash*, and is intended to serve the practical purpose of lighting the others.

Besides the menorah, the joyous nature of the modern incarnation of Hanukkah is borne out in its appeal to children. Songs are sung, games are played, gifts are exchanged, and a customary meal of latkes (potato pancakes) and other thoroughly fattening delicacies is consumed. Tradition being a tradition in Jewish culture, there is even a time-honored toy to play with on the holiday, the dreidel.

How appropriate, then, that somebody would have the

DOMINO

COMBINATION

idea of transforming the menorah—the physical emblem of Hanukkah—into an object of play as well? The Agayof Collection of reconfigurable menorahs does precisely that. Rather than taking the form of a fixed and static piece of cast metal, as most menorahs are, the Agayof designs break down the candelabra into its constituent parts, and then invites the celebrants to find their own joy in making the menorah of their choosing.

Fabricated in the Agayof studio in Jerusalem of lightweight anodized aluminum, which renders the colors permanent and the finish highly durable. Designs come in attractive wood cases or pouches.

THE CREATIVITY CATALOG

DOUGHNUTS

DREIDEL

PUZZLE LILI

WALL

SHEMEN

44

Discover these items at thecreativehome.com

MENORAHS BY LAURA COWAN (2009-2012)

Israeli Judaica designer Laura Cowan brings the traditional Hanukkah menorah into the 21st century. Outfitted with stainless steel bases and colorful magnetic candleholders fashioned out of anodized aluminum, her movable menorahs invite the kind of play and celebration of freedom that has come to be associated with this joyous and child-oriented Jewish holiday.

Slide Magnet and Travel Magnet Menorahs reflect Laura's signature style even as they express contrasting formal directions. Where Slide's base takes the shape of a slender and sinuous linear curve, Travel Menorah's plate is emphatically planar, square, and straight. As its name suggests, Travel is designed to be mobile, coming in a pouch with a see-through test tube and cork for compactly storing your candleholders when the holiday finds you on the road; the elongated proportions of Slide, on the other hand, suggest a piece that would prefer to remain stationary on a shelf, where it could stay on display throughout the year as an attractive ornament to any space.

Speaking of travel, let Laura's Saturn Menorah and Dreidel Set elevate you to new heights of design bliss and holiday enjoyment. The menorah is a circular disk made from stainless steel, on which removable magnetic candle holders can be placed as the holiday progresses. The center of the disk is open and sized to hold the dreidel. Unlike the bodies of most traditional dreidels, which are faceted cubes, this one is round and flat, its ring shape perfectly in harmony with the circular motion it undergoes during play.

Sets come with Aqua, Gold, or Silver dreidels. For younger kids there's also a Smart Dreidel Set, in which the top is suitably made from plastic. Pieces can also be ordered separately.

Saturn Menorah is 5½ inches diameter (13.9 cm), its dreidel 3 inches across (7.6 cm).

All Laura's pieces are signed by the artist and handcrafted by her in Israel.

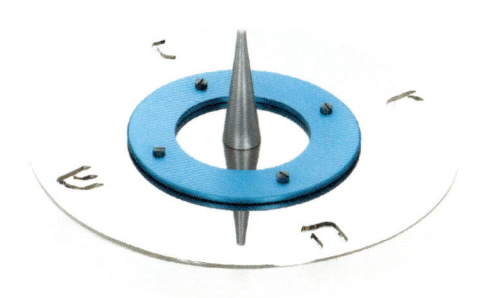

SATURN MENORAH AND DREIDEL SETS

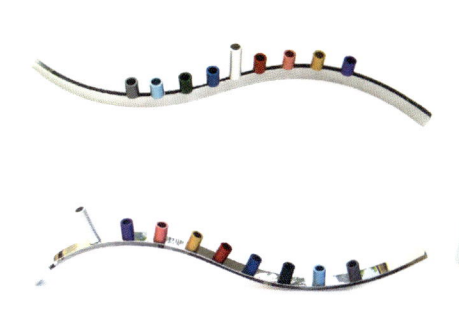

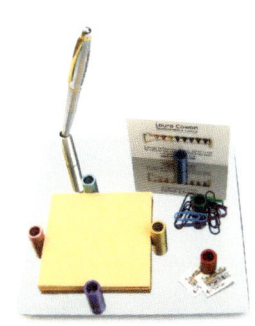

SLIDE MAGNET MENORAH

TRAVEL MAGNET MENORAH

THE CREATIVITY CATALOG

MODULAR MAGNETIC MATZO PLATE BY LAURA COWAN (2012)

If Frank Gehry designed a polished stainless steel matzo plate, it might well have looked like this—had not Israeli Judaica designer Laura Cowan beat him to it. While the wavy silhouette (inspired by views of the Tel Aviv waterfront) echo Mr. Gehry's curvilinear aesthetic, the use of hidden neodymium magnets and movable pieces is all Cowan.

Since the pieces can be placed in any arrangement, you can use the bowl in all sorts of ways—as a matzo plate during the Passover Seder, a base for tea lights during Hanukkah, a fruit bowl, or beautiful tabletop sculpture year round.

Available in an 11 by 11 inch Square (27.9 by 27.9 cm) and a 6 by 10 inch Rectangle (15.2 by 25.4 cm).

All pieces are signed by the designer and made in Israel.

MODULAR SCREEN BY MOORHEAD & MOORHEAD FOR LERIVAL

Inspired in part by camouflage patterns, award-winning architects Moorhead & Moorhead's Modular Screen is a space-defining system of perforated panels. Comprised of four panel configurations rendered in subtly graduated gray tones, the panels overlap each other when connected together to give the screen a distinctive three-dimensional quality unusual among space dividers. The result is a flexible hanging partition in which the layering of individual pieces de-emphasizes its modular nature while still allowing for the unlimited compositional possibilities that modular design provides.

Sets can be added together to form larger assemblies.

Screens are digitally fabricated in durable and cleanable polyethylene. The dimensions of each panel measure approximately 30 by 60 by ¼ inches (76.2 by 152.4 by .6 cm) and, depending on connections, can cover an area of about 4 by 6 feet (1.2 by 1.8 m). Connecting pieces come with the panels; hanging apparatus is not included.

Discover these items at thecreativehome.com

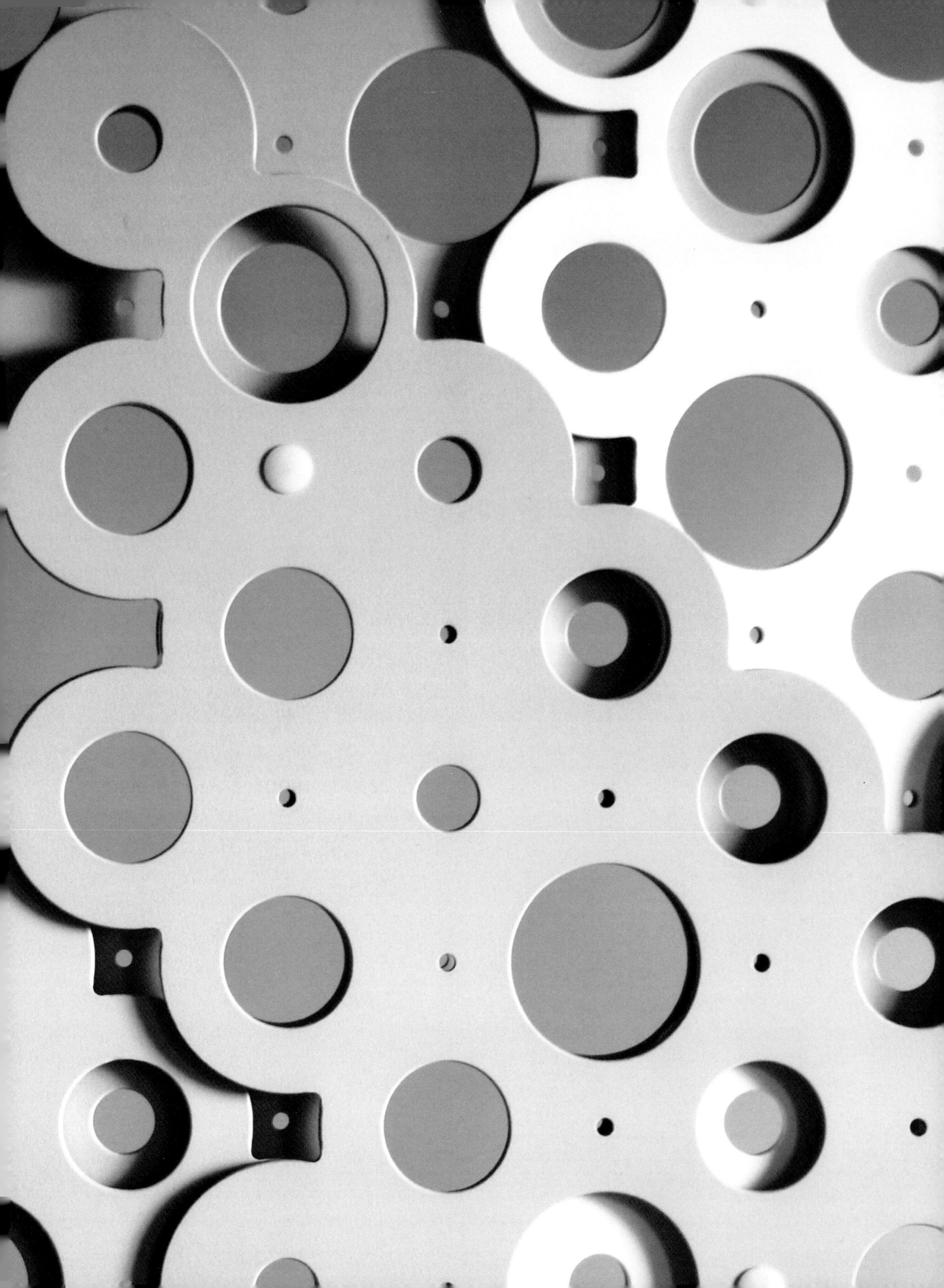

THE CREATIVITY CATALOG

MODULON BY JO NIEMEYER FOR NAEF (1984)

Designer's Jo Niemeyer's 4½ inch (11.5 cm) wood cube is divided into sixteen building bricks on the basis of the Golden Ratio. Thought to have been developed in antiquity, the Golden Ratio is arrived at by dividing a line so that the shorter part of the line has the same relationship to the longer part as the longer part has to the whole. In numeric terms the Golden Ratio is quantified as approximately 0.618.

The ratio exhibits remarkable and unique mathematical properties and has been applied to artistic and architectural production for centuries. Twentieth-century architect Le Corbusier made it the basis for his proportional system Modulor, which he embodied in the figure of the Modular Man. Now you or your precocious offspring can explore similarly creative paths among the limitless number of possible configurations embedded in the beautiful Modulon.

48

MOLECULE BUILDING SET BY FERM LIVING

Teach yourself and your children about the molecular basis of life using this delightful wood toy from Denmark. The Molecule Building Set comes in an attractive wood box making storage easy and suitable for gifting. Each set consists of twenty-four molecules in six colors and a slew of wooden sticks that connect the spheres in infinitely varied configurations—just like nature herself.

Please note that the Molecule Building Set is a decorative object not suitable for children under the age of three, but great for mad scientists in the family older than that.

Discover these items at thecreativehome.com

HOUSEWARES AND DECOR

MONDRI 3-IN-1 VASE BY FRANK KERDIL FOR PO

A vase with style, or should we say, with De Stijl? Clearly inspired by the work of Dutch artist Piet Mondrian (1872–1944), the Mondri 3-in-1 Vase is a three-dimensional evocation of the simple geometries and color palette favored by the modern master. But with a twist—unlike Mondrian's canvases, the vase breaks down into three separate compartments that can be grouped in different ways to suit your setting or tastes, or to accommodate differently sized flower arrangements.

Made of acrylic, Mondri measures 9½ inches wide by 3 deep by 7½ high (24.1 by 7.6 by 19.1 cm) when grouped together. The containers can also be used separately.

MORPHEO CRYSTAL CANDLESTICK BY SELAB FOR SELETTI (2008–2009)

This gorgeous crystal glass candlestick consists of several modular components which can be stacked in different sequences working from the bottom up. Simply slide each piece down the stem in whatever order you fancy to create lively and diverse silhouettes.

The candlestick comes packaged in a stunningly beautiful box, making it a winning gift for people with impeccable taste (that means you!).

Available in Clear Crystal and Multicolor. Candlesticks stand approximately 10 inches (25.4 cm) tall without candle. Candles not included. One candlestick per box.

THE CREATIVITY CATALOG

MOSAIK BY KATHRIN KIENER FOR NAEF (2002)

Three different mosaic cubes form the basis of this firework of colors. As no two surfaces are alike, eighteen distinct colors are visible, six of which are separated diagonally into two color tones. This subtle form, in combination with a clarity and pureness of color, is an invitation to create countless new variations to please the eye anew each day.

The dimensions of the cube are approximately 1 inch (2.5 cm) in each direction. A container frame for laying Mosaik on a tabletop surface or displaying it on an easel is included and measures 6¾ square inches by 1¼ inches (17 cm^2 by 3 cm) for the 36-piece set and 10⅝ square inches by 1¼ inches (27 cm^2 by 3 cm) for the 100-piece set.

MY BRICKS BY SELAB FOR SELETTI (2008-2009)

Did you know that the predecessor of modern-day LEGOs was actually made of wood? The use of plastic came a little later, when the concept of toy building bricks was more fully fleshed out by the Danish company that has made them since the 1930s. And that's how nearly all of us know them today.

Until now. Move up the material food chain with a set of interlocking building bricks made from white porcelain (a substance made from fired clay, just like real bricks). An elegant representation of a classic child's toy, but recast for grown-ups in a grown-up world.

Each set comes in a beautiful gift box and includes twelve square bricks and thirty-four double-square bricks. A rectangular brick measures 3¼ by 1⅝ by ¾ inches (8.2 by 4.1 by 1.9 cm).

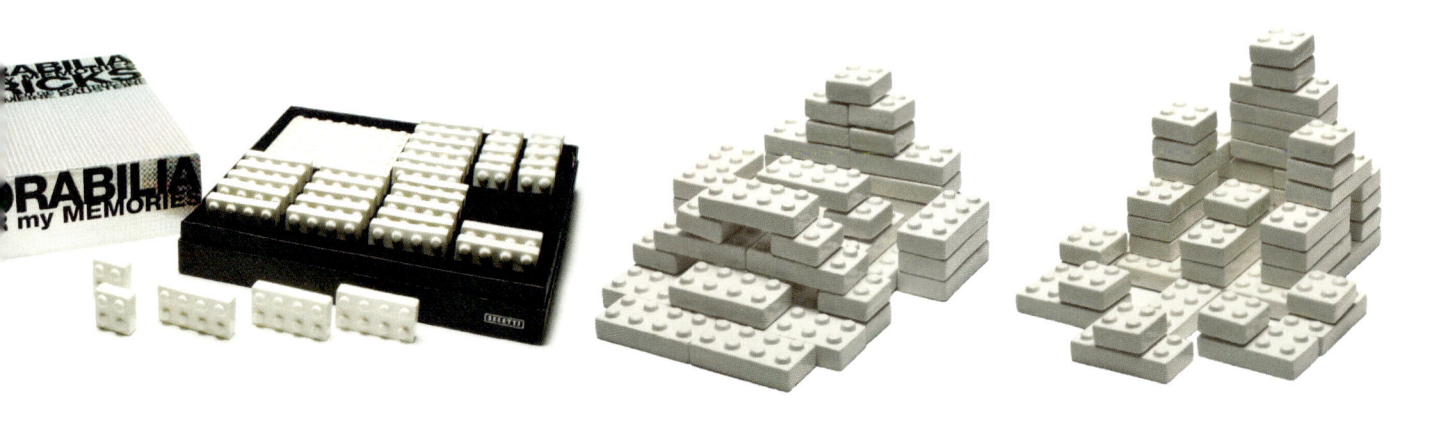

Discover these items at thecreativehome.com

HOUSEWARES AND DECOR

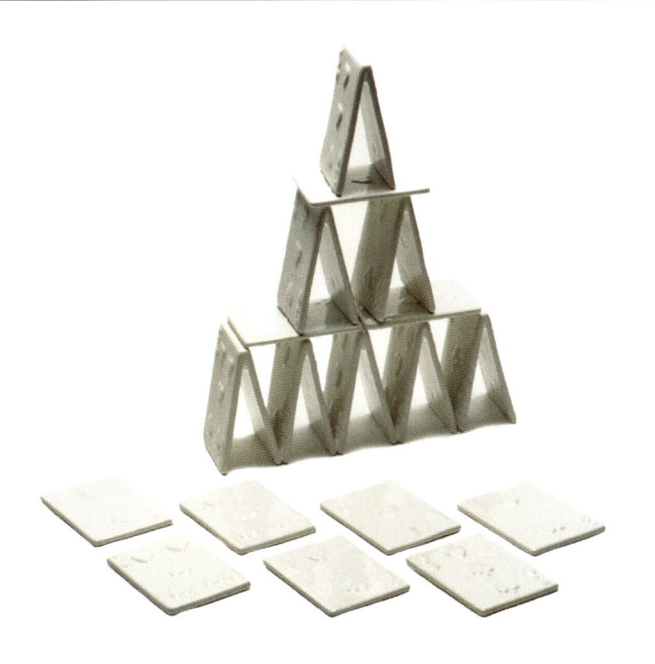

MY HOUSE OF CARDS BY SELAB FOR SELETTI (2008-2009)

The phrase "house of cards" is commonly used as a metaphor to describe something that appears substantial but is in actuality unstable, built on flimsy foundations and likely to come apart under the slightest stress.

Then there's My House of Cards, by Selab for Seletti. Rather than building blocks made from paper-thin card stock, this recreation of a universal metaphor uses a substantial white porcelain for constructing its modular units. You still need to stack the pieces up to make houses of your own design, but they're definitely not going to blow over at the first wind!

Beautifully boxed for gift giving and display. Each box contains eighteen cards. Good deal!

NOLASTAR MODULAR SCREEN BY ANA MOTJÉR, OLIVER SCHNEIDER, AND ROYAL FAMILY DESIGN LABOR (1999)

Nola Star has various functions as a curtain, wall paneling, room divider, or as a transparent accent element in rooms. With their play of solid and voids the screens diffuse natural and electric light in a gentle wash. The Nola Star system of attachment is simple and encourages the development of screens in a variety of heights, widths, and colors. It's a lightweight building system that invites creativity.

The Nola Star module is a 7½ inch (19 cm) square plastic panel that hangs from a rod or track when assembled. The squares have rounded corners and holes on all four sides through which they can be easily connected with the lightweight metal rings provided. With the proper track apparatus, screens can be folded back on themselves when you want to open up the space or bring in the outdoors.

One box holds twenty-five squares in a single color, which covers approximately 10½ square feet (1 m^2). Boxes include connecting rings. Rod and other hanging apparatus not included.

Available in packages of Wood Grain, Translucent White, and a Transparent Blue, Red, Green, and Yellow.

THE CREATIVITY CATALOG

NOMAD MODULAR SCREENS BY JAIME SALM AND ROGER C. ALLEN FOR MIO (2007–2011)

Made from recycled, double-wall cardboard, Nomad is a modular architectural system that can be assembled into free-standing sculptural screens, temporary partitions, rooms, or even displays without hardware, tools, or damage to existing structures. Simply slip one module into another, then another, then another; before you can say "module," you've got an attractive room divider right in front of you.

One 24-module package creates about twenty square feet with the open configuration, and about fourteen square feet with the closed configuration. Mix the available colors however you want, or stick to a monochromatic palette—the canvas is yours.

Available in a variety of colors. Twenty-four modules to a package.

Nomad and Nomad Butterfly modules can be combined in one assembly or used individually. Made in America.

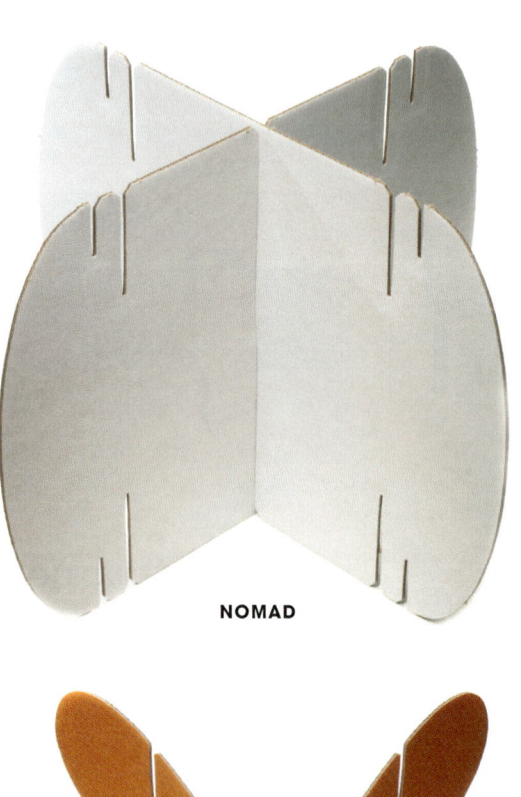

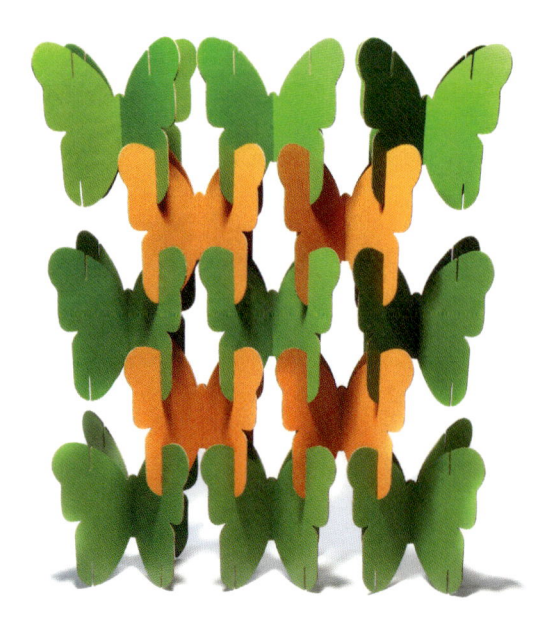

NOMAD

NOMAD BUTTERFLY

Discover these items at thecreativehome.com

HOUSEWARES AND DECOR

NORDIC LIGHT CANDLEHOLDER BY JONAS GRUNDELL FOR DESIGN HOUSE STOCKHOLM

Being a 1986 graduate of a Stockholm design school, Jonas Grundell probably burned more than a few candles pursuing his love of design through the night (which can be really long in that part of the world). Maybe that's why one of his most iconic creations is the Nordic Light flexible candleholder.

Shape the candle arms in any way you like: arms wide open, folded away, or radiating at various angles. Dynamic, beautifully made, and exuding warmth, the Nordic Light comes in 7-arm and 4-arm versions.

Available in Black, Gray, Red, and White. Dimensions of the 4-arm version when folded are 8 by 5 by in 1½ inches (20.5 by 13 by 4 cm). Dimensions of the 7-arm version are 12 by 8 by 1½ inches (30 by 19.5 by 4 cm).

NUMBERS CUBE CLOCK BY JONAS DAMON FOR AREAWARE (2006)

An alarm clock consisting of four 2-inch (5 cm) cubes. Each cube displays one glowing LED digit to make up the time display. Unlike static boxes usually associated with alarm clocks, this interactive collection of changing numbers can be arranged in any configuration. But be careful that you don't confuse yourself and oversleep by putting the cubes in the wrong order!

Available in Black and Red.

THE CREATIVITY CATALOG

NUMERO CLOCK BY ROOST

A lot of graphic design these days involves mashing up different typefaces in the same design. Ride the wave of typeface art, salvaged sign letters, and other contemporary graphic techniques with the customizable Roost Numero clock. Each cast-aluminum number is in its own typeface and can be placed anywhere on the wall, as can the battery-powered timepiece. Numbers and clock attach by screw.

For those who just like their numbers in a regular circle, a handy mounting template is included. Installed, that design measures about twenty-four inches (60.9 cm) in diameter.

Numbers average about 2½ inches square by ¾ inches deep (6.3 cm^2 by 1.9 cm).

OPALINE GLASS MODULAR VASE BY SELAB FOR SELETTI (2009)

From the Italian design house Seletti, this modular ten-piece vase set can be put together in a variety of arrangements using the elastic bands that come in three different sizes. Customize each grouping to work with your flower arrangement. Put all the pieces together in one big group or break them up into singles and multiples. And you don't have to use it only for planting material—they're also a nifty and stylish organizer for anything that can fit inside their variously dimensioned openings.

Made out of an Italian type of opaline glass, a beautiful material which originated in Napoleonic France before being lovingly adopted by the people who brought you Michelangelo! Available in Black and White sets. Nested the set measures 3⅛ inches in diameter by 4⅜ inches high (7.9 by 11.1 cm).

Discover these items at thecreativehome.com

HOUSEWARES AND DECOR

PANTONE FOOD TRAYS BY ROOM COPENHAGEN

We really admire this modular food tray system because it manages to combine some very diverse design traditions and be elegantly practical at the same time. Its minimalist detailing and use of low-profile rectangular rather than circular plates evokes an oriental sensibility, whereas its Pantone color schemes and cool, nearly unbreakable melamine construction conveys a more cosmopolitan, international style.

No matter what your aesthetic, Pantone Food Trays work well for a variety of foods and occasions. Sushi or tapas, brunch or cocktails, the proportionally sized trays can be placed together in all sorts of alignments and combinations, as well as individually. Stack them snugly when not in use for space-saving storage. And speaking of storage, consider using the trays as organizers for desktop, bath, and other non-food-related items—their durability and flexibility knows no bounds!

You can collect the trays as a four-piece set or as individual pieces ordered a la carte. Overall the four-piece set measures around 6¼ inches square by 1½ inches (16 cm^2 by 3.9) when stacked. Individual trays run from about 3 to 12½ inches (8 to 32 cm) in either direction.

Available in several delicious Pantone-branded colors.

THE CREATIVITY CATALOG

PAPERFORMS WALL PANELING BY JAIME SALM FOR MIO (2004-2013)

Transform a room in minutes with environmentally friendly MIO PaperForms sculptural wall tiles. Add color and texture to a single wall or surround the space with them. Leave them in their out-of-the-box finish, or paint them in your favorite color, or in several colors, to add even more character. Orient the tiles in different relationships to each other to produce strikingly different three-dimensional effects until you find the pattern you like. Some people have also used PaperForms to create art pieces that float on a wall.

The lightweight modules are recycled and recyclable. They can be installed with double-stick tape, Velcro, wallpaper paste, or tacks.

PaperForms are a new concept in surface coverings that gives individuals the ability to affordably customize and redefine space.

Available in Acoustic Weave, Cube, Ripple, and V2 patterns in a White finish. Tiles are 12 inches square (30.4 cm^2) and come twelve tiles to a pack; ergo each pack covers 12 square feet (1.1 m^2).

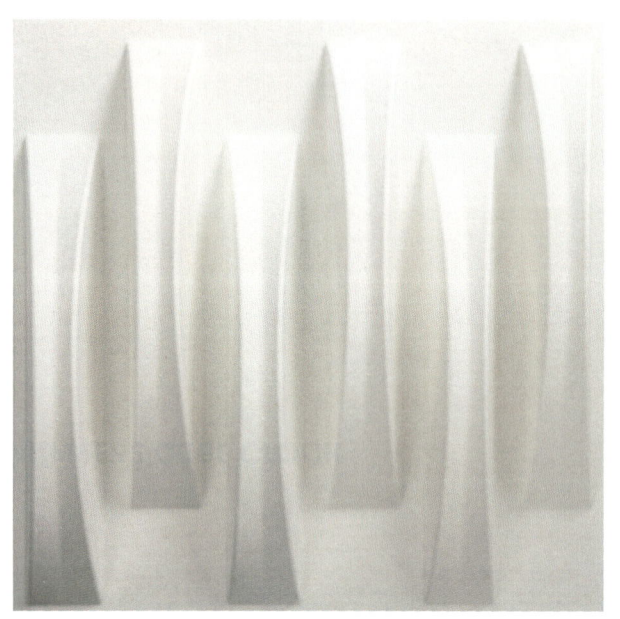

ACOUSTIC WEAVE

CUBE

Discover these items at thecreativehome.com

HOUSEWARES AND DECOR

RIPPLE

V2

POLYHEX BY INCORPORATED FOR LERIVAL

Bees do it . . . with hexagons. And so did creatives like architect Frank Lloyd Wright and sculptor Tony Smith, who drew on this quintessentially modular shape found in nature to create their art. PolyHex takes the concept of endlessly additive cells and recasts it in rotational-molded polyethylene to make a totally flexible design unit.

Hollow, yet strong enough to support anyone who might sit on it, PolyHex can be used as a seat, umbrella stand, flowerpot, or pretty much in any way you can think of. Perfect for both indoor and outdoor use, for adults and kids alike.

Available in Cobalt, Crimson, and Canary. Each unit is 17½ inches (44.4 cm) high and 13 inches (33 cm) across.

57

THE CREATIVITY CATALOG

PRESEPE NATIVITY SET BY MASSIMO GIACON AND LAURA POLINORO FOR ALESSI (2007-2010)

Porcelain figurines are among the great traditions in European decorative arts, but that doesn't mean contemporary designers can't make their own contributions to this rich legacy. Case in point: this charming Nativity set from Alessi.

Designed between 2007 and 2010 by comic strip artist and illustrator Massimo Giacon and Alessi designer Laura Polinoro, the basic set comes with five hand-decorated figures (Baby Jesus, Joseph, Mary, and two animals) and a wonderful manger available in Blue, Red, and White.

For an expanded scene you can collect additional figure groups, including the Three Magi, a pair of sheep, angels playing musical instruments, and Amir and Camelus (a camel).

The manger measures 6¼ by 5 by 5¼ inches (15.8 by 12.7 by 13.3 cm). Figures range in size from ¾ inches (1.9 cm) to 2 inches (5.0 cm) in height.

PROGRAMMA 8 TABLEWARE BY FRANCO SARGIANI AND EIJA HELANDER FOR ALESSI (1975-2009)

The Programma 8 series was originally designed in the 1970s by architect Franco Sargiani and industrial designer Eija Helander after five years in development. It was reissued in 2005 with additional pieces. The series consists of interchangeable containers, plates, and kitchen implements incrementally sized to fit snugly on specially designed stainless steel trays in a variety of configurations. The fluid nature of the Programma 8 system allows you to choose whatever combination of pieces will best satisfy the occasion at hand. It's a very architectural approach to product design: create a structural framework (in this case, the trays) and then freely place objects within it to meet fluctuating practical requirements. Think of it as a miniature equivalent of a modernist postwar skyscraper, only instead of an open floor plan organized by a grid of steel columns within which people and furniture are floated around at will, you have steel trays with pieces you can put in, shuffle, and take out as needed.

Besides containers, bowls, plates, and trays, Programma 8 includes salad, condiment, and cheese sets, cutting boards, a fish grate, and utensils. Containers are stoneware, ceramics, or glass, trays are 18/10 stainless steel with mirror polished edges. Aside from the sets, pieces are sold individually.

The standard module, represented by the 1×1 container (fig. 00), measures about 3 inches square by 2½ inches high (9 by 9 by 6.5 cm). Components increase in size in modular units, the largest measuring four by six modules.

Besides their work on Programma 8, Sargiani and Helander played an important role in Alessi's evolution as a premier global brand. The company was started in Italy in 1921 by Giovanni Alessi, a skilled metalworker who crafted tabletop objects. He was later joined by his son Carlo, who did most designs of the 1930s and early 1940s. By the latter decade Alessi began to work with outside designers as well, a practice continuing to the present day.

Eldest son of Carlo, Alberto Alessi joined the firm in 1970 the day after he finished law school. One of his first initiatives was to redo the company's corporate identity, tapping Sargiani and Helander to work on graphic design and packaging as well as the company's offices. Issued in the first decade of Alberto's stewardship, Programma 8 is the culmination of the trio's collaboration, and an expression of Alessi's current mission to create affordable household objects imbued with artistic quality.

Discover these items at thecreativehome.com

HOUSEWARES AND DECOR

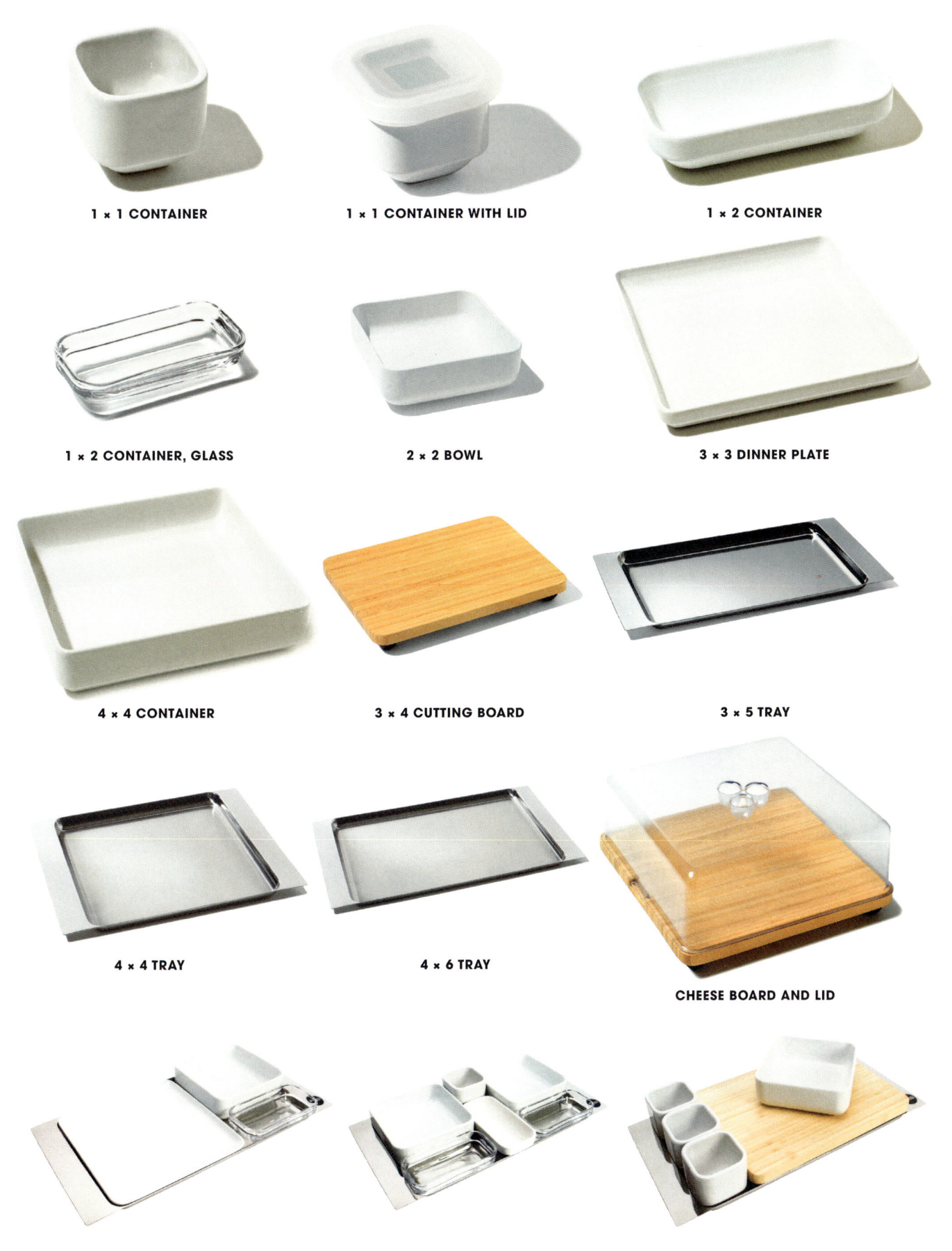

1 × 1 CONTAINER

1 × 1 CONTAINER WITH LID

1 × 2 CONTAINER

1 × 2 CONTAINER, GLASS

2 × 2 BOWL

3 × 3 DINNER PLATE

4 × 4 CONTAINER

3 × 4 CUTTING BOARD

3 × 5 TRAY

4 × 4 TRAY

4 × 6 TRAY

CHEESE BOARD AND LID

59

CHEESE SERVER SET

SALAD SERVER SET

HOUSEWARES AND DECOR

PUZZLE WINE RACK BY GIDEON DAGAN (2005)

Attractive and functional, this unique modular wine rack adds form and color to any space. Multiple units storing nine bottles each are easily combined to form larger racks accommodating the cellar of a modest user as well as a major boozer. Choose either Amber or Orange, or combine the two for a mottled look. You can rest them on one of two sides, and they can be stacked vertically as well as horizontally. They also look great standing alone in one or two units. Perfect for home, permissive workplace, restaurant, or hospitality environment.

Created in 2005 by Gideon Dagan of Dagan Design, the Puzzle Wine Rack was selected for exhibition in that year's California Design Biennial, a show representing the most innovative and creative design in the state.

The rack is injection-molded from transparent ABS recyclable polymer. Dimensions are 18½ by 18½ by 8½ inches (47 by 47 by 21.6 cm).

RHOMBINS DESKTOP STORAGE AND PLAY BY ERIC PFEIFFER AND SCOT HERBST FOR AMAC (2011)

Rhombus (noun):
   A parallelogram with opposite equal acute and obtuse angles and four equal sides.
   And
   Any parallelogram with equal sides.

Rhombin (proper noun):
   A really cool modular system based on the rhombus shape, used for creating an organized and playful desktop. Arrange the modules in flexible configurations to meet your ever changing storage needs, while making a graphic statement that will make your desktop smile. Place the modules side by side, in a line, or go vertical in stacks—the possibilities are endless.

A module measures 7 inches long by 4 inches across and high (17.7 by 10.1 cm). Made in California using Cereplast, a plant-based bioplastic. Good for the environment, good for your stuff, good for you.

THE CREATIVITY CATALOG

SCRABBLE PEARL EDITION BY WINNING SOLUTIONS FOR HASBRO

The perfect gift for people who love Scrabble (hey, consider yourself eligible too!). Take their game up a notch with this handsome special edition board and tile set. The tiles are an attractive white to harmonize with the pearlescent rotating game board, silver foil stamping, white sand timer, and tile stands. Play with this set once and you'll think you went to Scrabble heaven.

Comes with pencils and tile pouch. Board measures a standard 16 inches (41.6 cm) square by 1½ inches (3.8 cm). Recommended for ages eight and up.

PS: Did you know Scrabble was invented by an architect?

STACT WINE WALL BY ERIC PFEIFFER (2012)

STACT isn't just a wine rack. It's an interior decor piece that stores wine in a beautiful way.

Transform your wine collection into wall art with an elegant modular wine wall that expands and adapts to fit your unique space. Mix and match the space-saving STACT wine storage panels to create your own unique design. Crafted from aircraft-grade anodized aluminum, it's easy to assemble and install on any drywall surface, and suitable for home and commercial applications.

Brought to life by award-winning designer Eric Pfeiffer, STACT is a modular, flexible, and visually enticing way to enhance your space while celebrating your wine collection.

Modular means infinitely expandable too, letting you add panels as your wine collection grows or location changes.

Each panel measures 11 by 14 $^{15}/_{16}$ (28.8 by 37.7 cm), is sold individually, and includes supports for nine standard-sized bottles (wine and bubbly). For each two panels you can support up to twelve bottles. Mounting hardware included. Available in Electric Orange, Piano Black, Pure White, Walnut, and Zebrano.

Discover these items at thecreativehome.com

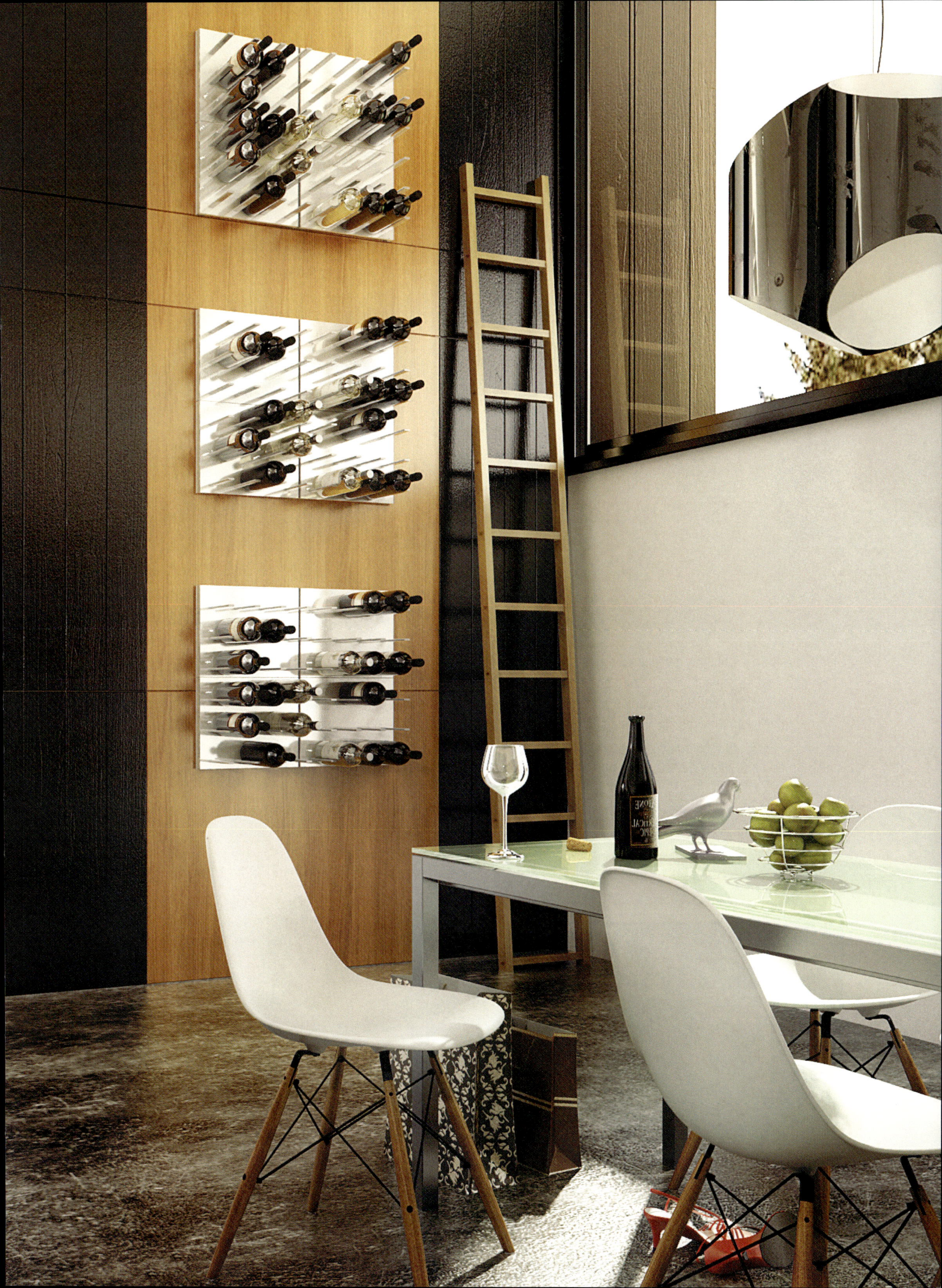

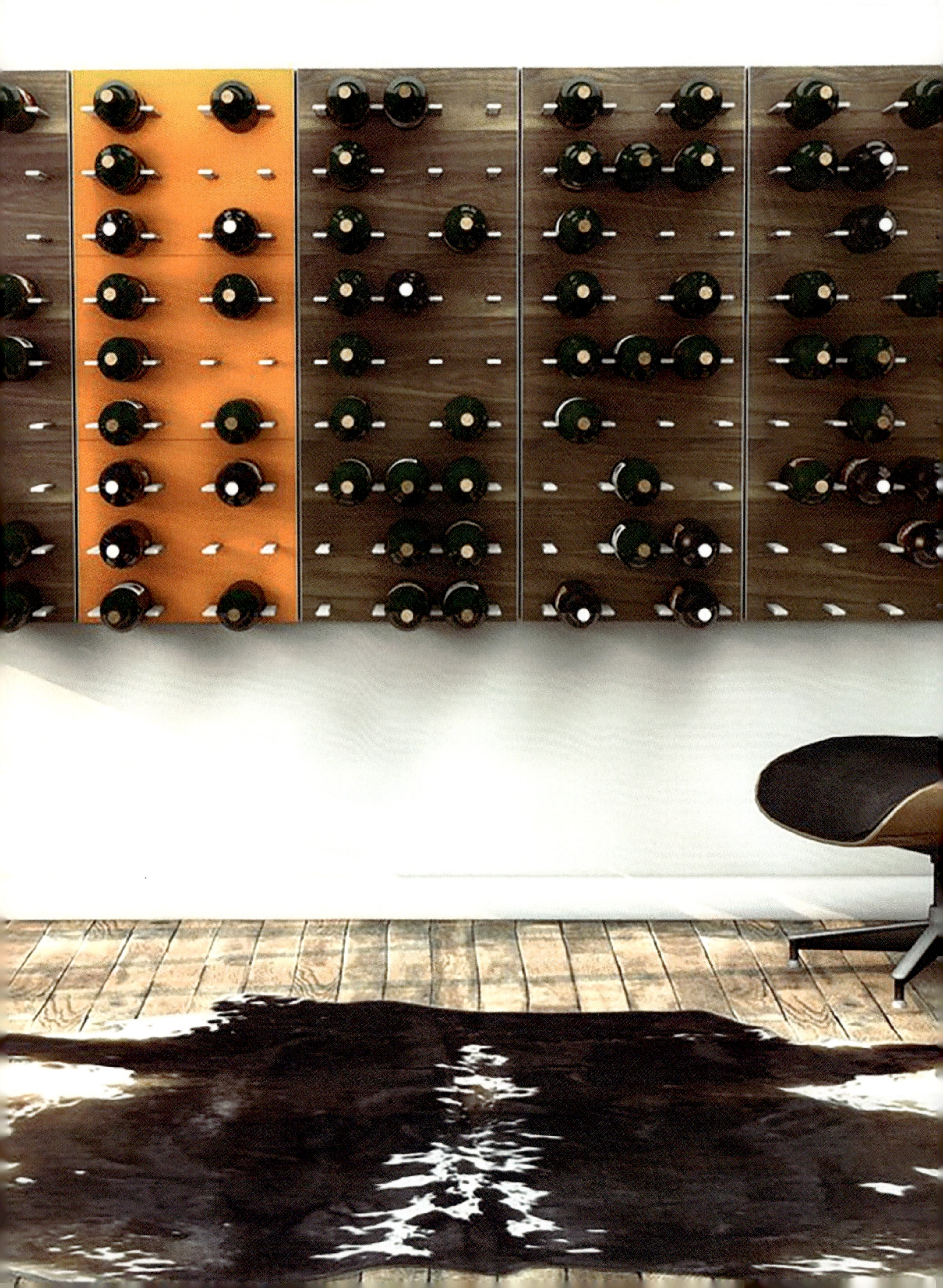

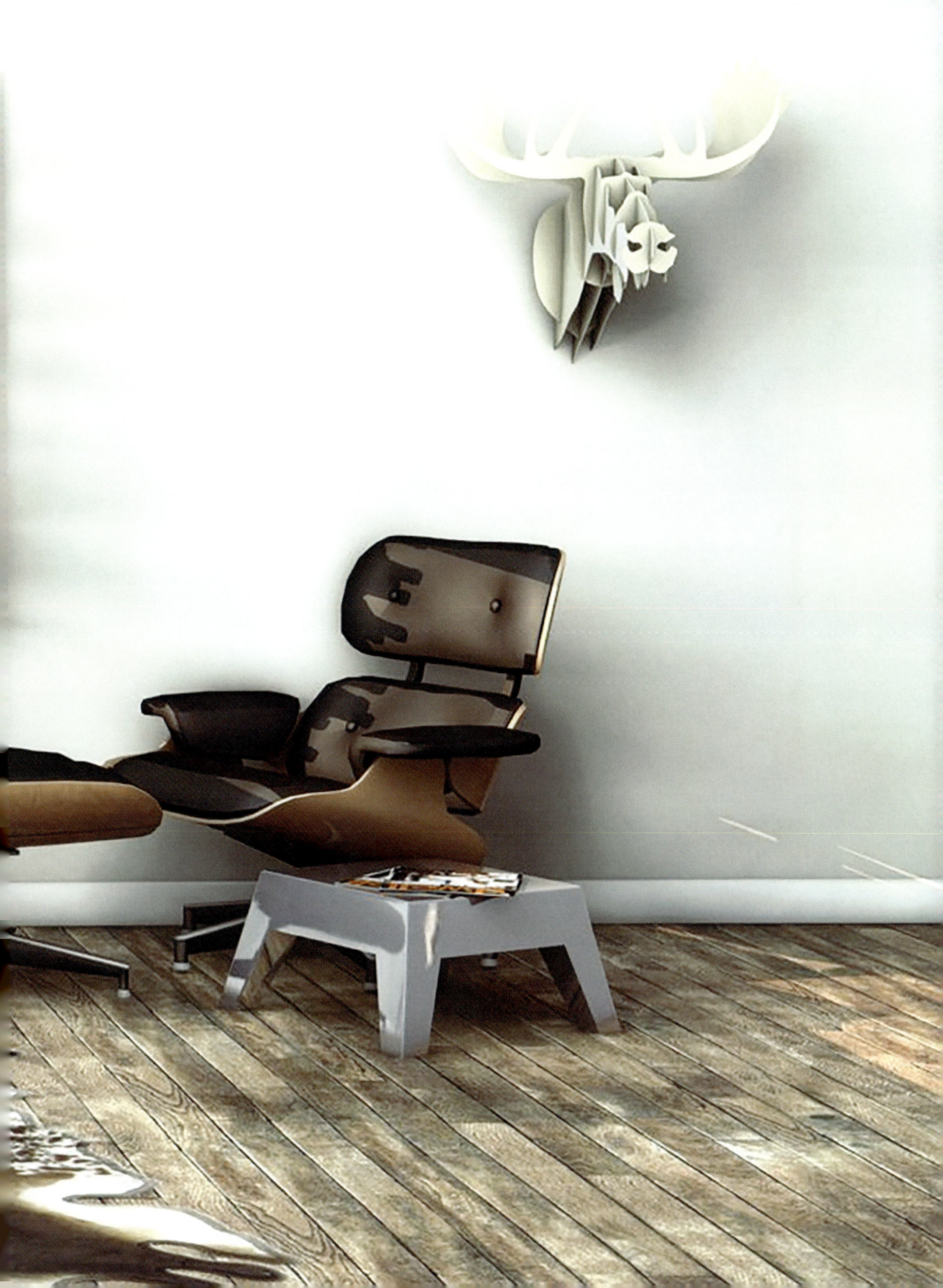

THE CREATIVITY CATALOG

STITCH INTERLOCKING RUG
BY NAURIS KALINAUSKAS (2005)

Finding the right rug can be difficult, especially when you need it to be a particular size, in a particular color scheme, within a particular budget, and in a look you like. Rather than spend your time combing through piles of rugs, wouldn't it be more fulfilling to make it up yourself?

No, you don't have to know how to operate a loom or have a degree in design to make this possible. The Stitch Interlocking Rug system gives you the power of customization without needing either. Simply choose the colors that work for you from the available palette, figure out how big an area you need, and order. The funnest part is putting the pieces together however you want them.

Made from polypropylene, which is a durable material well suited to areas with significant traffic and use. The material makes the rugs easy to keep clean and are nonfading. Both their look and durability make them suitable for grown-up spaces as well as kids' rooms.

Each piece measures approximately 15¾ by 17¾ inches across (40 by 45 cm) and about ⅜ inch thick (0.8 cm). A box comes with ten pieces in one color. One box covers around 8 square feet (0.7 m^2).

Colors include Aqua, Black, Light Gray, Dark Gray, Orange, and Red, as well as Beige, Fuchsia, Ivory, Lime, Pink, Taupe, and Yellow.

Discover these items at thecreativehome.com

HOUSEWARES AND DECOR

TABLE TABLE BY MOS ARCHITECTS FOR LERIVAL (2010)

Table Table is an exploration into folded aluminum that tests the limits of material str configuration. The result is a single L-shaped unit that can be secured to other units possible configuration, each of which can then be dismantled and reconfigured to serve

Table Table presents an ideal solution for the type of user who demands multifunc shifting priorities. By encouraging continuous reconfiguration, Table Table manages to ness, and individuality into the otherwise commonplace activities of everyday life and w

Made from powder-coated bent aluminum. Standard colors are Eggplant, White, and surface texture and is recommended for outdoor use. Custom colors and an anodized fin of five leaves.

Dimensions per unit are 25 by 24 by 29½ inches (63.5 by 61 by 74.9 cm).

TABLETALK TRIVET BY NEL LINSSEN FOR GOODS (2000)

This flexible trivet is made of sixteen linked heat-resistant adjustable polyamide discs so it can be shaped to accommodate serving dishes of varying sizes and configurations. Think large forms for big platters and stockpots and small, compact forms for saucepans and little serving dishes. After dinner you can just play around with it by shifting the discs around into various patterns. You'd be surprised by how much fun a trivet can actually be when it's transformable.

TableTalk can handle cookware up to 425° F (220° C). That's hot stuff.

Available in Lime/Black. Each disc is 1¾ inches diameter (4.4 cm). Designed by jewelry artist Nel Linssen and made in The Netherlands.

THE CREATIVITY CATALOG

TECTUS BY JO NIEMEYER FOR NAEF (1996)

This 4½ inch (11.5 cm) maple wood cube is subdivided in adherence to the Golden Ratio, a proportion thought to lie at the foundation of many examples of ancient and modern architecture. Become an architect yourself (without the long office hours) as you arrange and rearrange the seventeen pieces and half-dozen black planes in similarly harmonious relationships. Because of the remarkable powers of this ratio, you'll find it's actually hard to create something that isn't beautiful!

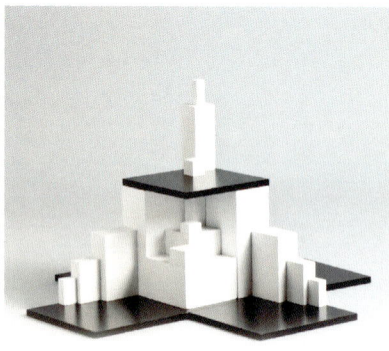

TERRAIN VASE BY STEPHAN JAKLITSCH FOR MOMA (2010)

Drawing inspiration from puzzles and organic landscapes, architect and designer Stephan Jaklitsch of Jaklitsch / Gardner Architects designed the Terrain Vase as an assemblage of eleven interlocking dividers and one water reservoir. Connected, the intersecting slats that form the vase provide multiple openings in which to place flowers. A single vase can be constructed in two different configurations, and multiple vases can be joined to each other to create a larger undulating silhouette evocative of rolling terrain—a perfect metaphor for the natural ground out of which flowers grow.

Made of biodegradable cornstarch-based PLA plastic. Pieces disassemble for cleaning. Hand-wash recommended. A single vase measures 8½ inches long by 5 inches wide by 7 inches high (21.5 by 12.7 by 17.7 cm).

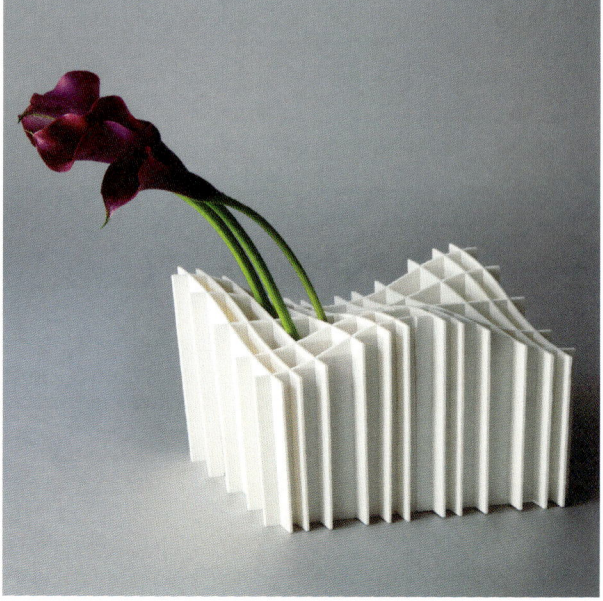

Discover these items at thecreativehome.com

TETRIS MIRROR BY JULIA DOZSA FOR FIAM (2010)

Mirror, mirror on the wall, who's the most modular of them all? Why, that's easy—the Tetris Mirror of course!

The Tetris Mirror is a sophisticated system of mirrored modules that interlock to form larger compositions of reflective glass. For once you can shape the mirror to suit its surroundings, rather than search endlessly for the right alignment of shape, size, and looks. Don't settle for something you happen to find—design something that is unique to your space.

Choose from three different styles, and between clear mirror and a combination of clear and red-tinted mirror components. An ingenious system of magnetic backs joins the modules together.

Dimensions range from 15¾ wide to 31½ inches high (39.9 to 79.8 cm).

TRASK LAMP BY JAIME SALM AND ROGER C. ALLEN FOR MIO (2009)

Maybe you can't bend the world to your will, but you certainly can do it to the Trask Lamp. It's a plug-in LED tabletop light set into a powder-coated steel housing that comes flat-packed. You insert the LED strip into the 42-inch-long (106.6 cm) housing, then bend the steel with your bare hands to achieve the look and lighting direction that suits you. Trask makes LED lighting affordable and truly customizable.

Trask is an environmentally conscious design: its steel casing is fully recyclable; its powder-coating has a durable, low VOC finish; and the approximately 350-lumen LED lamps are energy efficient.

Available in Chartreuse, Silver, and White.

THE CREATIVITY CATALOG

TRY IT TRIVET BY DROR BENSHETRIT FOR ALESSI (2009)

The recurring reconfigurable trivet theme has this time attracted the talents of Dror Benshetrit, a gifted creator who reinterprets this historically humble device to produce a conceptually novel and interactive version. Try It is made up of three detachable circular arcs, each of which can be used as a trivet by itself. The smallest can easily handle an espresso cup, for example, while the largest can hold a medium-sized casserole.

But where it really gets interesting is when the pieces are used together because they can be magnetically connected in a variety of sinuous and concentric patterns. That can make for some rather eye-catching ornamentation on your table, not to mention giving support to objects of all shapes and sizes.

Made of polished 18/10 stainless steel. Fitted together, Try It measures 9¾ by 7½ inches (24.7 by 19 cm).

TY DIY SHOWER CURTAIN BY GRAIN

DIY means Draw It Yourself, at least when it comes to the Ty DIY Shower Curtain. A very unusual product, Ty lets you create your very own shower curtain by drawing whatever you want on it with permanent marker. It's like having a blank canvas in your bathroom, a place for you to express your inner artist and decorate a space in a uniquely individualized way.

Ty is a 60 by 72 inch (152.4 by 182.8 cm), 100% high-density polyethylene, white shower curtain with nickel-plated brass grommets. Unlike other shower curtains made of vinyl, Ty is PVC-free and will not off-gas in your home. In fact, Ty breathes, making it less likely to grow gross mold and mildew. It's also stronger than vinyl, and will last a very long time before being recycled.

Comes with your choice of Black, Blue, or Green permanent marker made from 74% post-consumer waste. And when we say permanent, we mean permanent—even after you wash the curtain in cold water with a mild detergent and hang it to dry, at which stage it will take on a soft, linen-like texture.

Designed and made in America by creative-minded people.

Discover these items at thecreativehome.com

HOUSEWARES AND DECOR

URBIO MODULAR GARDEN AND WALL ORGANIZER BY ENLISTED DESIGN

Ah, Kickstarter—where would the world be without this incubator of promising design concepts? Okay, so civilization survived a few millennia before it showed up, but still! It's thanks to them that we now have Urbio, a magnetically modular urban garden that works equally well as a wall-mounted organizer. Simply attach the backplates to your wall in whatever arrangement works best for you, then place your collection of containers anywhere on the grid. Don't worry; powerful neodymium magnets will hold them in place. At least, until you pop them off for watering, cleaning, or because you want to change their placement.

Urbio comes in two kit sizes. The Big Happy Family Kit includes six 10-inch-square wall plates and six containers. As a rectangle it measures 20 by 30 inches (50.1 by 76.2 cm), but you can position the backplates in any pattern. The Happy Family Kit comes with two plates and three containers, and measures 10 by 20 inches side by side (25.4 by 50.1 cm). Both kits come with all the brackets, screws, and sheetrock anchors you'll need, and a handy-dandy template for easily mounting the plates. Kits can be combined as needed, of course.

Great for kitchen and bath, office, living areas, garage—pretty much anywhere you go, now that we think of it. Made of lightweight, recyclable, and durable polypropylene.

URSA THE BEAR BY DAVID WEEKS FOR AREAWARE (2009)

This reconfigurable wooden animal figure is so much fun we can hardly . . . bear it. Ursa's powerful hardwood frame can hold many poses, and her elastic-band muscles and durable wood limbs make her almost impervious to breakage (unlike those quick-to-destruct plastic thingamajigs that come and go). An enduring classic that will give the pleasure of play to generations of fun-loving owners.

Designed by Brooklyn's own David Weeks. Made from sustainably harvested new-growth beech wood. Dimensions of Ursa Minor are 5½ by 10 by 4½ inches (13.4 by 25.4 by 11.4 cm). Papa Bear is 13½ by 6½ by 5¾ (34.3 by 16.5 by 14.6 cm). Winner of several prestigious design awards. Recommended for children and adults ages three and up.

THE CREATIVITY CATALOG

VASEMAKER BY RON GILAD FOR DESIGNFENZIDER

VaseMaker divides the classic vase into its two functional elements: support for a flower and a container for the water that nourishes it. Then it leaves off the container and gives you the opportunity to recomplete the form by placing your own vessel below the remaining part of the vase. You and designer Ron Gilad become co-creatives in the act of vase making. Pretty nifty of you!

What's more, you can vary the choice of vessel any time you want, which replaces the classical stability of the traditional vase with the fluid and dynamic imaginative processes characteristic of contemporary design. Pretty nifty of you too!

VaseMaker is part of the Tel Aviv Museum of Art collection, a winner of a Red Dot International Design Award, and a Conduit National Design Award of Distinction. It's so novel, it's patented.

Made of porcelain. The base measures 6 inches square (15.2 cm^2), and rises to a height of 2½ inches (6.3 cm).

HOUSEWARES AND DECOR

WALL FRAMES BY WEXEL ART (2010)

Most of us don't wear the same clothes day after day, or drive the same car year after year, or even paint our walls the same color forever and ever—so why should the photos, documents, and family artwork we display in our home and workplace be fixed for eternity? Well, it often is, if no other reason than because it's a pain in the posterior to change it out of conventional frames (the scientific term for this condition is "inertia").

May we introduce you to the Art Wall Picture frame concept? It's a quite ingeniously simple method for creating a permanent display of consistently rotating artwork. It works like this: you mount a beautiful clear acrylic panel to your wall by means of four hardware mounts that attach a frameless acrylic panel 1½ inches (3.3 cm) from the wall. You then slide your artwork behind the panel, and fix it in place using small round magnets.

When you're ready to swap it out for something else, simple move the magnets aside and slide in the new artwork. No dismantling or rehanging of the frame, no recutting of mats.

Since the panels are designed for the artwork to float within their perimeter, you have enormous flexibility in what you can display. Show several small pieces at once or a single larger one, then do something completely different. Of course, you can also leave those prize pieces in the frame for a permanent exhibition.

Art Wall frames come in a wide range of sizes and several special shapes, including a trio of curvilinear frames commissioned from famed designer Eva Zeisel (1906–2011).

Frames come with four pairs of magnets. Extra magnets can be ordered separately.

EVA ZEISEL

RECTANGULAR AND SQUARE

THE CREATIVITY CATALOG

YUKI SCREEN BY NENDO FOR CAPPELLINI (2006)

This elegant modular screen by Cappellini is made from components whose shape is inspired by hexagonal snowflakes. Just as snow gathers depth as more flakes are piled on top of others, the Yuki Screen is formed by piling components on top of each other. The interconnection of various basic modules allows you to create compositions of varying dimensions and silhouette. Great for adding a visual accent to a space, or dividing it without the dense obstruction of material walls.

One set contains thirty-six individual modules, which can form a screen approximately 71 by 39 by 12 inches (180 by 99 by 30.5 cm). Being modular, your screen can be shaped to any equivalent set of dimensions. Individual modules measure 16½ by 14¼ by ⅜ inches (41.9 by 36.1 by .9 cm). You can also combine sets for larger assemblies.

Made of durable and cleanable ABS plastic, available in Anthracite. Created by the internationally recognized Japanese design firm Nendo.

Discover these items at thecreativehome.com

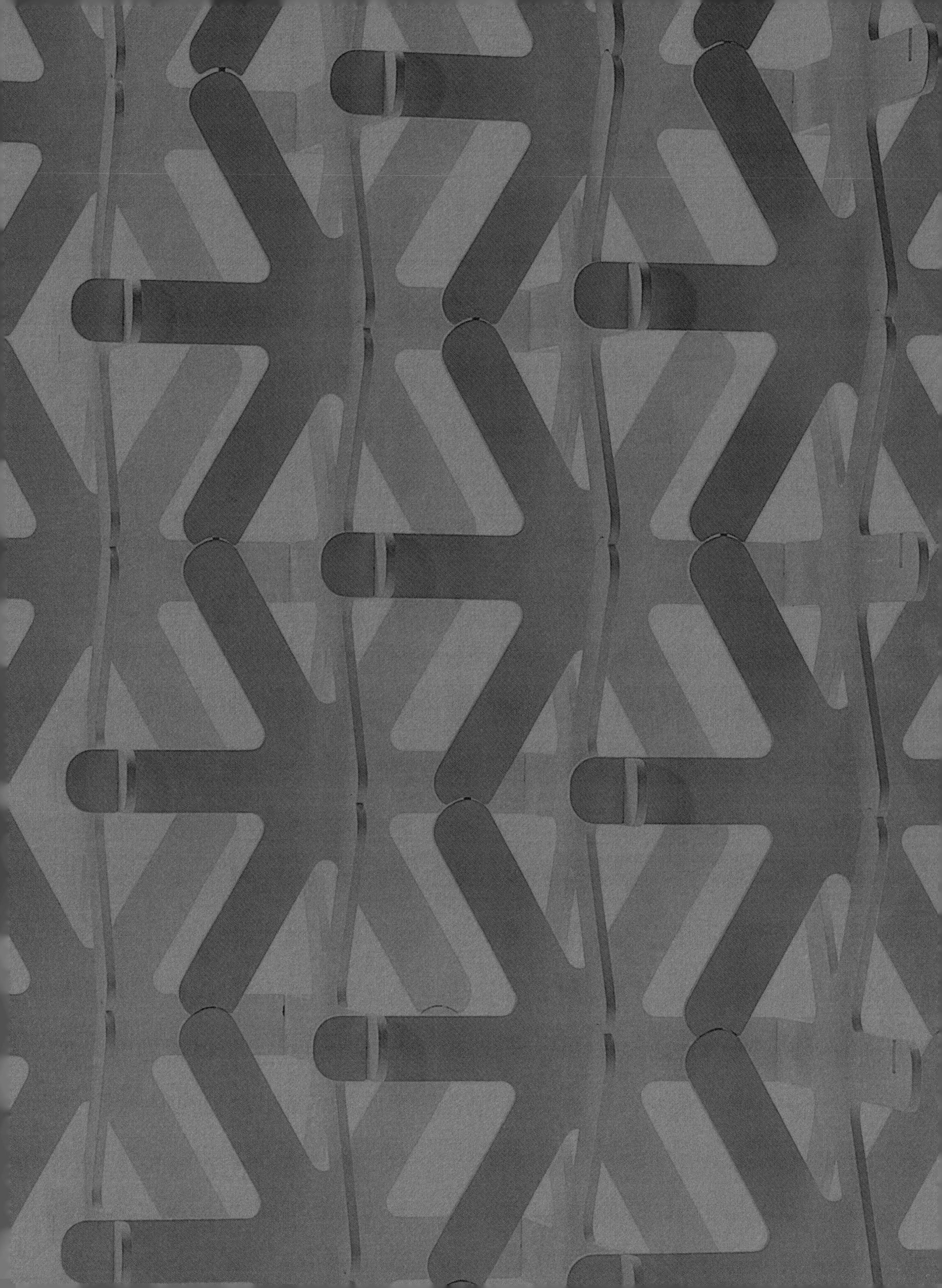

JEWELRY AND APPAREL

KISHUT MODULAR JEWELRY
BY HILA RAWET KARNI (2009)

U.K.-based Hila Rawet Karni is a jewelry designer whose works have been featured throughout the world, from Tokyo and Design Basel in Miami to Tel Aviv, Milan, and London. Combining her background in industrial design, her knowledge of origami, and her impeccable fashion sense, Hila incorporates unusual materials to create unique, wearable pieces. Her Kishut Collection is notable in utilizing individual modules rendered in an industrial material, in different colors, and with assorted connection hardware to form an unlimited number of necklace, earring, and brooch designs.

Each package comes with enough pieces to form one of three necklace designs created by Hila: the Isabelle, Mod, and Tulip. All three are available on Clear, Red, and Black. Take them out of their package and they're ready to wear. Or, you can reconfigure them to your own designs at any time (and back again). You can keep the colors solid or mix them up among the various designs—being modular they'll interconnect with no problem.

The Isabelle necklace comes with fourteen modules, the Tulip design comes with twenty modules, and the Mod has twenty-six.

The colored elements are injection-molded silicone, and the metallic buttons are stainless steel.

Discover these items at thecreativehome.com

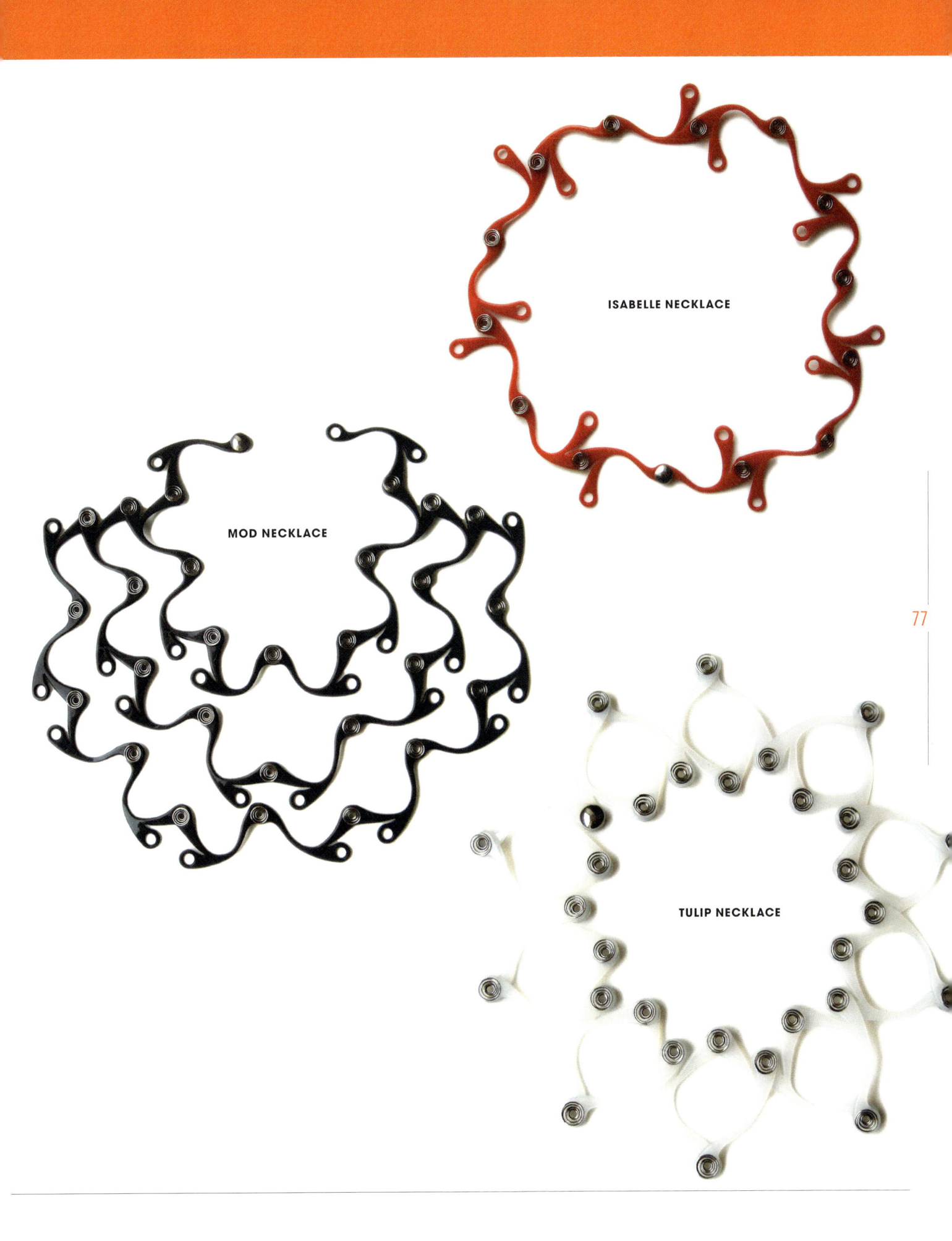

ISABELLE NECKLACE

MOD NECKLACE

TULIP NECKLACE

77

THE CREATIVITY CATALOG

SPORTIVO LINKABLE JEWELRY BY ITALIANISSIMO

Sportivo Linkable Jewelry lets you be your own designer without ever going to jewelry school! Simply connect the colorful bands using nickel-free metal links to make ankle and wrist bracelets, necklaces, chokers, and belts. Layer multiple pieces on top of each for eye-catching adornment. Then take everything apart and make something completely new for your next outfit—after all, tomorrow is another day!

The bands are 100% made in Italy and come in a rainbow of colors. They're hypoallergenic, flexible, and soft to the touch. Build a collection of assorted colors and lengths to meet the needs of every occasion. You can even cut the bands down for special sizes.

Necklace bands are ¼ inch thick (0.6 cm) and 18 inches long (45.7 cm). Bracelet bands are ¼ inch thick (0.6 cm) and 9 inches long (22.9 cm).

STIX+STONES NECKLACE BY BRANDON PERHACS (2007)

Stix+Stones is a line of jewelry that gives the wearer the ability to create a diverse array of sculptural compositions using the two fundamental geometries of sphere and rod. The innovative design potential of Stix+Stones is hidden inside the hand-brushed stainless steel rods, dubbed "stix" by the designer, which contain invisible magnetic stops positioned at precise intervals along their length. The magnetized design allows the user to play freely with the components, while at the same time ensuring that the parts array themselves in elegant proportions.

Designed by Brandon Perhacs and made in America. Available in a six-piece set with two stix and four spheres, and a 14-piece set with eight stix and six spheres. The neck cord in both versions is 16 inches long (40.6 cm).

Discover these items at thecreativehome.com

JEWELRY AND APPAREL

SWITCH GEAR INTERCHANGEABLE JEWELRY BY LISA MONAHAN (2008)

Switch Gear Interchangeable Jewelry was created by Massachusetts architect and metalsmith Lisa Monahan. Lisa designed the collection so that you can make all sorts of custom arrangements from the pieces that come in each set. So many that after a while your friends will think you have a walk-in jewelry closet at home—only you'll know that it all comes out of a travel case no bigger than the palm of your hand.

Sets typically include everything you'll need to customize your own earrings and necklaces, including hoops, loops, drops, and chains. All contents are American-made or found, and feature a rich array of unique materials, among them sterling silver, red agate, silver pewter, glass, bright and polished brass, anodized aluminum, colored glass, and one-of-a-kind vintage and industrial pieces.

Collect multiple Switch Gear sets and you'll never run out of something unique to wear!

CHICKIT EARRINGS AND NECKLACES

DAY TO NIGHT EARRINGS AND NECKLACES

TEEN EARRINGS AND NECKLACES

THEWRAP BY ROXI SUGER FOR ANGELROX (2006)

Okay, people, it's a wrap—literally! Thewrap by Roxi Suger for Angelrox is a Brooklyn-designed, transformable knit that gives versatility new meaning. It's a skirt, a dress, a tunic, a shawl, a vest, a kimono, a top—come to think of it, it's all of them. Which makes getting dressed not only fun, but creative too.

Each wrap is lovingly crafted in America from bamboo and rayon, which are sustainable, biodegradable, plant-based fibers made from trees. The knit is incredibly comfortable and smooth on the skin, and creates an elegant drape and flow.

Thewrap comes in one size that will fit just about everybody (yes, every body) thanks to its very flexible material and clever shape. Spot clean when possible to save water and the environment; otherwise hand or machine wash on a delicate setting.

THE CREATIVITY CATALOG

UNO MAGNETIC JEWELRY BY LUIS PONS

UNO, meaning "one" in Spanish, is an interactive magnetic jewelry design that can take the form of a necklace, bracelet, ring, or anything your imagination and a mirror can conjure up. Created by well-known architect and interior designer Luis Pons, UNO Magnetic was born in the course of an architectural project in Miami where Luis was compelled to think outside the building envelope (that's what architects call "the box"). The result was not only a work of architecture, but an innovative idea for jewelry that was both a personal statement about Luis's own cultural identity and a flexible platform for others to make one for themselves.

The structure of UNO Magnetic is deceptively simple, consisting of a specially designed ball chain accompanied by a spherical magnet. Together, however, the possibilities grow more complex, as the two components yield infinitely creative opportunity when working in concert.

In addition to the ball and chain, UNO offers magnetic ornaments like spheres, hearts, rings, and stars to personalize and accentuate the strands. A line of charming magnetic earrings fills out the collection nicely.

At the end of the day, take your UNO jewelry off to store overnight, then combine your pieces in entirely new arrangements the next. That's the magic of magnetism!

This is UNO.

This is u, no?

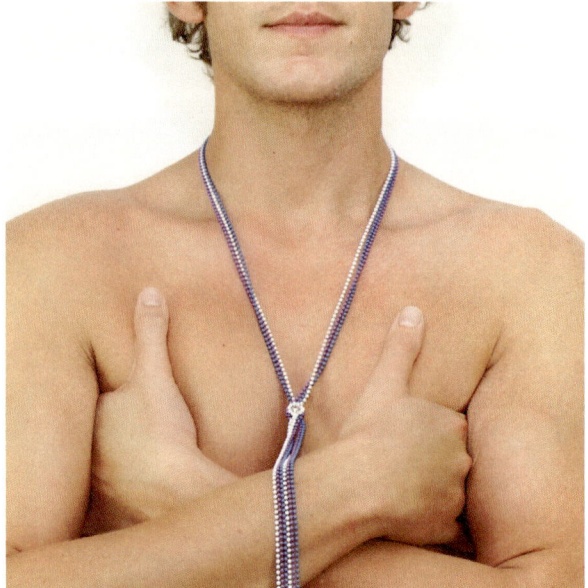

Discover these items at thecreativehome.com

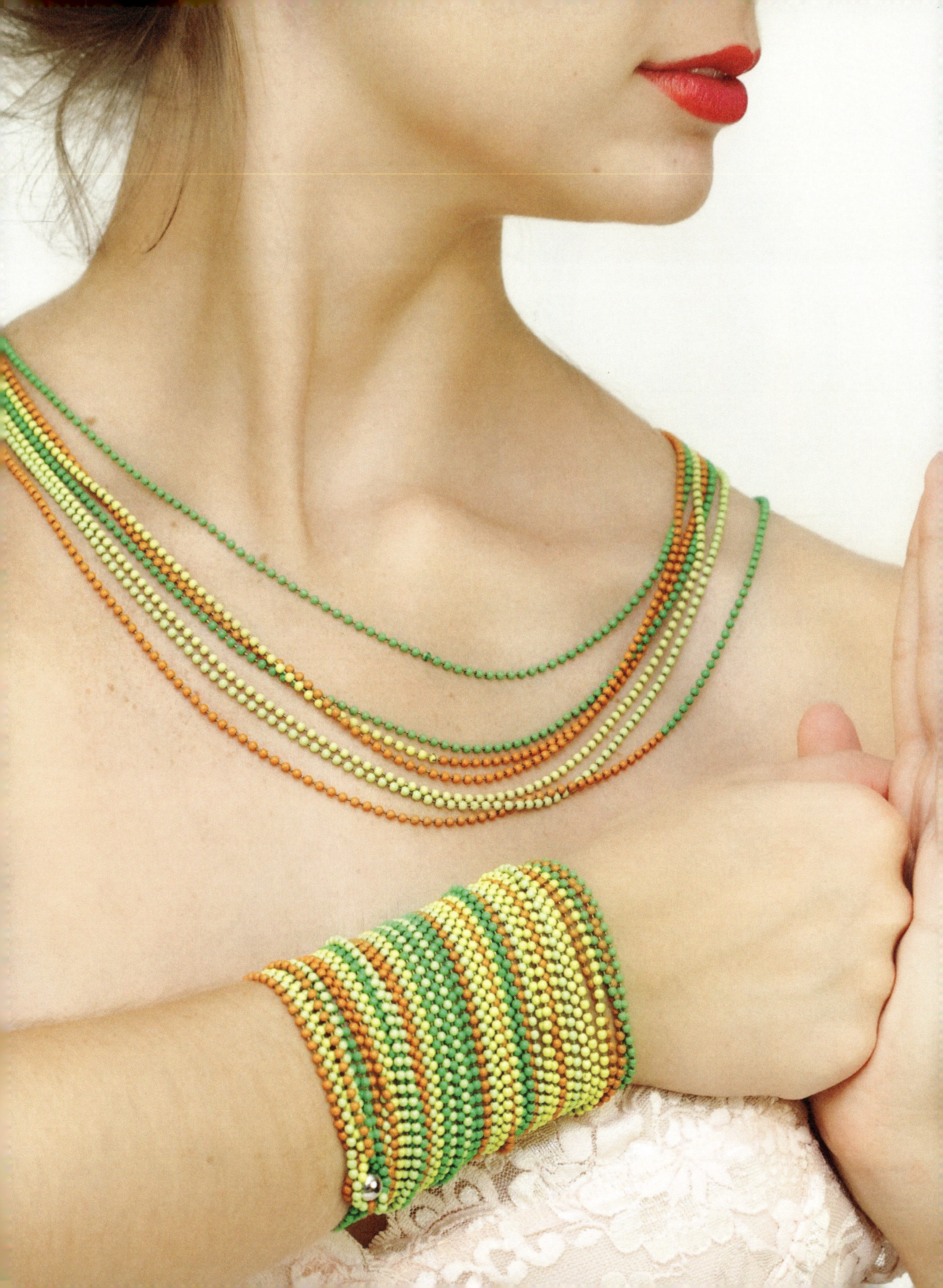

SHELVING AND ORGANIZATION

BOOGIE WOOGIE SHELVING
BY STEFANO GIOVANNONI FOR MAGIS (2004)

Boogie Woogie is right! A term first used to describe a particular style of dance-inducing music in the 1930s and 1940s, it aptly describes the distinctive undulating facade of this modular shelving unit from Magis Design. Assembled in multiple units, the piece produces a unique sculptural effect worthy of Italian Baroque architecture and unlike almost any other shelving system on the market.

The modules are made in Italy of injection-molded ABS plastic, and come in either an open or closed back. They can be stacked on the floor up to four units high and for as long as you've got room. Place them against a wall or use them as room dividers as well as for storage, in which case you might want to place modular groups back to back for a two-sided facade.

Available in a high-gloss Black, Red, and White. Two modules per package.

Each square module measures 20½ inches by 11 inches deep on the outside (52 by 20.7 cm); the clear opening inside the module is about 15 inches square by 11 inches deep (38.1 cm2 by 20.7 cm).

Discover these items at thecreativehome.com

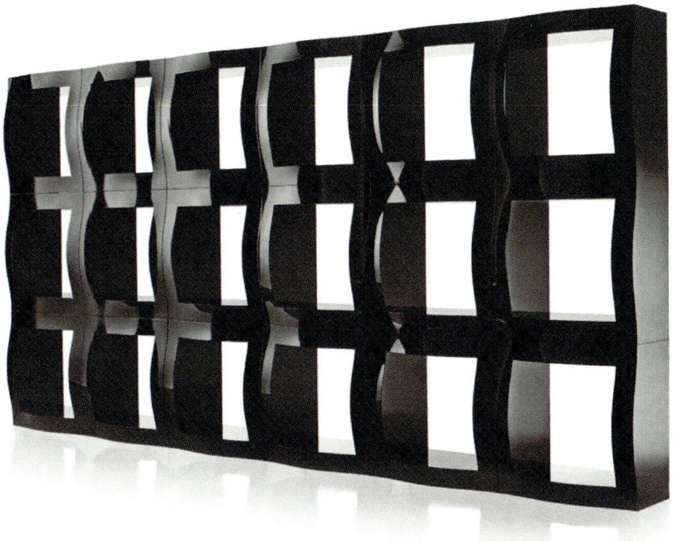

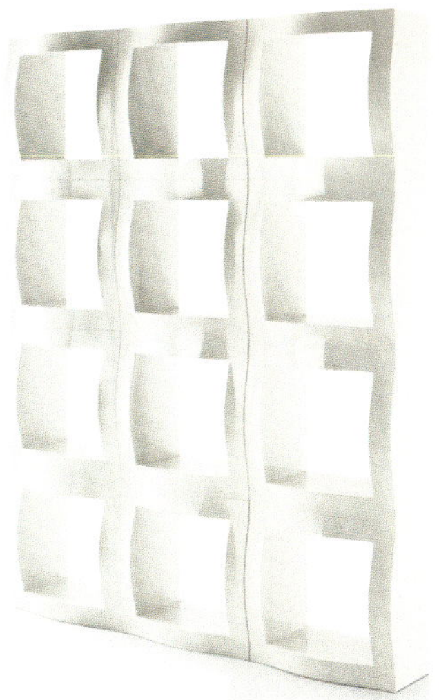

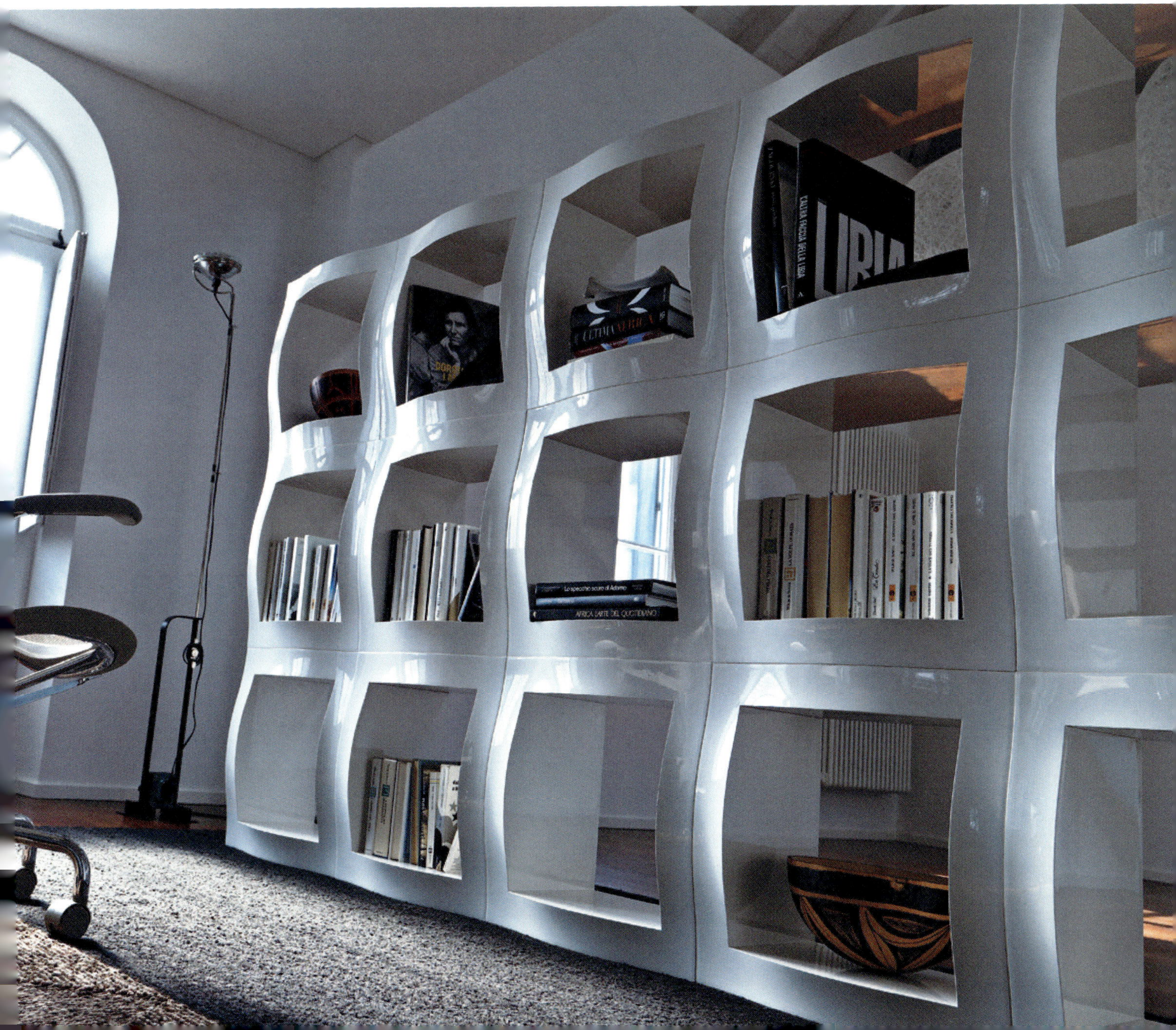
Lo specchio scuro di Adamo
AFRICA L'ARTE DEL QUOTIDIANO

THE CREATIVITY CATALOG

BOOKWORM BY RON ARAD FOR KARTELL (1999)

Not every bookcase needs to play it straight, or so thinks world-renowned designer Ron Arad. Arad clearly threw out the standard playbook when he designed this wall-mounted, customizable shelving system in 1999. It was his careful analysis of extrusion technology which enabled him to create a bookcase that can be bent to assume an unlimited number of curved shapes without compromising strength and functionality.

That means you can create an installation entirely your own. Transform the mundane fact of storing books and objects into a sculptural focal point and accent piece in your space.

Made from batch-dyed, fire-retardant PVC. Each shelf length can support as much as 20 lbs (9 kg) when properly installed.

Available in Short, Medium, and Long lengths and in five colors: Matte Aluminum, Matte White, Opaline Cobalt, Opaline Black, and Opaline Wine Red.

All Bookworms have 7⅞ inch deep shelves (20 cm). Lengths run from 126 to 323 inches long (320 to 820 cm).

CLOUD MODULAR SHELVING BY RONAN AND ERWAN BOUROULLEC FOR CAPPELLINI (2004)

Made of a high-density polystyrene, the Cloud Shelving System has garnered much attention thanks to its modular, original form and innovative materials. Clouds can be stacked and aligned to create large shelving and display units, room dividers, or sculptural installations. There is no limit to the size of a structure you can build with these components other than the size your space. The units, fabricated using a rotational molding technique, are joined by means of snap-on clips.

Cloud is on permanent exhibit at New York's MoMA.

An individual module measures 73¾ by 41½ by 15¾ inches (187.5 by 40 by 105.2 cm).

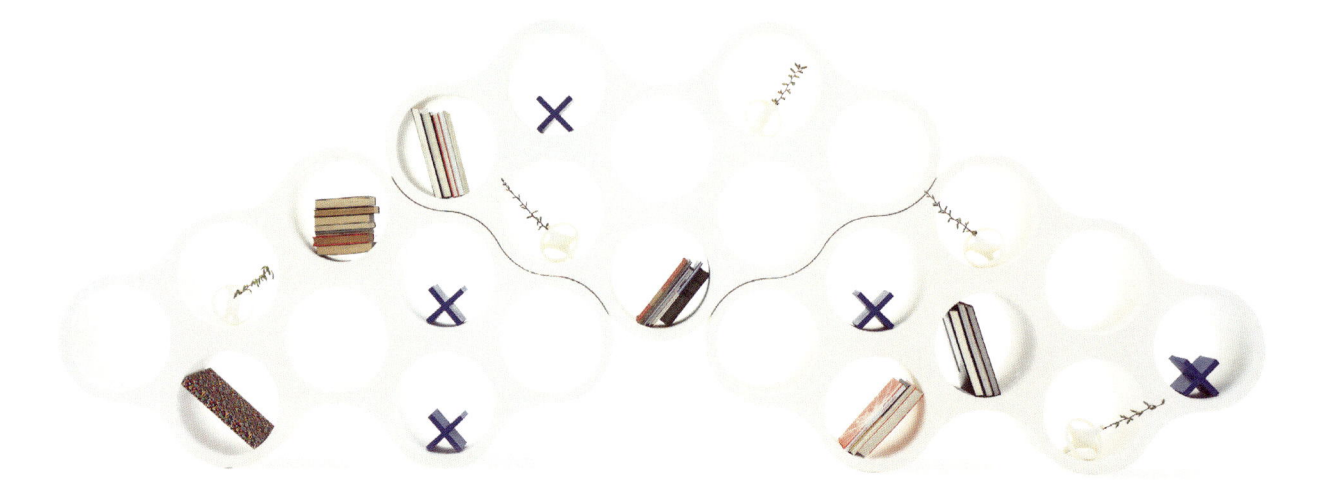

Discover these items at thecreativehome.com

SHELVING AND ORGANIZATION

COMPONIBILI STORAGE SYSTEM BY ANNA
CASTELLI FERRIERI FOR KARTELL (1969)

Flexible, functional, and practical, Kartell's Componibili storage modules have been in production since the 1960s and have been widely recognized for their innovative design. But don't just take our word for it: take a trip to MoMA in New York or the George Pompidou Centre in Paris, where you can view Componibili in their permanent collections.

The series come in Large, Round, and Square units. Each design offers different options for tailoring the design to your specifications, including size, color, and accessories. Select the components in the quantities you need from the available options, then simply stack the pieces together to make your own modular storage grouping. The pieces will just as easily break down and reassemble should you ever need to add to or reconfigure your group.

Slip a set of casters under the bottom unit and your Componibili will go where you go. Or they can sit directly on the floor if you prefer they stay put.

Made in Italy of durable ABS plastic. Square modules are available in White; Large Round comes in Silver and White. Units range in height from 9 to 15 inches (22.9 to 33 cm).

Componibili were designed in 1969 by Anna Castelli Ferrieri (1918–2008), a pioneering architect associated with the postwar period of Italian modern design, and a cofounder of the Kartell brand with her husband.

LARGE ROUND UNITS

SQUARE UNITS

THE CREATIVITY CATALOG

CUBIT AND CUBITEC SHELVING BY DORON LACHISCH FOR DLP PLASTICS

Cubit and Cubitec are award-winning modular shelving systems that give you the ability to create a storage unit tailored precisely to your needs. Put the panels together in the arrangement of your choice, and you're good to go. At least, until the day arrives when you need to expand, change, or relocate your shelving; then it's a snap, as in 1) snap the pieces apart; 2) add, subtract, or reassemble, and 3) reuse.

With shelf modules able to support up to 55 lbs (24.9 kg), both systems work equally well as bookshelves, display pieces, or storage furniture. Despite their strength and durability, Cubit and Cubitec are lightweight and transportable, being made of 100% recyclable injection-molded polypropylene.

The standard Cubit unit comes with open backs and fronts. Doors and back panels can be added and are purchased separately.

Available in Orange and Transparent White. Mix and match colors or stay all in one hue.

Overall dimensions vary with the configuration. The inside dimensions of a single Cubit compartment is 15½ square by 13½ inches deep (39.3 cm^2 by 34.2 cm). Cubit differs in having a depth of 10 inches (25.4 cm), and chamfered corners. By the way, if you want extra deep shelving you can combine units front to back in part or all of your storage piece.

Cubit and Cubitec are the brainchildren of Israeli industrial designer Doron Lachisch, who founded a plastics company in 1979 which continues to manufacture the product today.

CUBIT SHELVING

CUBITEC SHELVING

Discover these items at thecreativehome.com

CUBITEC SHELVING

THE CREATIVITY CATALOG

DRAWERDECOR LINER SYSTEM BY KMN HOME (2010)

The DrawerDecor system is a sleek way to custom organize your kitchen drawer with modern style and a splash of color. No more utensils sliding and banging around inside your drawers. No more holes in your fingers as you jab yourself with a shish kebab holder while rummaging in search of something else. Now the inside of your kitchen drawers can look just as nice as the outside of your kitchen (after you've cleaned up, of course).

DrawerDecor is a four-piece system using a nonslip rubbery material that is tacky to the touch, completely adjustable, and easily rinsed clean. Simply trim a base mat to the size of your drawer bottom and insert. Add dividers where needed to keep utensils in place, and you're done. Need to add something new later, or replace a utensil? No worries—everything in the system is repositionable and reconfigurable, which means less waste and landfill.

Each kit comes with sixteen pieces, including one 14-by-20-inch base mat (35.5 by 50 cm), five 3-inch dividers (7.6 cm), five 1½-inch dividers (3.7 cm), and five ¾-inch triangular dividers (1.9 cm). Available in Iris, Lime, Red, Sky Blue, and Tangerine.

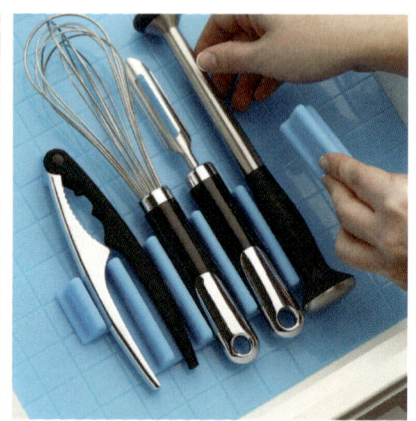

IVY MODULAR COATRACK BY MOS ARCHITECTS FOR LERIVAL

"A doctor can always bury his mistakes. An architect can only advise his client to plant ivy," said the sharp-tongued Frank Lloyd Wright. Ivy is a modular wall hook system—a coatrack for people who hate stuffy old coatracks and wall art for people who hate any coatrack. Arrange the sixteen Y-shaped pieces provided in each package to create an abstracted pattern of a climbing vine or a geometric arrangement of repetitive form. Then hang your hat on it. And gloves. And other stuff.

Available in Charcoal, Green, Pink, and Yellow. In addition to the modules, a package contains all the connectors, wall screws, and anchors needed for installation. Packages can be combined and colors can be mixed. Sixteen modules cover an area equivalent to about 24 by 36 inches (60.9 by 91.4 cm) depending on configuration. Each hook is 5 inches wide by 6 inches long by ½ inch deep (12.7 by 15.2 by 1.2 cm).

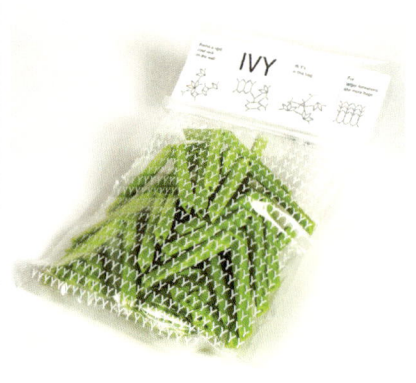

Discover these items at thecreativehome.com

SHELVING AND ORGANIZATION

JOINT VENTURE SHELVING BY MATT GAGNON
FOR RS BARCELONA

Designer Matt Gagnon's Joint Venture Shelving System starts off by questioning whether shelves need to be always straight across. Responding with an emphatic "no," Gagnon steps down his metal shelf unit along its length, and then devises a support system that allows the shelves to be adjusted vertically and bays to be added horizontally. Thanks to the unique shape of the shelves, you can create some pretty interesting visual effects as you position and orient the shelves in various ways.

Not only does this versatility mean you can customize your unit to work with your physical space, it also means that your shelf arrangement could well be unique. We suppose that's why Mr. Gagnon called it Joint Venture—you collaborate with the designer in determining the final configuration of the unit, rather than being a passive consumer who simply takes it as it is. And is stuck with it the same forever.

Assembly is super-easy, requiring no screws or fancy hardware. Start with a pair of vertical supports either 42 or 84 inches (106.6 or 213.3 cm) high, then slide the metal shelves into any of the predrilled slots along their height. That's it! The unit will stand comfortably on the floor with no additional anchoring needed.

Add as many shelving bays as needed, now or in the future. Units break down as easily as they go up, so you can always reconfigure them if you move or redecorate later.

Made in Spain of steel and painted White in durable polyester paint. Shelves are 10 inches (25.4 cm) wide and tall, and 10¼ inches (26 cm) deep.

KEY MODULAR STORAGE BY HOUSEFISH (2008)

Ever experience a sense of dread as you pick up the assembly instructions for a product you purchased? Do you get visions of parts strewn all over the floor and hours of mystification as you analyze the hieroglyphics that pass for a manual these days?

These are just a few of the reasons to make stackable Key Modular Storage by Housefish your shelving and storage of choice. Housefish may well turn out to be the easiest furniture you ever put together. First choose from a menu of sizes, colors, finishes, doors, and open units to create your design. Then gather your modules, assemble them with aluminum keys inserted at each end, and stack. Voila! A super-strong, handsome, and flexible storage piece is yours.

Made with love and care in Denver from 100% USA-sourced material and parts, including FSC-certified wood, and zero-VOC finishes.

LOOPITS STRETCH AND STORE BY HEATHER O'DONAHOE FOR QUIRKY (2013)

We're pretty loopy for Loopits, a fun way to keep things within arm's reach. Think of them as giant elastic bands that wrap around circular mounts you can place just about anywhere, giving you a completely customizable, reconfigurable, and expandable storage solution. Hang all sorts of stuff from the loops—desk supplies at your workstation, utensils in your kitchen, tools in the garage.

Mounts attach to surfaces with either adhesives or screws, and are as easy to install as they are to remove. You can combine multiple sets to expand your storage of network at any time.

Each set includes three small bands and three large bands, and six mounting disks. Disks measure 1 inch diameter by $5/8$ inches deep (2.5 by 1.5 cm); unstretched, the large loop is 12½ inches long (31.7 cm) and the small band 8 inches long (20.3 cm).

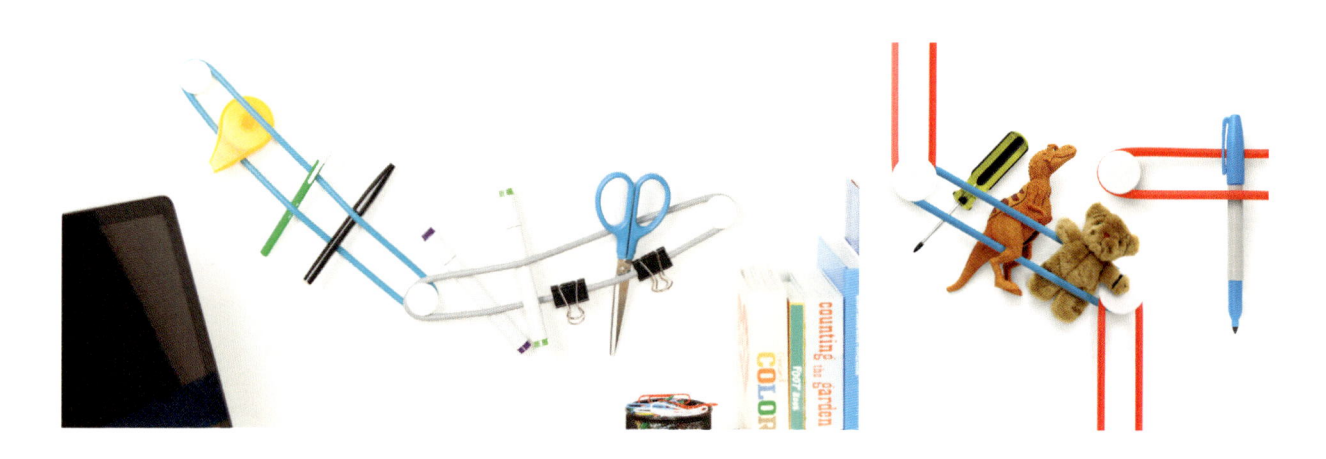

Discover these items at thecreativehome.com

SHELVING AND ORGANIZATION

MIX BOXES BY THE UTILITY COLLECTIVE (2010)

The Mix Boxes return a lo-fi interactivity to a world made busy by complex devices and objects. The set includes six well-crafted boxes of varying size that allow you to create compositions based on your unique design and storage needs.

The Mix Boxes allow for spontaneity and change. The set encourages interaction and allows your own personality into the product. Life is fluid: when circumstances change, the Mix Boxes can change with them.

These products are not mass-produced on an assembly line in some faraway place, then shipped across an ocean. Instead, each Mix Box is numbered and made especially for you in the U.S.

Dimensions for width and height range from 5½ to 38 inches (13.9 to 96.5 cm). Boxes are between 10½ and 15½ inches deep (26.6 to 39.3 cm).

MODULAR BOOKSHELF SYSTEM AND BINS
BY GIULIO POLVARA FOR KARTELL (1974)

Like the building blocks we used to play with as children, this modular bookshelf system from Kartell lets you create an unlimited number of shelf arrangements from just a few simple pieces. When we were kids, blocks meant hours of fun and brain development. Now that we're adults and our brains are done developing, it means getting a shelf unit that suits our space, our budget, and our needs exactly.

Components come flat-packed and ready for assembly: just press the pieces together to lock them in place. There's no need for tools or connecting hardware, which means fewer bruised thumbs and calls to the handyman.

Made from ABS plastic, the shelves are sturdy and durable. Their streamlined cubic geometry works in almost any context, from urban loft to contemporary workspace, from the casual home to a public space. Thanks to their open backs, they can even do double duty as attractive space dividers.

Components are available in Black or White. When assembled, each compartment measures 14 inches (35.5 cm) in height, width, and depth. Add 1⅜ inches (3.4 cm) for each divider.

For even greater versatility, cubic containers designed to slip snugly into any opening let you store loose objects, papers, and other items that are otherwise challenging to keep organized. Made from lacquered polyurethane, the bins are available in Black, Light Blue, Red, White, and Yellow.

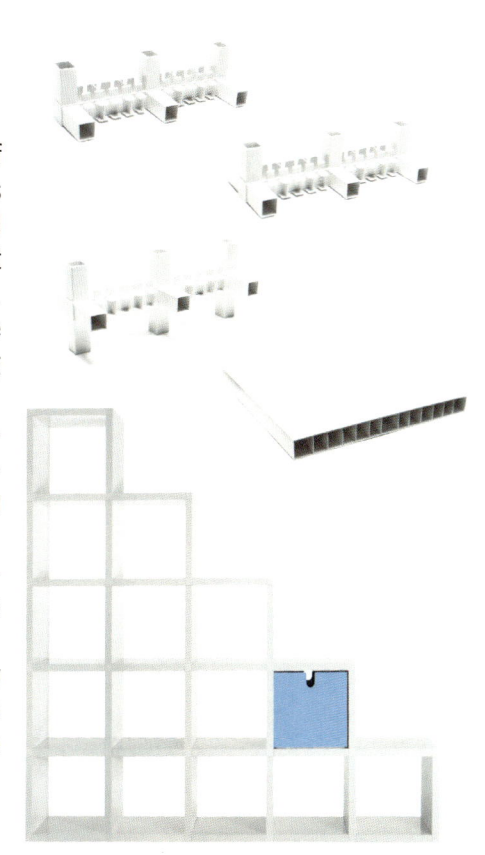

OPTIC STORAGE CUBES BY PATRICK JOUIN FOR KARTELL (2006)

The beautifully made Kartell Optic Storage Cube is notable for the diamond-faceted transparent and reflective surfaces that make up its sides and top, all of which produce a subtly shimmering optical effect when viewed under light.

Each unit has four integral corner supports for placing a cube directly on a floor; the same supports serve as a positioning mechanism for stacking cubes on top of each other. Combine as many units as you want by mounting them vertically or side by side; they'll look right in just about any type of space, from kitchens and baths to living and hospitality environments.

Made from very strong PMMA, the Optic Cube is available with a matching door or an open front, and comes in Crystal, Matte Black, Purple, Red, Smoke, and Yellow.

Dimensions are 15¾ inches (40 cm) in each direction.

OTO 100 STORAGE SYSTEM BY PIL BREDAHL FOR MUUTO (2000)

Muuto's OTO 100 Storage System is a visually distinct shelving unit. Its barrel shelves come in successively larger diameters and hold together by a large heavy-duty elastic band. The narrow profile of the fiberglass barrels and bands give the piece an exceptionally airy look without sacrificing strength and durability.

The pieces all come nested inside each other and are easily assembled in whatever configuration you choose. They'll disassemble just as easily when it's time to move to the next location.

Designed by Phil Bredahl, the OTO 100 Storage System works great for housing books, display pieces, or clothing—not to mention serving as a really cool multi-tier nap place for your cat.

Available in Graphite Black and Warm White. Depending on how you stack the barrels, the dimensions of the unit will fall somewhere around 63 by 11¾ by 41½ inches (160 by 29.8 by 105 cm).

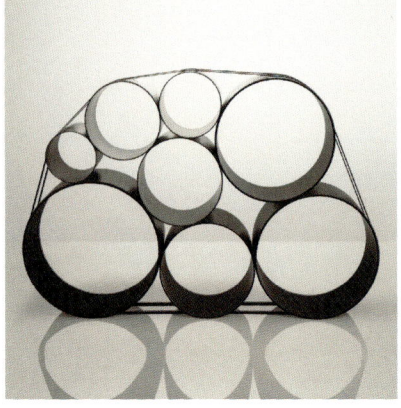

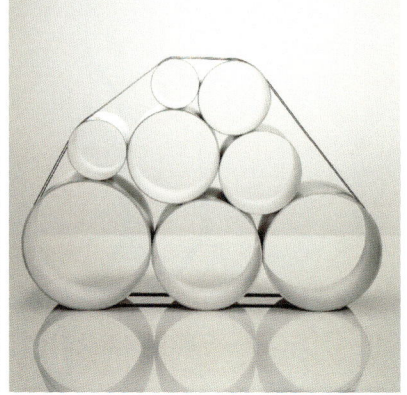

Discover these items at thecreativehome.com

SHELVING AND ORGANIZATION

STACKED SHELVING SYSTEM BY JULIEN DE SMEDT FOR MUUTO
(2007)

If the 21st century is defined by mobility, both physical and communicational, then Muuto's Stacked Shelving System must be the design of the century.

Versatile, flexible, modular, the Stacked Shelving System is made of up three different-sized container modules, white steel clips to bind them together, and an optional podium on which to place them. By varying the number of modules, their orientation and configuration, selecting modules with or without backs, choosing finishes and colors, and deciding what goes inside them, you have almost limitless freedom in shaping your space.

Shelves with backboards include a wall mounting kit, which can be purchased separately for shelves without backboards. Podium and additional clips also sold separately.

Modules are made of White pigmented ash veneer or White paint over MDF. Shelf dimensions range from 8¾ to 25¾ inches wide (22.2 to 65.4 cm) and are 13¾ deep by 17¼ high (34.9 by 43.8 cm). The podium measures 51½ by 13¾ by 8 (130.8 by 43.8 cm).

93

THE CREATIVITY CATALOG

TETRAD SHELVING BY BRAVE SPACE DESIGN

Did you know the word tetrad means a figure made from four squares, at least one of which is connected to another on one or more sides? And that the inventor of the legendary 1980s computer game Tetris coined his name by combining "tetrad" with his favorite game, which happened to be tennis? Neither did we, until we discovered the Tetrad Shelving System from Brave Space Design.

Tetrad Shelving is a modular, lightweight shelving solution comprising five differently shaped units reminiscent of the famed computer game. Create a customized storage piece by stacking the pieces in any arrangement you want (subject to the laws of gravity and physics, of course). Combine multiple sets to produce larger pieces. Then, when you've lived with it long enough, take it down and make a totally new configuration. Life is short, why live with the same old same old?

Tetrad comes in three styles. Tetrad Flat Shelving is most easily recognized by its multicolored metal backs, though it is also available with white backs. Boxes come in Natural Maple or White ¾-inch ply (1.9 cm). Units are 9 inches deep (22.8 cm). Tetrad Bamboo features identical pieces, now constructed from natural and amber bamboo. Tetrad Mega is pretty mega, with shelves that measure 11 inches deep (27.9 cm) and sides 1½ inches thick (3.8 cm). A beveled edge on all sides adds an attractive layer of detail and a unique optical effect when viewed at an angle. Mega is fabricated from walnut and ash veneers. Unlike the first two designs, Mega units have an open back for a transparent effect.

Made to order in America.

BAMBOO SHELVING

MEGA SHELVING

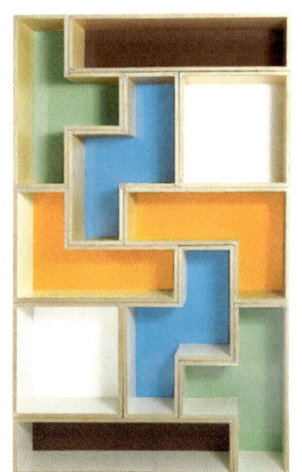

FLAT SHELVING

Discover these items at thecreativehome.com

SHELVING AND ORGANIZATION

USM MODULAR FURNITURE BY FRITZ HALLER (1963)

In the early 1960s, Swiss architect Fritz Haller was commissioned by metalwork manufacturer Paul Schaerer to create a flexible shelving and storage system based on modular architectural structures. Reflecting his professional background, Haller made it a goal to marry technical perfection and durability with design elegance. The result of his efforts was the USM Haller furniture collection. Today the USM line is celebrated as a design classic, and is one of the jewels of MoMA's permanent design collection.

Being streamlined and contemporary in styling, USM furniture works as well in the private home as it does in office, commercial, and other environments. And since it's modular, pieces retain their intrinsic aesthetic qualities no matter how the units are grouped together.

The key component in the USM system is a chrome-plated brass ball joint to which metal panels and chrome steel tubes are attached. These elements provide the supporting structure and the exterior envelope for the components and materials contained inside the modular units.

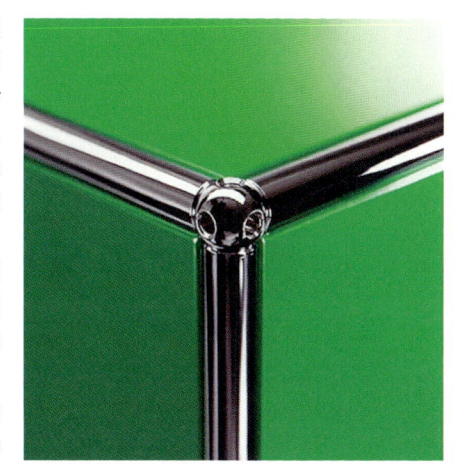

Metal panels are powder coated and available in a range of colors. Finishes are applied using environmentally friendly coating processes.

To meet the high quality and technical standards of USM furniture, pieces are shipped fully assembled to their destination. White Glove delivery means the piece will be delivered to your location, uncrated, and put in place for you.

You can order from a catalog of Quick Ship products, which can be on their way in as little as one to two weeks. Other preconfigured assemblies ship in ten to twelve weeks. Or you can work with USM-trained designers to create your own custom unit to fit your needs and vision exactly, using the modular system Haller devised over a half-century ago.

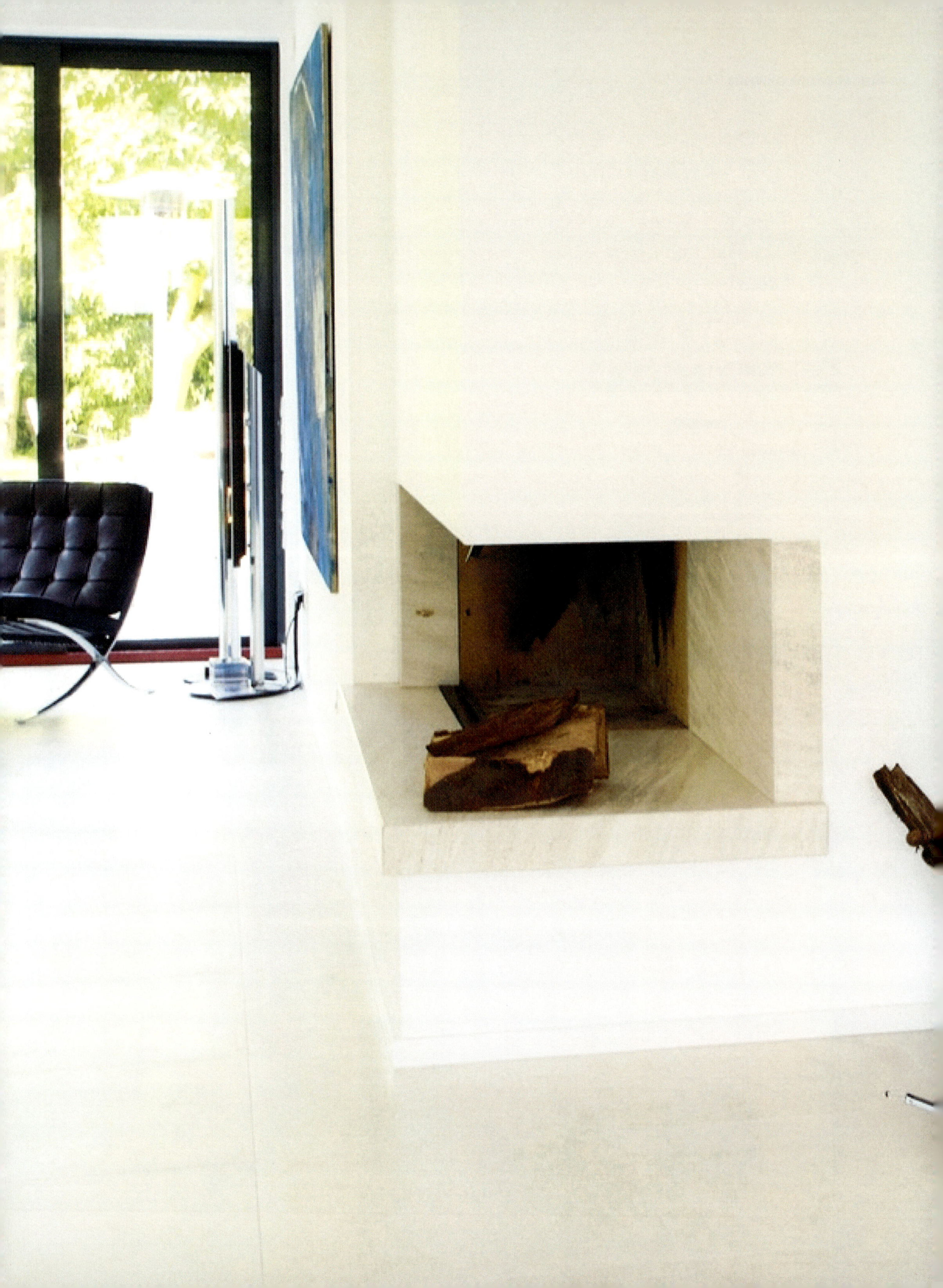

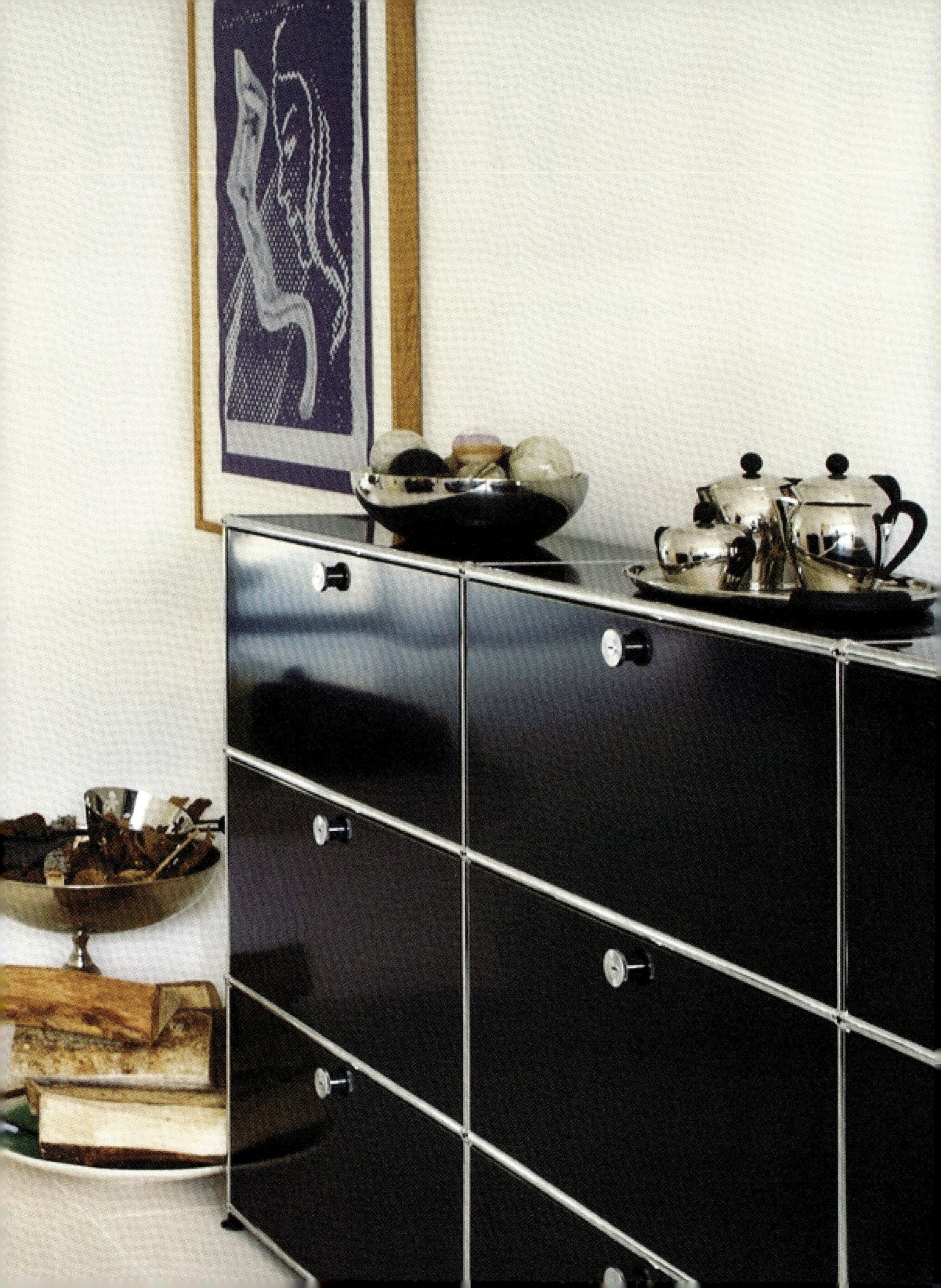

WAY BASICS STORAGE CUBES

These economical yet attractive storage cubes are made of zBoards, an environmentally sustainable product formed from 99% post-consumer recycled paper. zBoards go together without tools or hardware. Super-strong 3M brand adhesive strips let you fit the pieces neatly together. Just peel, stick, and you're done.

Honest. Holds up to 50 pounds (22.6 kg) per cube, which makes them pretty darn strong. Stack a few of them on top of each other or run them along the floor—go ahead, they can take it!

Cubes come in two sizes. The Cube Plus is plus-sized: 13½ by 15½ by 11¼ inches (34.3 by 39.3 by 28.5 cm). The regular Cube measures about 13½ by 12½ by 11¼ inches (34.3 by 31.7 by 28.5 cm).

Cubes come in Green and Orange (good for kids), and Black, Blue, Espresso, Green, Natural, Orange, Pink, and White (good for the rest of us).

Discover these items at thecreativehome.com

SHELVING AND ORGANIZATION

YUBE CUBE MODULAR STORAGE

The Yube Cube is a totally new kind of modular furniture and storage system based on three core concepts:

Easy: Four sides snap together quickly with a slide-in back; steel frame locks and corner clips push into place to make a rigid structure.

Personalized: You can get exactly what you want by outfitting your cubes with additional features like doors, shelves, bins, and support feet in just the assortment you want. Need to change your arrangement later? No problem—it can all break down and reassemble in another configuration just as easily as it went up.

Sustainable: All materials used in the Yube are recycled, recyclable, or biodegradable. The Yube outer panels are made from compostable sugarcane, the frames from Woodlite, a proprietary compound of nontoxic moldable plastic mixed with bamboo, the planet's fastest growing renewable wood resource. Woodlite utilizes 20% to 30% less nonrenewable resources than similarly molded products. It even smells good and, unlike regular plastic, there is a pleasing, lightly sweet aroma to remind you this is no ordinary material.

There are lots of accessories to outfit your Yubes with, including feet, shelves, canvas bins, and doors. Cubes are 14¼ inches (36 cm) in all outside dimensions.

CHILDREN

3DOODLER PRINTING PEN
BY MAXWELL BOGUE AND PETER DILWORTH (2013)

Traditional Old World draftsmanship meets New World technology in the 3Doodler, the world's first 3D printing pen. Unlike many technologically conceived devices, however, this one is easy to use out of the box. In fact, if you can trace, scribble, or sign your name; you can use the 3Doodler to create three-dimensional drawings in the air or build up sculptures on a tabletop.

Fundamentally, the 3Doodler is like a 3D printer except you hold it in your hand and it's powered by your mind instead of a computer file. Just plug it in, insert a supply of colored plastic, heat it up, and you're ready to create with the press of a button and the movement of your hand.

This is one of those ideas that seem outwardly simple, yet only occurred to a small group of creative people just a few years ago. Mind you, so excited was the world about this invention once it was announced that the Doodler team raised an astonishing $2.3 million on Kickstarter—after asking for just $30,000 in seed money. And no wonder: the 3Doodler is a unique item that appeals to hobbyists and artists, grown-ups and children, the technologically literate and the digitally disinclined.

A starter kit includes a 3Doodler pen, power cord, and a choice between two types of plastics. Additional packets containing fifty strands in a variety of colors can be purchased separately.

Discover these items at thecreativehome.com

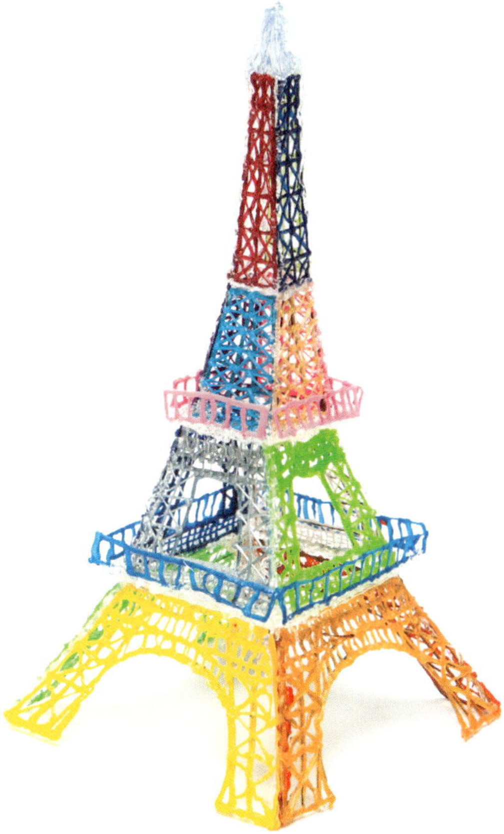

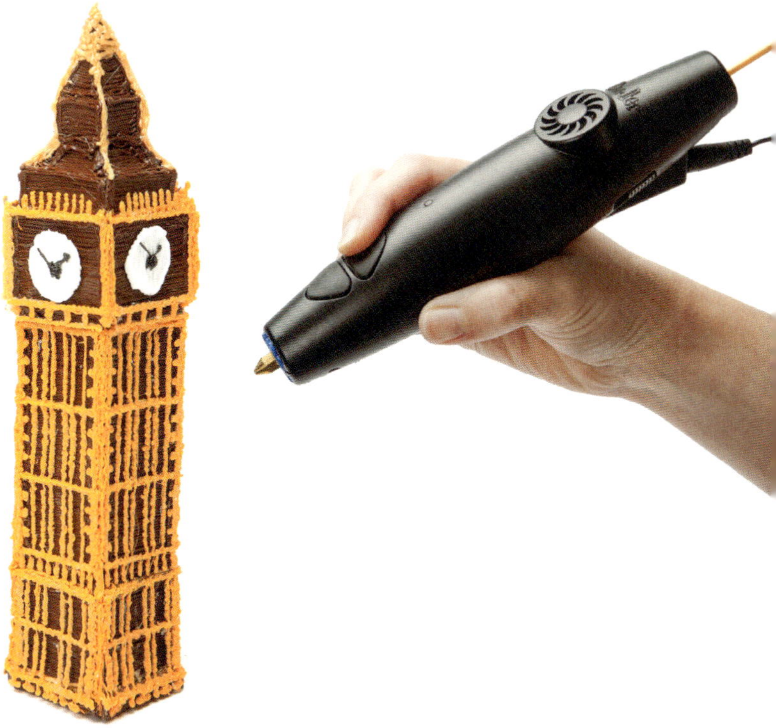

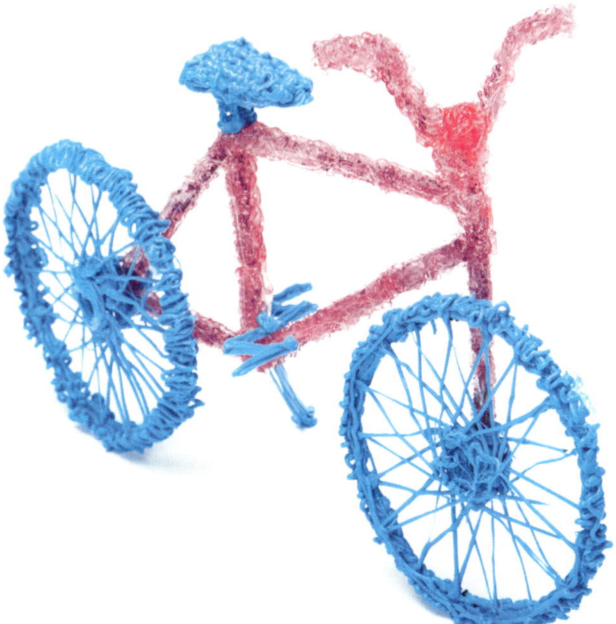

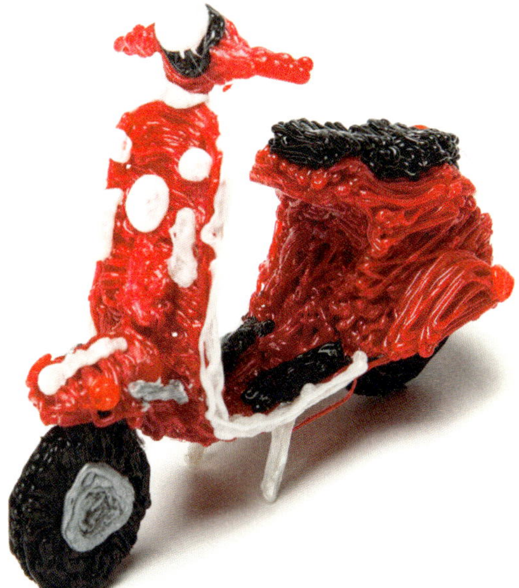

THE CREATIVITY CATALOG

ALPHABET FACTORY BLOCKS BY HOUSE INDUSTRIES FOR UNCLE GOOSE (2012)

House Industries was formed in 1994 as a font foundry specializing in handmade typographic designs. So it's entirely fitting that the equally talented alphabet block company Uncle Goose would collaborate with them to produce the Alphabet Factory blocks set.

Inspired by the original House Industries factory logo and featuring a selection of letters, numbers, and symbols from House's renowned font collections, the blocks are not only played with by hand, but they are made by hand as well. In other words, this is an analog product through and through.

Made in America from basswood, each set contains twenty-four cubes 1¾ inches square on each face (4.4 cm^2). For ages three and up, and later stage people who admire a post-industrial aesthetic.

ARCHITECTURAL STANDARD UNIT BUILDING BLOCKS BY MELISSA & DOUG

Give a child the chance to design architectural masterpieces with this set of forty-four hand-scrolled and -turned wooden blocks in eleven different shapes. Columns, pediments, voussoirs (the wedge shapes in traditional archways)—it's a veritable treasure chest of classic architecture.

The natural finish, smooth-sanded hardwood block set is packaged in a handsome wooden storage crate for easy storage. Packaged dimensions are 4½ by 15 by 12 inches (11.4 by 38.1 by 30.4 cm).

Recommended for ages three and up.

Discover these items at thecreativehome.com

AUTOMOBLOX BY PATRICK CALELLO (2004)

Many parents are familiar with the childhood impulse to pull things apart, often to their chagrin. Well, this toy may be the solution to the problem. Automoblox is deliberately designed for children to engage in unstructured action play with a collection of modular car and truck designs whose pieces are actually meant to come apart. Only now, kids are encouraged to put them back together so they can play with the cars, or better yet, to interchange them with other models for a vehicular mash-up. Think of Automoblox as creative destruction for the pre-entrepreneurial set.

Models include sports cars, utility vehicles, hot rods, trucks, and vans. Automoblox come individually in full-sized versions as well as in sets of miniature vehicles for people with smaller hands, or smaller garages, or who just like smaller things.

Beautifully designed by founder Patrick Calello, the products stand out for their visual quality, ingenious interlocking part system, and predominantly wood construction. Calello came up with the concept while still a student at Rhode Island School of Design; ever since then he's been driven to bring his idea to market, to the joy of miniature motorheads everywhere.

Automoblox is recommended for ages three and up, although we caution grown-ups from hogging them too often.

M9 SPORT VAN

C9P SPORTS CAR

C9-R SPORTS CAR

THE CREATIVITY CATALOG

T9 PICK-UP

104

T900 TRUCK

X9-X SPORT UTILITY

Discover these items at thecreativehome.com

BALANCING BLOCKS BY FORT STANDARD FOR AREAWARE (2012)

We can't tell which is a better analogy for these distinctive balancing blocks: the great sculptor Isamu Noguchi or the Flintstones. Depends on your cultural frame of reference, we guess. Either way, you can't help but admire the unexpectedly novel way of thinking about blocks that notable Brooklyn design firm Fort Standard brought to the task.

Instead of conventional cubic forms, each block is carved into a multifaceted shape that appears irregular at first glance, yet carefully distributes the mass of the block around a central axis to facilitate stacking. Build 'em up, tear 'em down—the solid wood blocks can take it, because they're handmade from repurposed hardwood salvaged from old furniture.

Available in Multicolor and White, finished in a nontoxic paint that allows the natural grain to show through. Comes as a set of ten blocks in a nice cotton drawstring bag and handsome packaging suitable for gifting. A hands-on treat for children and grown-ups alike.

BALL OF WHACKS BY ROGER VON OECH FOR CREATIVE WHACK COMPANY (2006)

Rubik has his cube, van Oech has his equilateral quadrilateral, or more precisely, a spherical shape formed by thirty rhombi held together by powerful rare-earth magnets. Not so powerful, however, that you can't pull them apart and recombine them into an infinite number of configurations. Abstract geometric shapes, representative animal, vegetable, and mineral figures, celestial bodies—you'll never lack for new combinations to explore.

This is one of those rare toys that work as well for adults as it does for younger folk (you know, the ones who figure out the Rubik's Cube in about half the time you do). Do it while watching late night comedy shows, waiting at the airport, driving through midtown (as a passenger, of course), or pretending to work. Actually, in stimulating brain activity and hand-eye coordination you may well find yourself zipping through the rest of your day after just a little activity with the Ball.

Available in Black, Blue, Multicolor, and Red. Comes with a creativity guide full of tips and exercises written by Mr. von Oech. Multiple sets can be combined to form larger figures.

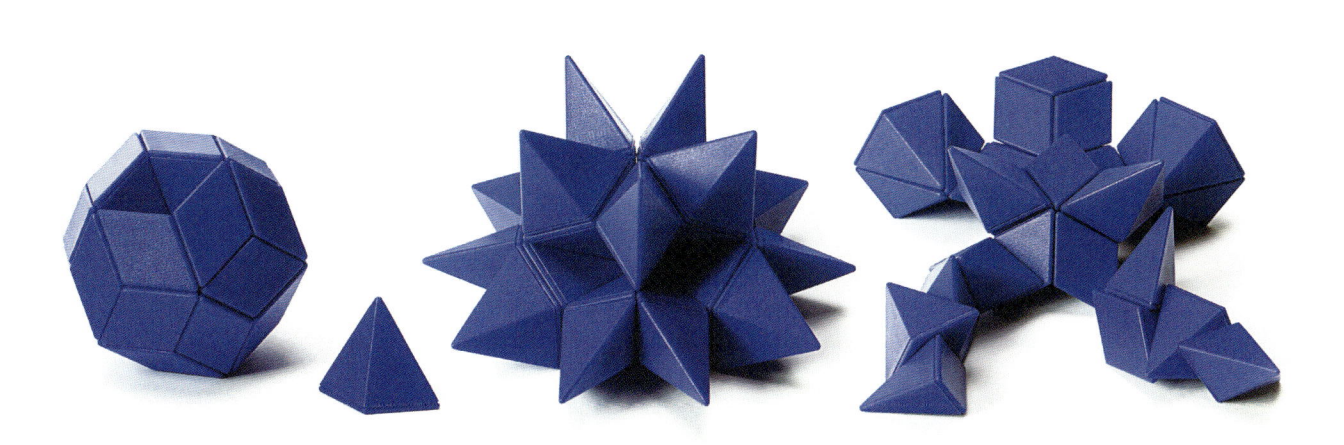

THE CREATIVITY CATALOG

BAUHAUS OPTICAL TOP BY LUDWIG HIRSCHFELD-MACK (1923), REISSUED BY NAEF

Bauhaus graphic artist and educational toy specialist Ludwig Hirschfeld-Mack (1893–1965) designed this Optical Color Mixer Top in 1923. Sold as one of several successful toy products executed by Bauhaus workshops and instructors, the piece was eventually discontinued, only to resume regular production in 1977. The toy is not only fun but instructive as well because it shows how form and color are optically transformed under the effects of motion. Having seven interchangeable discs to play with means way more fun than just the same old top going round and round. They also hold helpful information on the back side explaining the optical phenomenon brought about by each disc.

Made of wood, the top has a diameter of approximately 4 inches (10 cm). Recommended for children and other people three and up.

106

BIMODAL BLOCKS BY TIM BOYLE FOR BRINCA DADA (2012)

We hesitate to call these blocks because . . . well, because they look like no other block set we've seen. Whereas most blocks are a series of identical cubes with printed or carved decoration, these are undulating, irregular, nonrepetitive, and let the natural wood grain be the decoration. Which may be why they're so appealing, fun, and exceptionally stimulating to the imaginations of child and grown-up alike.

Hand-carved BiModal Blocks will last a lifetime, or more realistically, multiple lifetimes. As stunning in the playroom as they are in the living room or office. Twenty-two pieces per set.

Oh, and did we mention that you can also use these blocks to play games? It's true—in fact, a total of four different games with up to three players, as described in the booklet provided.

Not for children under the age of three.

Discover these items at thecreativehome.com

CHILDREN

BUILDING BLOCK MENORAH BY DECOR CRAFT

Be the first on your block to build a menorah with interchangeable building bricks! The colorful snap-together pieces will stack and join in a limitless number of possible arrangements, which will delight kids (and grown-ups who are kids at heart) by giving them an outlet for creativity and imagination. A joyous holiday just got even better!

The set includes forty building blocks and twelve removable stainless steel cup inserts for the candles. Each block measures 1¼ inches square (3.2 cm^2).

CHANGEABLE LUNCHBOXES BY WHIPSAW FOR YUBO (2007)

In an eco-conscious world, it's difficult to rationalize using disposable food holders for your kids' lunch day after day. Neither is it fun for kids to have their food squashed into a mushy mess because they're packed in a soft pouch and buried under a lot of other lunches at school. Oh, and did we mention the hassle of trying to clean out lunch pouches when they can't go in a dishwasher?

Time to bag the baggies and the pouches, parents! This adorable modular lunchbox and container system solves all these problems, and more. Each set comes with one large and two small lidded containers, detachable front and back lids, and an icepack. Add some medium-sized containers and an attachable drink holder for even more food flexibility.

And we saved the best for last: your kids can decorate their boxes with removable cover plates illustrated with kid-friendly themes, from dinosaurs to cupcakes. Collect different plates and swap them out to keep the look as fresh as the food.

All pieces are dishwasher safe, except the cover plates, which are easily removed for cleaning. Outside dimensions are 10 by 7 by 3½ inches (25.4 by 17.7 by 8.8 cm).

THE CREATIVITY CATALOG

CHILD'S CHAIR BY KRISTIAN VEDEL (1957), REISSUED BY ARCHITECTMADE

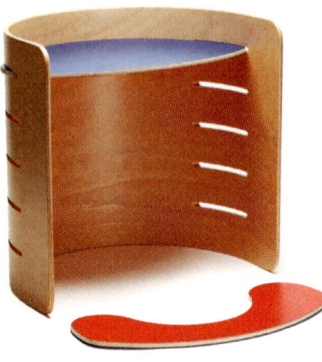

Architect Kristian Vedel (1923–2003) designed children's furniture in a simple, modern style that grew out of a child's nature, rather than as miniature versions of "grown-up" pieces. He thought about the ways a child moves, and incorporated their inclination to use furniture for playing as well as for its stationary purpose into his designs.

Vedel's reconfigurable Child's Chair of 1957 exemplifies his design principles. It's a semicircular bent plywood form, with horizontal cutouts to accommodate adjustable pieces of laminated plywood. The adjustable curved pieces are held in place by friction, resulting in a perfect design for a safety-conscious child's chair, without the use of any potentially abrasive screws, nails, or bolts, or sharp corners.

Thanks to the removable pieces and abstract geometry, Vedel's chair can be utilized for various ends, from a seat, table, rocker, or highchair, to something entirely imagined—in other words, a toy.

"My purpose was to create a combination of a child chair and a tumble stool, appealing to the children's own fantasies and their varying psychological and physical needs. A tool, to support single as well as group of children, which in size, form, weight, and character, fits as many situations and ages as possible," wrote Vedel.

The architect designed the chair to be useful during all phases of a child's development, from crawling to sitting to standing up and eventually to walking. Nor does the potential value of the chair end with adulthood; it can still be used as a stool or side table even after childhood is just a memory. That memory can live on even longer by giving the piece to a grandchild or family relation to enjoy as an heirloom piece spanning generations.

The dimensions of the upright chair are 17 by 12¼ by 16 inches (43.1 by 30.7 by 40.6 cm).

Discover these items at thecreativehome.com

CHILDREN

COLOREM CHALK CUBES BY MIRJAM HÜTTNER FOR NAEF (2010)

Dot-dot-comma-dash and the smiley face is finished. So what's next? Five water-soluble chalk crayons enable children to draw their imaginary world on the twelve maple wood cubes, which are varnished with high quality blackboard paint to give them a beautiful and erasable drawing surface.

In no time, colorful cats or fabulous magical fishes are created. Maybe then you untie the elastic cord that holds the cubes together and rearrange them to create fantastical images of never imagined creatures. Or turn over a few cubes at a time and fill in the missing parts for some really interesting brain development exercises. Wow, the blackboard at school never did that!

The set includes five water-soluble chalk crayons (White, Green, Red, Blue, and Yellow), an elastic cord to tie the cubes together, and a sponge for cleanup.

DADO CONSTRUCTION TOYS BY FAT BRAIN TOYS (2007-2010)

DADO CUBES

Dado is a free-play creative construction toy that combines art and science as you and your child explore the architectural principles of proportion, balance, structure, and color. Unlike many traditionally stackable construction toys, Dado toys utilize slotted pieces to facilitate the stable assembly of a nearly limitless array of potential three-dimensional structures. Not only does this make Dado toys fun to play with, but it also encourages the development of all sorts of mental and manual skills in your child. Build things, build minds could well be the Dado motto.

Dado Planks comes with 106 planks in five bright colors. Dado Squares features thirty-five 3-inch-wide slotted plates that can be used to create structures as much as 36 inches high (91.4 cm). A set of Dado Cubes contains ten nested cubes, scaled from 1 to 5 inches (2.5 to 12.7 cm). All are made in America (yes, America) of durable, heavy-duty plastic.

Since their debut, Dado toys have been recognized as an exceptional learning toy, with so many awards and commendations that we couldn't possibly list them all here!

Recommended for ages three and up.

THE CREATIVITY CATALOG

DADO PLANKS

110

DADO SQUARES

Discover these items at thecreativehome.com

DR. LAKRA'S MUTANT LABORATORY FOR GENERAL MONSTERS (2012)

Dr. Lakra's Mutant Laboratory includes eighty-four recycled cardboard paper triangles that form cartoon characters created by the Mexican artist Dr. Lakra, whose work is represented in the collection of New York's MoMA. Recombine the cards to create another 190,000 or so fun and freaky mutant characters of your own (that should keep folks busy for a while!).

The set includes an instructive booklet and Dr. Lakra's fifty favorite mutant combinations.

Ages three years and up, and for grown-ups who may never grow up.

EAMES HOUSE BLOCKS BY HOUSE INDUSTRIES FOR UNCLE GOOSE (2010)

Charles (1907–1978) and Ray (1912–1988) Eames were among the most important designers in mid-century America. In the late 1940s, they were invited to design a model home as part of the famous Case Study program held by the magazine *Arts & Architecture*. Set back from a cliff overlooking the Pacific Ocean, and assembled within a matter of weeks of prefabricated steel parts intended for industrial construction, the structure ultimately became the home and studio where they would spend the rest of their lives. Today it stands as a milestone of 20th-century American architecture and has been designated a National Historic Landmark.

Tours of the exterior of the Eames House and studio are available if you travel to California; otherwise you can bring this iconic piece of residential architecture to the convenience of your own home with these beautiful printed wood blocks (and for a lot less, we might add). Each set of thirty-six sustainable Michigan-grown basswood blocks represents twenty-nine separate hand-pulled screen passes. In the true Eames spirit of modular design, the blocks disassemble and recombine in a multitude of patterns.

An heirloom accessory as well as a beautiful tool for teaching young people about their design heritage, these blocks will be declared a landmark of their own by anyone who has the pleasure of viewing them.

Made in America for ages two and up. Hip, hip hooray!

THE CREATIVITY CATALOG

ECO-DOUGH BY ECO-KIDS (2008)

This play dough looks good enough to eat! And no wonder, because Eco-Dough is made from all natural ingredients, such as plant, fruit, and vegetable extracts. Essential oils keep the dough soft and pliable while providing a light aroma. And the colors are absolutely mouthwatering (there we go again). Not surprisingly, Eco-Dough was first sold in farmer's markets, and since then has become the leader in the natural dough market.

Just check out these ingredients to understand why: natural and organic fruit, plant and vegetable extracts from annatto seed, beets, blueberries, carrots, paprika, purple sweet potato, red cabbage, and spinach, flour, salt, cream of tartar, organic rosemary oil, vitamin E oil, soybean oil, coconut oil, potassium sorbate, and citric acid. All natural means peace of mind for your kids' safety as they develop their imagination through creative play.

Each pack of Eco-Dough contains five four-ounce containers (113.4 g). Manufactured in the great state of Maine by a family of five. Great for kids two to eight years old, and older.

EXTREME STUNT KIT BY WALL COASTER (2009)

Stick it to the wall and let their imaginations roll! The Wall Coaster Extreme Stunt Kit has interchangeable parts so kids can build all sorts of rolling marble runs up to 13 feet (3.9 m) long while learning principles of gravity, how weight can affect speed, spatial reasoning, and all sorts of brain developments.

Pieces are made of lightweight ABS plastic, and adhere with reusable adhesive that peels off easily. Kids can use the kit on almost any surface, and can change the design as many times as they like for new and different marble runs.

A kit includes two three-quarter change-ups, four half-circle zigzags, one extra-large catcher, two three-hole crazy circles, six 10-inch coaster tracks, three 4-inch coaster tracks, ten 1-inch coaster tracks, two 6-inch coaster tubes, two coaster bands, one package of reusable non-marking coaster tack, and four blue lightweight crystal marbles. And here's a bonus: the marbles are glow-in-the-dark!

Invented by a twelve-year-old (with help from Dad), and made in America with 90% recycled materials. For ages five and up.

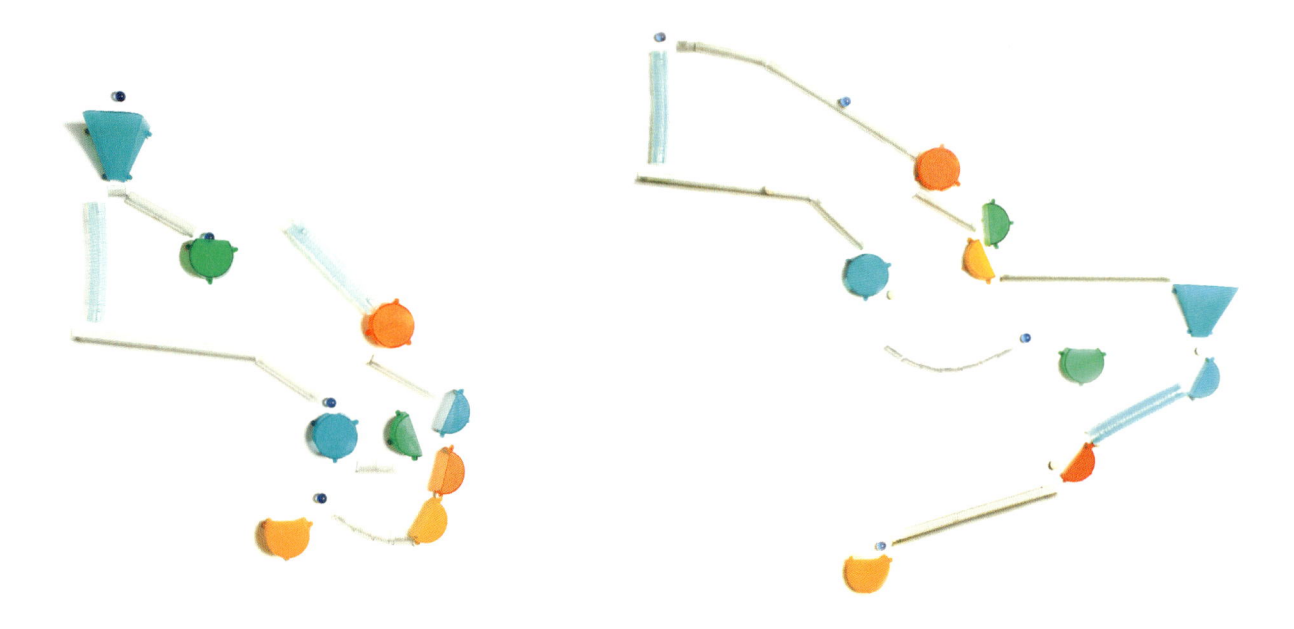

Discover these items at thecreativehome.com

FRACTILES MAGNETIC TILING TOY

Create snowflakes, starbursts, fireflies, or beautifully abstract patterns with the Fractiles art and design toy. It's fun that's guaranteed to never end, because there really is no limit to the number of different arrangements you can make out of these magnetic, multicolored, diamond-shaped tiles. For us, the best part is that Fractiles is a versatile toy with no right or wrong solution (unlike conventional puzzles having only one correct answer), so creativity will never succumb to perceptions of failure.

When it's time to close out the day's play, the toy can be safely tucked away without worrying about pieces falling off, thanks to the firm magnetic hold of the tiles. The next day, just pick up right where you left off by moving tiles around with simple, easy hand motions.

Fractiles are an excellent tool for nurturing creativity, pattern recognition, social collaboration, and compositional technique. Kids will get pleasure from using them whether they're on their own or in a group, at home or on a road trip. Did we say road trip? The Travel set is a handy 8-inch square (20.3 cm^2) package with ninety-six tiles. The Fridge gives you forty-eight tiles while the Large Set weighs in at a hefty one hundred and ninety-two pieces.

Suitable for ages six and up (and when we say up, we mean grown-ups). Made in America.

FREE UNIVERSAL CONSTRUCTION KIT BY F.A.T. LAB AND SY-LAB FOR ADAPTERZ LLC (2012)

The great open-ended construction toys we all know and love—LEGO, Duplo, Fischertechnik, Gears! Gears! Gears!, K'NEX, Bristle Blocks, Lincoln Logs, Tinkertoys, Zome, and Zoob—are largely closed systems, meaning they can't be used in connection with other products. Now imagine this all changed, and you could create the world's first construction toy mash-up where pieces from one design can connect to the others. Makes a creative toy builder salivate with possibilities!

Drool no more, friend. The Free Art & Technology Lab (aka F.A.T.) and Sy-Lab (aka Sy-Lab) have jointly come up with an ingenious solution to the problem: make connectors to connect the disconnected! That's right, the eighty pieces in their Free Universal Connector Kit are designed to marry modules from one system to another so you can be free to explore the nirvana of uber-interoperability.

It's easy to make your own set of connectors. First, download the free Construction Kit file. If you own or have access to any of the open-hardware desktop 3D printers, such as the Makerbot, RepRap, Ultimaker, or Printrbot, you can use the file to output your connectors. Another option is to upload the file to an online 3D printing service bureau (Ponoko, Sculpteo, or Shapeways for example), who will make and ship the kit back to you (for a few bucks).

If none of these are in the cards, you could console yourself by downloading the Free Universal Connector Kit poster and hang it on your wall. Think of it as a pinup for the toy crowd!

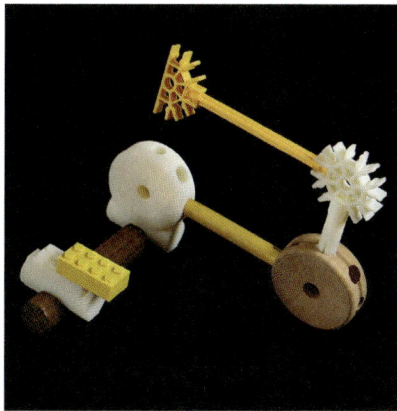

THE CREATIVITY CATALOG

FROEBEL GIFTS REISSUED BY RED HEN BOOKS AND TOYS

In the 19th century Friedrich Froebel changed the way we think about early childhood education. He and his followers designed a collection of educational toys to demonstrate that children learn by playing. Known around the world as the Froebel gifts, these objects were an important aspect of the pedagogic concept he named kindergarten (a garden where children can grow). The Froebel gifts have been widely imitated and adapted by educators and toy makers ever since.

Gifts two through six comprise a suite of variously shaped wood blocks. All but one begin with the form of a cube, which is then subdivided according to specific proportional relationships. The beautiful wood boxes in which the gifts are stored encourage the return of the blocks back to their original cubic whole when the play ends. To help the novice navigate their educational journey through the numbered sequence of gifts, Froebel expert Scott Bultman has prepared the booklet *A Guide to Froebel Blocks*, which can be purchased separately.

It is famously recounted that architect Frank Lloyd Wright was given a set of the Froebel blocks at age nine (thanks Mom!), and in his autobiography declared that he learned the geometry of architecture in kindergarten play. Could the next great architect be just waiting for their blocks?

Discover these items at thecreativehome.com

GRIMM'S SPIEL UND HOLZ DESIGN CREATIVE TOYS

Founded in 1978, Grimm's Spiel und Holz Design is a relative newcomer to the German toy industry, given the country's role in defining modern childhood play. For it was there that Friedrich Froebel introduced kindergarten in the mid-19th century, and promoted the value of specially designed wood objects as teaching tools.

Froebel's advocacy of hands-on learning heavily influenced later school movements, such as Waldorf and Montessori. Motivated by similar principles, Grimm's toys are intended to encourage kids to engage in open-ended manual play using simple yet visually compelling wood objects. Pieces are hand-cut and sanded, and colored with nontoxic water-based dyes that meet American and European safety standards. No lacquer is used in order to preserve the natural feel of the wood through the dyes and enhance the tactile experience. A little bit of tooth also helps keep stacking blocks stacked.

Grimm's stacking and nesting toys, like the Large Pyramid and Elements series, help strengthen hand-eye coordination as well as reasoning skills essential to problem-solving. (These two toys are eloquent symbols of our dual nature: the proportionally graduated and prismatically shaped Pyramid blocks represent the coolly rational half of our brain that seeks to quantify, align, and organize, whereas the nonrepetitive and irregularly shaped Elements collection evokes our emotional and intuitive side.) The company's line of magnetic toys is oriented toward more two-dimensional activities, such as composition and picture-making.

Other Grimm's products include puzzles, baby rattles, doll houses and furniture, mobiles, decorative items, roll-along animals, and vehicles.

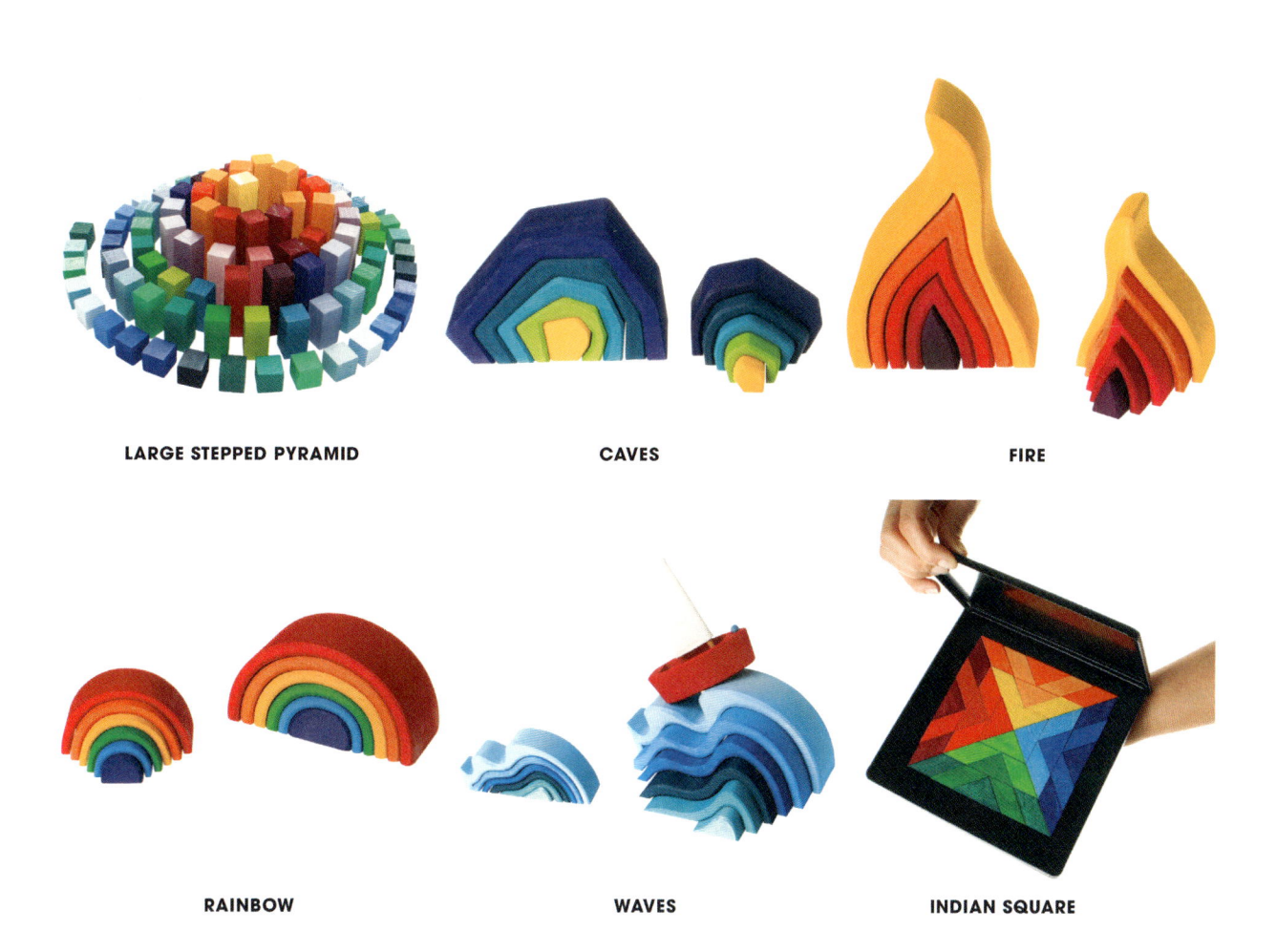

LARGE STEPPED PYRAMID

CAVES

FIRE

RAINBOW

WAVES

INDIAN SQUARE

THE CREATIVITY CATALOG

FOUR ELEMENTS

GRAPHIC CIRCLES

HEXAGON STAR

GRAPHICAL

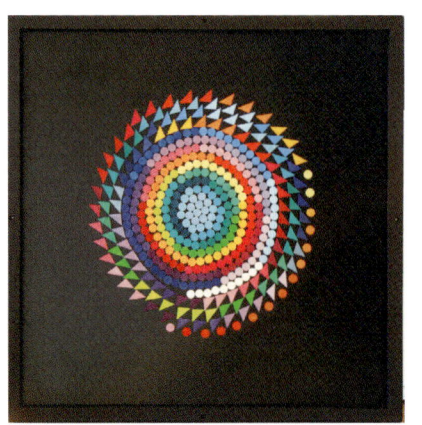

TRIANGLES

MAGNETIC DISPLAY BOARDS

Discover these items at thecreativehome.com

RED CIRCLES

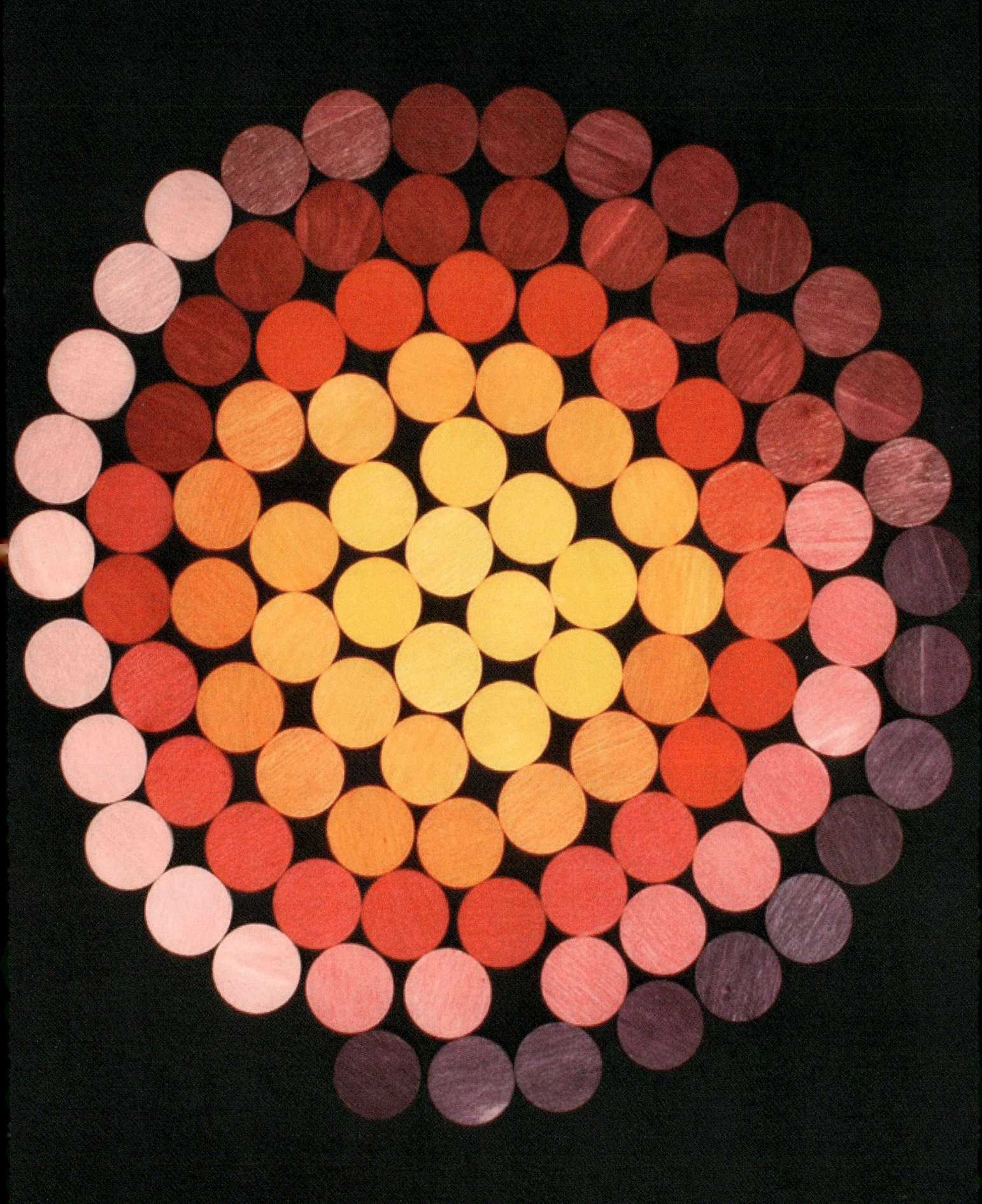

THE CREATIVITY CATALOG

IMAGINETS BY MINDWARE

Boost children's fine-motor and visual thinking skills. The sturdy wood carrying case features durable hinges and rope handles that are perfect for little hands to grasp. Do we hear road trip? Inside, forty-two brightly colored magnetic blocks can be arranged on the boards to replicate any of the fifty full-color design challenges printed on durable cards, or just make up your own. Plus, the magnetic board surface doubles as a dry-erase board, so kids can decorate a backdrop for their creations.

Imaginets has received the following awards: Parents' Choice Gold, Major Fun, Parenting for High Potential, Tillywig Top Fun, Creative Child Magazine Preferred Choice, and iParenting Media Award.

The dimensions of the case opened up are 23 by 14 by 1½ inches (58.4 by 35.5 by 3.1 cm). Recommended for ages three and up.

JIX STRAW CONNECTORS BY PATRICK MARTINEZ (2012)

Jix is a Kickstarter success story. Conceived by French-born visual artist Patrick Martinez, Jix is a modular connector that lets anyone turn conventional drinking straws into sculptures simply by joining them together. Build anything from small tabletop structures to stadium-sized installations, highly geometric constellations to free-form organic webs. Great for children motivated to exercise their imaginations, and equally great for grown-ups who want to do the same.

Made in America of post-consumer plastic. Comes 125 to a pack.

Discover these items at thecreativehome.com

LINX
BUILD WITH STRAWS

THE CREATIVITY CATALOG

KALEIDOGRAPH PATTERN DESIGN TOY
BY KALEIDOGRAPH DESIGN (2011)

We all went through kindergarten, but did you know the very concept was invented by a fellow named Friedrich Froebel in the middle of the 19th century? Until then adults didn't believe children of that age were capable—which shows you how much grown-ups know.

Now, Froebel did a lot more than just give this grade a name. He also developed a whole series of teaching tools to foster child creativity and growth, his wood blocks being perhaps the most famous. Inspired by Froebel, now comes Kaleidograph, a deceptively simple toy made up of cutout colored cards that will generate billions of different visual patterns when variably stacked and rotated.

Made in America from durable, nontoxic paperboard, each card measures 4¾ inches square (12 cm^2) and comes in a 12-card set that includes a two-sided poster with over 150 example designs to challenge and inspire. Available in Flora and Crystal patterns.

For ages five to adult, because some of us never want to stop learning how to be creative.

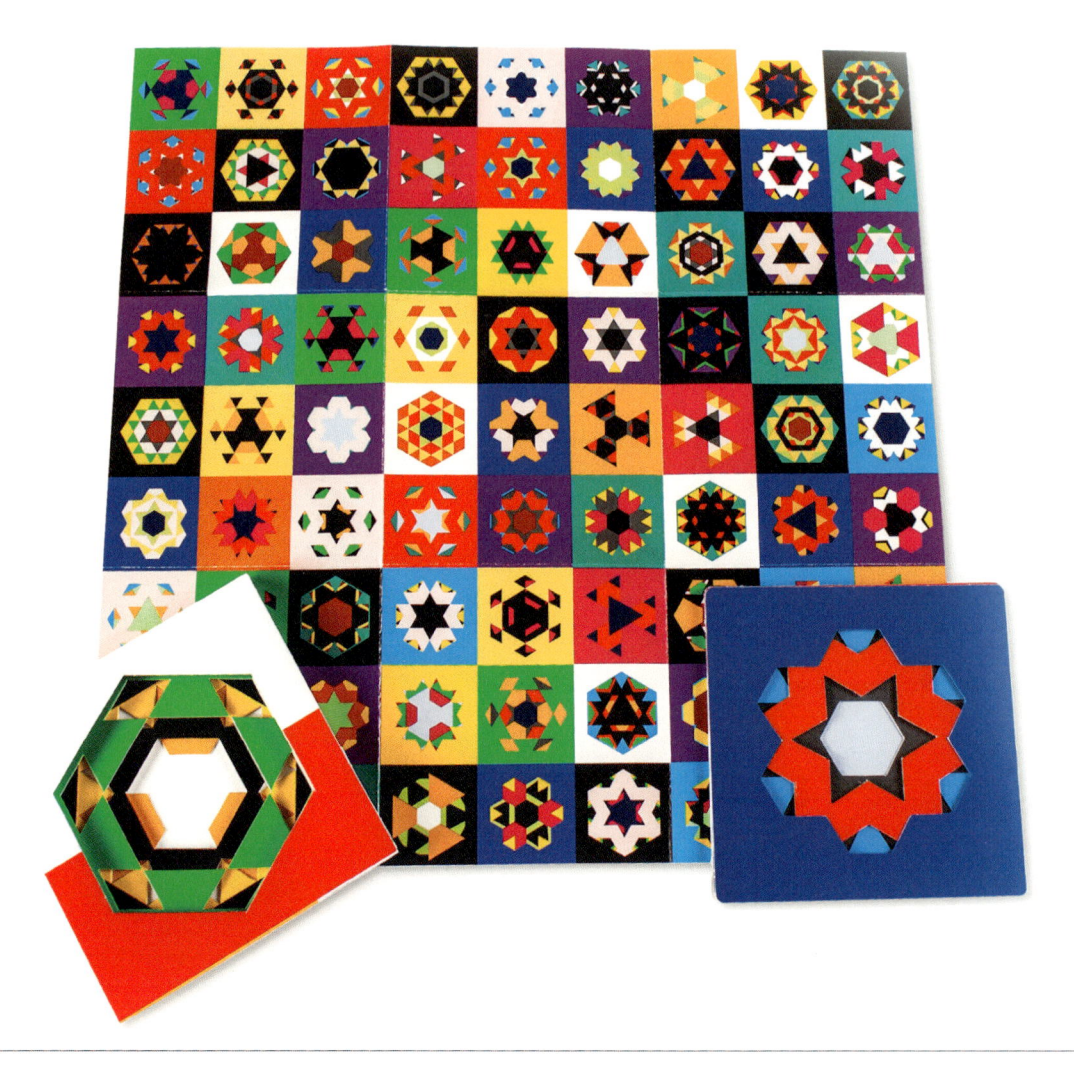

Discover these items at thecreativehome.com

CHILDREN

KIDZ PAINTABLE PLACEMATS BY MODERN-TWIST

Let's face it: kids love to draw, and only sometimes like to finish their meals. So why not encourage both by bringing art to the table? These hand-silk-screened placemats are delineated with playful line drawings that children can color in with dry-erase or washable markers. Simply wipe clean with a damp cloth or rinse with soap and water to return them to their original state for the next meal. Made from food-grade silicone, the sturdy mats won't crease or rip no matter how many times they get a wash of color from the little ones.

A unique product that encourages nutrition while nurturing creativity, these reusable and recyclable mats are nonporous, germfree, and free of BPA, lead, latex, phthalates, and other harsh chemicals. Heat-proof to 425°F (250° C).

Paintable Placemats can be purchased individually or as a gift set for birthdays and other occasions. The gift set comes in a handsome box and includes a placemat and a box of four dry-erase markers.

Available in a variety of different patterns and images. Mats are approximately 16 by 14 inches (40.6 × 35.5 cm).

ALPHABET ANIMALS

DAY AT THE POND

FARM BUDDIES

FARM TO TABLE

FARMER'S MARKET

KIDZPUZZLE CUSHION BY BUZZISPACE (2009)

The BuzziSpace KidzPuzzle Cushions make sitting a pleasure for adult eyes and kids' bottoms—although who says grown-ups can't have fun plopping down on them either? Like Buzzi's other delightfully soft products, these poufs are made from gorgeously colored recycled felts and environmentally safe foam cores. They're beautifully made to order by Belgians and will last longer than it takes for your kids to grow up.

Each cushion measures 33½ by 21⅝ by 11¾ inches (85 by 55 by 30 cm) and interlocks with other cushions, so you can use them individually or in groupings that you can change as the need or whim strikes you. Flexible, versatile, fun-ky; this isn't a puzzle, it's a no-brainer!

LADRILLOS SHELVING BY JAVIER MARISCAL FOR MAGIS (2005)

The Ladrillos Shelving System is a wonderfully whimsical design utilizing very colorful characters from the imagination of Javier Mariscal to serve as supports. The playful pieces, made from polyethylene, range in heights from 9¾ to 15¾ inches (24.7 to 40 cm). The characters attach to the specially designed shelves with butterfly screws; for units four or more shelves high, a wall hook is required for additional lateral stability.

Shelves are white laminate with a black edge and are 78¾ inches long by 14½ deep (200 by 36.8 cm). The shelves are routed in the center to provide for attaching the supports. Supports come two to a pack.

You can create your own assembly by ordering supports and shelves à la carte.

A truly charming design that can brighten any room. Oh, by the way, what does Ladrillos mean? It's the word for "brick" in Spanish. Gracias, Javier!

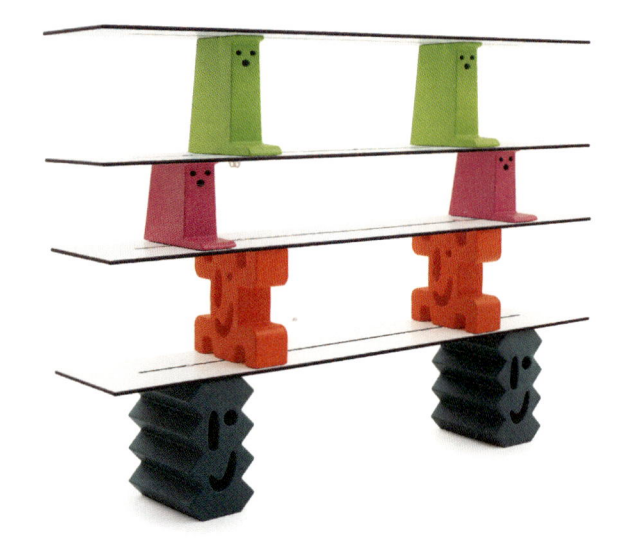

Discover these items at thecreativehome.com

LEGO STORAGE BRICKS AND HEADS BY ROOM COPENHAGEN (2012)

It's a parent's dream come true: motivating kids to tidy up their stuff by making it fun! These oversized LEGO bricks are designed to stack and interlock just like the originals, except that their tops come off to reveal generous storage space within. Kids can stash their goods (including their LEGO collection) inside one moment, then build a really awesome structure the next.

And who says grown-ups can't have fun with these too? They're beautifully made and come in classic LEGO colors, which means they'll look right at home anywhere in the home. Dorms too!

To go completely over the top, attach some LEGO Storage Heads to the bricks for extra container capacity. They're designed to hold firmly to the bricks, just like the real thing, and when you flip their lids you'll find still more space inside for things that would otherwise get away.

Made from polypropylene with no PVC. Bricks and heads are BPA- and phthalate-free too, so they're totally people safe.

Bricks run from 5 to 19¾ inches in various directions (12.7 to 49.5 cm). Heads measure from 6½ to 9 inches in diameter (16.5 to 24 cm).

LITTLE FLARE CUSTOMIZABLE TABLE BY MARCEL WANDERS FOR MAGIS (2005)

Encourage your child's artistic development with the Magis Little Flare Table. It's a stylish way for kids to host tea parties, do homework, or engage in arts and crafts. Best of all, the design doesn't just encourage kids to express themselves creatively, it actually provides a mechanism for doing it. Each leg is hollow and made from clear ABS plastic, which means whatever goes inside becomes part of the visible design.

To make the most of this opportunity to personalize, designer Marcel Wanders created the My Personal Table(t) Sketchbook filled with sheets of line drawings for kids to color in. Another ten blank sheets are provided for making artwork from scratch. After a drawing's done, simply roll up the sheet and insert it into the leg to show it off. When you're ready for a change you can remove the sheet and replace it with another. Kids will feel great about decorating their own personalized piece of furniture.

Alternatively, you can leave the Magis Little Flare table legs empty or fill them up with whatever strikes your fancy. Got a beach house? Put in sand and shells. Like colored marbles? Fill 'er up!

There are several table styles and sizes to choose from. Table tops are made of MDF and come in Small and Large Sets. The Large Set comes in White and accommodates eight legs without pen holders. The Small Sets come in White, in Circle and Salad decorative patterns, all with four red pen holders.

Legs are 21¼ inches high (54.1 cm). Tabletops are 39½ and 101½ inches long by 29½ wide (100 and 258 by 75 cm).

THE CREATIVITY CATALOG

MAGNA-TILES CONSTRUCTION TOYS
BY VALTECH (1997)

Here they are: Magna-Tiles, a creative construction toy that has reached almost cult status among the kinder cognoscenti. We had heard of them over the years, and after parents kept asking us about them we felt compelled to hunt them down and join the cult ourselves.

In case you're just being initiated, Magna-Tiles are colorful magnetic plates that come in various sizes, colors, and finishes. They attach and detach easily, so kids can play with them for hours of open-ended imaginative fun. But don't let that fool you—they're also educational, as they help the child develop patterning, shape recognition, constructive, and motor skills.

All Magna-Tiles are interchangeable, so kids can combine sets and exchange pieces with friends. They come in sets of 32, 48, and 100 pieces, in both solid and transparent colors.

The smallest sets contain tiles in the form of isosceles, right, and equilateral triangles, and squares. Intermediate sets add an arch, door frame, hinged door, a wheeled chassis, and other architecturally themed pieces. The largest set adds still more of the triangular and square tiles.

Recommended for ages three and up. That means you too!

124

MAKEDO CONNECTOR KITS (2009)

In an age when kids are often highly programmed and where learning is measured by standardized testing, it's refreshing to see a toy whose goal is to nurture pure free play and imaginative invention.

Makedo is a kit-of-parts that kids can use to construct things out of cardboard, paper, paint, string, old buttons, old socks, bicycle parts, and just about other scrap materials they can forage. What's inside their flagship product Kit for One are twenty-nine re-pins, twenty-nine re-clips, six lock hinges, one safe saw, and an inspiration poster. What comes out of these parts is unbounded creativity and infinite variety.

And because the parts are all reusable, kids learn the value of recycling materials and sustaining the environment.

Ages five and up, and that includes adults who still like to make stuff.

Discover these items at thecreativehome.com

MARBLE TRACK SYSTEM BY MATTHIAS ETTER FOR CUBORO (1985)

Marble-run toys represent building with a purpose—to make marbles go through a slotted course that you or your child creates out of modular building blocks. Since the blocks are interchangeable, the runs can be made serpentine or linear, low-profile or multilevel, fast or slow and steady. Since the blocks are interchangeable and can be combined with others sets, there are no conceivable limits on how many courses can be developed (okay, at some point we all run out of money and can't buy any more blocks, but that's a different matter).

The value of systems like this is that kids of all ages will probably never get bored playing with them because there will forever be new configurations to explore. And because the blocks are of varying complexity, the degree of difficulty in building a marble run can be properly self-calibrated to suit children of different ages and abilities, as well as multigenerational playing.

Cuboro offers three basic sets to start things off, and then another dozen or so supplementary sets which they recommend using to expand on the basic sets. There are also downloadable templates and guides to help players advance.

As a form of construction toy, Cuboro marble runs encourage spatial reasoning, logical thinking, fine motor skills, concentration, and of course, creativity. The Cuboro brand is notable for its award-winning, ecologically sensitive, and high quality production (after all, we're talking about people who manufacture famously precise watches). Blocks are made in Switzerland out of local beechwood in a specialized joinery operated by the same Swiss family for decades. Built to withstand hard knocks, Cuboro is a sustainable, open-ended toy conceived for generations of play.

CUGOLINO POP 13-PIECE   **CUGOLINO 37-PIECE**   **STANDARD 54-PIECE**

THE CREATIVITY CATALOG

MILLER GOODMAN WOOD TOYS BY ZOE MILLER AND DAVID GOODMAN

It only takes a quick glance at these delightful wood toys by MillerGoodman to know we're in the presence of some mighty powerful creative forces. Zoe Miller and David Goodman bring their talents and eye for design to the field of reconfigurable toys, and the world is better off for it.

It's equally apparent that the two share a passion for anthropomorphic content, with a particular focus on the face. Whether it's the block forms of ShapeMaker and FaceMaker, or the variously figured pieces that come with PlayShapes, the toys are designed so that children (and motivated adults) can continually generate images of fanciful animal and humanoid creatures by rearranging the pieces in ever shifting arrangements. As open-ended designs, they teach kids to explore multiple options in their search for answers, to recognize that just a few parts can yield a multiplicity of outcomes, and to appreciate the potentially vast capabilities of the human imagination.

ShapeMaker and FaceMaker each come with twenty-five blocks forming an 8¼ square by 1¾ inch tableau (21 cm^2 by 4.5 cm). PlayShapes comprises seventy-four pieces stored in a charming unbleached drawstring cotton bag. The toys are hand-printed on beautifully crafted hardwood blocks carved from rubberwood, which is sustainably harvested from plantation trees that no longer produce the latex needed for rubber production (no, the wood will not bounce). They come with booklets illustrating sample arrangements to inspire kids of all ages, starting at three years old.

PLAYSHAPES

FACEMAKER

Discover these items at thecreativehome.com

SHAPEMAKER

THE CREATIVITY CATALOG

MY SPACE DIVIDER BY BJÖRN DAHLSTRÖM FOR MAGIS (2005)

Little folk need their space, too. Magis Design's flexible My Space Dividers are easy to put together and very versatile; you can move the posts around to create different configurations, enlarge a divider by adding more posts and screens, mix and match different decorative patterns, and easily disassemble the whole thing when needed.

Screens come in three fun schemes: Jungle, Ocean, and Safari. The fabric is polyester so they're a snap to clean, and durable. The supports are made from blow-molded polyethylene and have spherical tops for complete safety.

Ready-to-assemble sets come with three screens and four posts. You can also purchase single screens and posts in sets of two or three for extending or customizing your screen.

My Space Divider is part of the Magis Me Too Collection, which is a pint-sized suite of super-tough objects that combine fun with fantasy and stimulate the senses of childlike curiosity. Designed by artists thinking with the mind of a child, "me too" is the voice of children demanding their own forms of expression.

Screens are 47¼ by 26¼ inches (120 by 67 cm).

128

ORGANECO BUILDING BLOCKS BY HAPE

Organeco are beautiful big bamboo blocks in bright colors and playful graphics. The combination of traditional building blocks, vibrant architectural illustrations, and the use of eco-friendly bamboo makes this product stand out from the crowded field of children's blocks. Thanks to the unique extra-large size, lightweight hollow design, and innumerable combinatory possibilities of Organeco, your children will be drawn to these early-age construction toys again and again.

What about the name? Well, Organeco is a synthesis of *organic* and *eco*, which just so happens to be the two core values underlining Swiss-based Hape's quality standards and social awareness. The company's name, by the way, is pronounced "happy," which pretty much says it all.

Recommended for ages 1½ and up.

Discover these items at thecreativehome.com

PAOLO CREATIVE TOY BY REMEMBER

Say hello to Paolo, one of the funnest, colorfulest, and imaginativest creative toys we've ever come across. Each box comes with 122 durable figure pieces and 50 plug-in connectors that let you or your kids concoct creatures of the most fantastic kind.

Make an army of kooky men, then a gaggle of goofy animals—then take everything apart and try something even crazier. It's open-ended creative play of the best kind, encouraging kids of all ages to exercise their visual skills and stimulate their imagination. Not to mention that it's a great way to detach young folks from their ubiquitous screens and give those fingers something else to do!

PLAYABLE METAL BY METAL ART

It's time to give your or your kids' inner engineer a chance to do some serious construction. The Playable Metal series of construction toys is a patented collection of aluminum blocks cast in modular shapes. The pieces are beautifully made of solid aluminum alloy, with high quality production and finish. Pieces bolt together using special screws and the special hex wrench provided. Several modules are designed to allow blocks to move and rotate within the figure. Follow the patterns provided with each set to build cars, figures, structures, and thingamajigs of your own creation. Playable Metal is the perfect open-ended creative toy for the young mechanic—or the seasoned executive.

The Car Set comes nicely boxed for gifting with ten blocks, rods, connecting screws, and a wrench. The Infinity Set comes the same, except it contains nineteen blocks. Available in several metallic colors. Combine sets for even more astounding creative construction. Recommended for any age.

CAR

INFINITY

THE CREATIVITY CATALOG

PLAYABLEART CREATIVE TOYS BY BERND LIEBERT

PlayableArt is a suite of beautifully designed creative and stress-relief toys. Each toy is made up of wood pieces with specially designed connectors that allow parts to be rotated multidirectionally and in nearly limitless configurations, without fear of pieces breaking apart or the toys losing their shape.

For children, PlayableArt offers the opportunity for open-ended and unstructured play, which helps them develop their visual and fine-motor skills, as well as concentration, spatial reasoning, and structural know-how. For adults, the repetitive and tactile manipulation of PlayableArt serves a therapeutic function that can reduce the stress of being adults (some of which has to do with our kids, if truth be told).

The gorgeous color finishes on these finely sanded pieces blend beautifully with the natural wood grain underneath to make them as suitable for the office desktop as for a child's playroom.

Angle, Art, and Stick are just some of the designs toy master Bernd Liebert has created for the PlayableArt family. Made from maple wood with nontoxic, water-based paints produced in Germany. Recommended for ages 9 to 99 years. Centenarians welcome too.

ANGLE

STICK

BALL

Discover these items at thecreativehome.com

CHILDREN

PLAYPLAX BY PATRICK RYLANDS (1966)

Patrick Rylands was an art student in England in 1966 when he came up with the concept of PlayPlax. A creative constructive toy, PlayPlax went on to sell over a million copies, and even won the Duke of Edinburgh's Prize for Elegant Design in 1970. Then it went out of production as other toys took over the marketplace.

Until now, that is. Lovingly resurrected by a group of admirers in the UK—who even got the original factory in Cheshire to make them with the same dyes that gave the first pieces their gorgeous color—PlayPlax is back for a new generation. And very likely, even in our age of batteries, bleeps, and bits, its value as a source of hands-on fun and creative development will be appreciated as much as it was half a century ago.

For ages three and up. Each box contains forty-eight squares in give colors. Made in the UK.

PS: curious as to how many different possible combinations you can make if you use all forty-eight squares? Glad you asked, because we calculated that there are 1.75×10 to the 75th power of them. Which is a lot!

THE CREATIVITY CATALOG

PLUS-PLUS BUILDING TOY BY GEARED FOR IMAGINATION (2012)

Have you heard about a construction toy from Denmark that has kids and grown-ups piecing together small bricks to make all sorts of fantastic creations? Fooled you! This time it's not LEGO—it's Plus-Plus, a creative new riff on the classic brick toy many of us have grown up with.

Plus-Plus's innovation is to recast the conventional brick from a simple rectangle to a toothed design. This deceptively simple change opens up huge new creative possibilities, in particular the ability to fabricate three-dimensional and multidirectional assemblies. If you thought LEGOs could make a multitude of things, wait till your kids get their hands on these babies.

Midi bricks are 2 by 1⅛ by ¼ inch (5.1 by 2.9 by 0.6 cm), and are available in 20- and 100-piece sets. There's also a smaller Mini brick version; they weigh in at ¾ by ½ by ⅛ inch (1.9 by 1.3 by 0.3 cm). Minis come in 300- and 600-piece sets, which should give you and your wards more than enough bricks to do great things with. Plus-Plus sets offer several attractive color palettes to choose from.

For children and grown-up children three years and up.

Q-BA-MAZE MARBLE RUNS BY ANDREW COMFORT FOR MINDWARE (2011)

Designed by architect Andrew Comfort, Q-Ba-Maze 2.0 is a unique system of colorful plastic cubes that interlock to form a marble run. Since the cubes are all interchangeable, there's no limit to what you can build—except maybe for the laws of gravity. Infinite creativity means you and your kids will never run out fresh design possibilities.

And with the balls able to take multiple routes as they careen through the run, there's the element of unpredictable action with every launch —quite unlike most runs, which compel each marble to follow a single prescribed track. It's like a live demonstration of probability, physics, and art all in one.

The Starter Set contains thirty-six cubes in your choice of a warm or cool three-color palette, plus fourteen metal marbles. Also available in a Big Box Set with seventy-two cubes and twenty marbles. For extra fun, there's an add-on Zoom Stunt Kit that gives you two coaster tubes, a marble vortex, a universal connector, and ten extra steel marbles.

Recommended for ages five and up; not for children three and under.

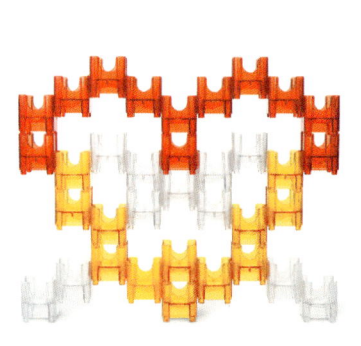

Discover these items at thecreativehome.com

CHILDREN

QUADROR BUILDING BLOCKS BY DROR BENSHETRIT FOR DECOR CRAFT (2013)

Talk about a eureka moment! Internationally known designer and architect Dror Benshetrit was puttering around in his workshop one day in 2006 (as people with creative minds like to do) when he came across an intriguing geometry. Four L-shaped pieces, Dror found, could be joined together in a way that the pieces could lie flat against each other or be folded out to form a structural support. Fascinated by its flexibility, stackability, and interlocking capability, he eventually dubbed his discovery QuaDror.

Since then Dror has been exploring all sorts of ways QuaDror could be used. And what better use than as elements of play? After all, they are blocks, even if they do things that no cube has ever thought of doing!

Pile them up, place them side by side, build walls, lay them flat—the creative possibilities of QuaDror are endless. Great for kids and grown-ups of all ages who like to think outside the blocks.

A set includes ten QuaDror blocks each measuring 3 inches square on the face (7.6 cm^2).

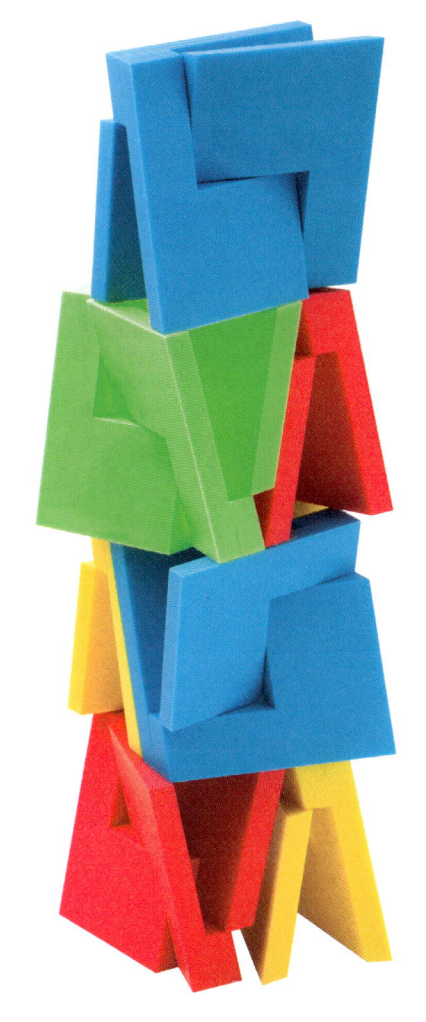

THE CREATIVITY CATALOG

SNAP CIRCUITS ELECTRONIC TOYS BY ELENCO

Snap Circuits is an award-winning, unique system of modular electronic components that lets children and adults build working models of battery-powered devices. Thanks to the interchangeable and interlocking nature of each component, and a base which allows for their flexible yet organized placement, there are literally thousands of possible projects to tackle.

You could start with the smallest set, which comes with a manual illustrating no fewer than 100 experiments, and work your way up to the largest one, which offers a stunning 750 projects. Along the way your child could put together such electronic marvels as an amplified musical bell, a screaming fan, a voice controlled burglar alarm, an AM radio, a photosensitive electronic organ, a lie detector, a remote controlled vehicle, and a two-finger touch lamp, to name just a few. With each project kids (and adults who might have skipped a science class or two) will have a chance to learn about many different aspects of engineering and science, including solar power, electromagnetism, computer interfacing, light generation, motors, remote control, motion detection, integrated and digital circuits, and switching.

Snap Circuits are a snap because that's how they connect together. No tools needed—just fingers and an inquisitive mind. We promise you'll never hear "I'm bored!" again, because your kids will be too busy experimenting and deciding what to build next. A great creative toy for the Age of STEM (Science, Technology, Engineering and Mathematics).

Batteries not included. Shockingly good fun for ages eight and up.

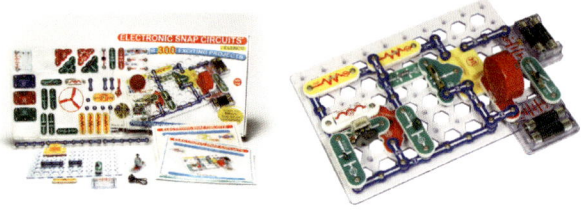

300-IN-1

EXTREME 750 EXPERIMENTS

JR. 100 EXPERIMENTS

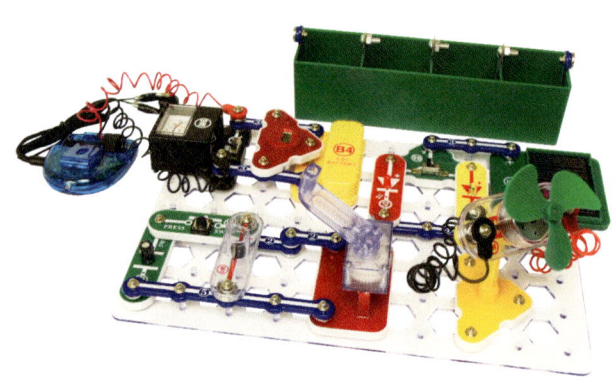

GREEN

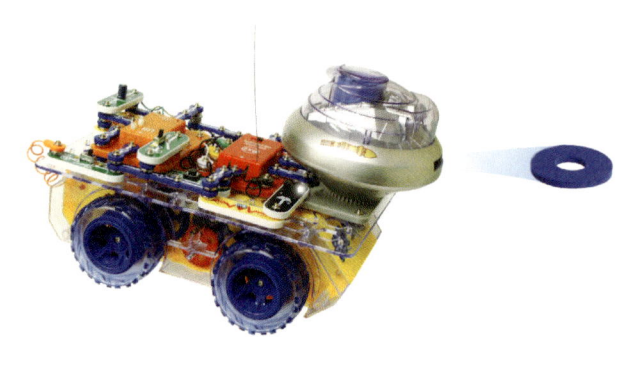

DELUXE SNAP ROVER

Discover these items at thecreativehome.com

SPIEL BUILDING BLOCKS BY KURT NAEF FOR NAEF (1954)

This faceted building cube system is one of the first designs by company founder Kurt Naef and is indicative of the principles behind his approach to play. The sixteen brightly colored cubes, each with eight angled teeth, can be wedged together to form staggered constructions, such as bridges and towers. For those who like to defy gravity with cantilevers and other engineering derrings-do, the brick's faceted design makes it possible to construct pieces wider at the top than at the base. Few building block systems let you do that, but then, Naef products often open up creative development in unexpected and unique ways.

The dimensions of an individual block are approximately 2 inches (5 cm) in each direction. Arrayed in a square, the blocks measure about 8 inches square by 2 inches (20 cm^2 by 5 cm). Available in Multicolor and Rare Woods, which consists of maple, birch, ash, chestnut, beech, elm, American walnut, and acacia.

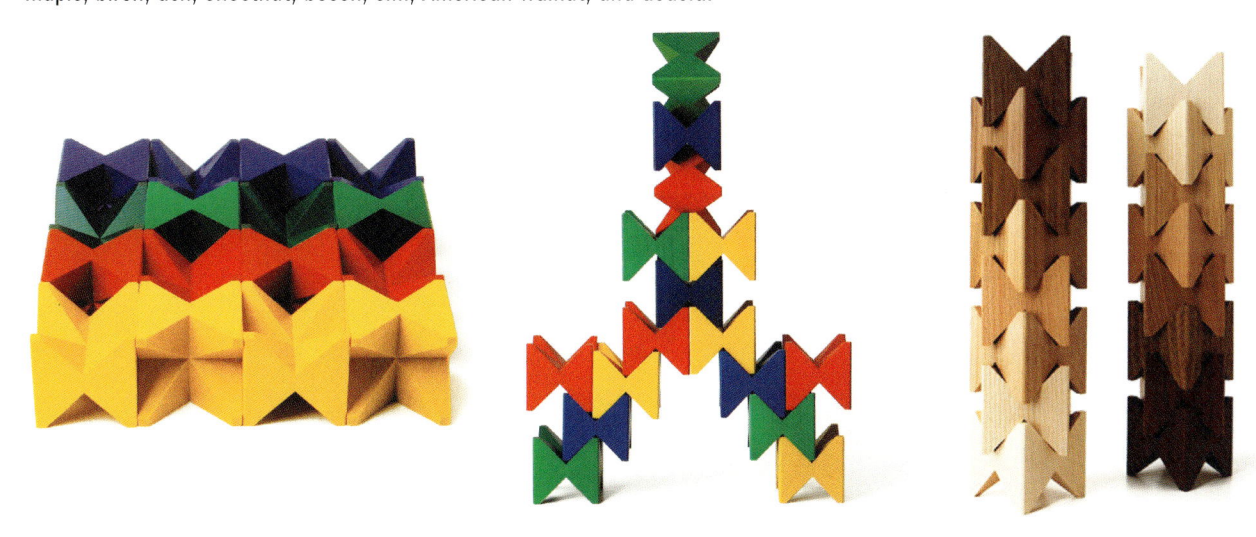

STRAWZ CONNECTIBLE DRINKING STRAWS BY NUOP DESIGN (2007)

Using Strawz Connectible Drinking Straws, you or your kinder can create dizzying sculptural contraptions for sipping or slurping your favorite drinks. Each set includes twenty flexible, rubbery connectors; twelve long and twelve short straight plastic straws; and an array of U-shaped connectors, elbows, T-connectors, straight joins, and 4-way intersections with which to design your fluid-ingesting network. Strawz are addictive, fun, washable, and available in multiple colors. Being modular, the creative enjoyment never ends (until the liquids run out).

Good for kids ages six and up, and just as good for adults who just don't want to go straight anymore.

Available in a mouthwatering Blue, Lime, Orange, Pink, Red, and Violet.

THE CREATIVITY CATALOG

SUSPEND BY MELISSA & DOUG (2012)

A family game of steady hands and tricky balancing acts. Try it and you'll be hooked, literally. Suspend comes with twenty-four rubber-tipped wire pieces that hang from a tabletop stand and each other by means of hooks running along their length. Sounds easy, eh? Now try adding piece after piece . . . oops, not as easy as it looks! Each time a bar is added, the balance shifts, the difficulty changes, and the rather attractive, mid-century modern–looking midair sculpture transforms itself.

Oh, and did we mention you have to roll a die to determine which color piece you need to add each turn? So can you do it? The suspense is killing us—time for you to find out.

For one to four players, eight years and up (adults get to play too, yay).

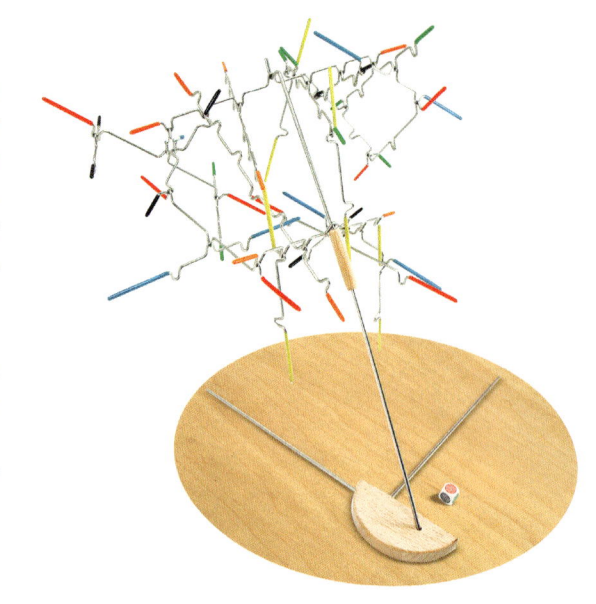

TEGU MAGNETIC BLOCKS (2009)

Tegu Magnetic Blocks are among the most beautiful of the recombinable playthings in *The Catalog*. Made from sustainably sourced, eco-friendly Honduran hardwoods and assembled by local craftspeople, Tegu provides limitless opportunities for open-ended and unscripted play and creativity. They're lead-free, non-plastic, nontoxic, and finished with a water-based lacquer to ensure play is safe as well as fun.

There's another side to the Tegu line that's just as important: the company is driven by a humanitarian mission to foster child education, employment, local empowerment, and the responsible stewardship of natural resources in Honduras. It was there that the company founder discovered the need for such an enterprise during a visit in 2006. Since then the company has worked tirelessly to make that vision a reality.

Tegu blocks come in a variety of colorways, sizes, shapes, and sets. There are starter sets of fourteen, six, and eight pieces, the last two of which come in handsome pouches suitable for executive giving and desktop play. Larger sets include twenty-four and forty-two piece versions, a classroom kit of 130 pieces, and the Ultimate Builder's Set containing a whopping 480 blocks. A Mobility collection lets kids build their own vehicular fantasies using magnetic car bodies and attachable magnetic wheels. Speaking of cars, the Tegu Tote is perfect for transporting blocks on road trips and vacations.

Because the magnets are fully embedded in the Tegu Blocks (we challenge you to figure out how), this product is suitable for play from infancy on.

6-PIECE PRISM POCKET POUCH

8-PIECE POCKET POUCH

Discover these items at thecreativehome.com

CHILDREN

24-PIECE

42-PIECE

MOBILITY SERIES

TRAVEL TOTE

THE CREATIVITY CATALOG

TOOBALINK BY METRE IDEAS AND DESIGN (2012)

Waste is a terrible thing to waste, so why waste it? Teach your kids a thing or two about caring for the environment by introducing them to Toobalink, the world's first modular creative toy using discarded paper towel and toilet tissue tubes. Construct all sorts of stuff, from animals to swords, using the connecting pieces that come with each package. It's open-ended, inexhaustible fun that stimulates the imagination and fosters creativity.

Designed in Brooklyn and almost entirely made in America. Recommended for ages five and up.

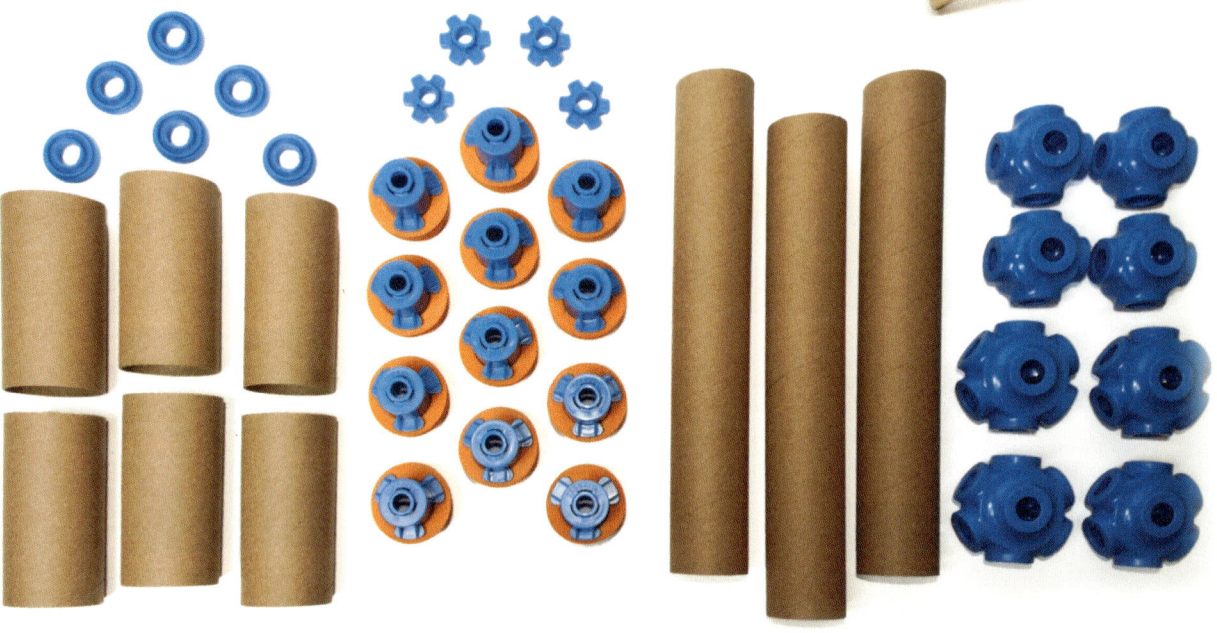

138

WALLCANDY ARTS WALLPAPERS AND STICKERS

WallCandy Arts designs, manufactures, and distributes stylish peel-and-stick, removable and reusable wall stickers, chalkboards, whiteboards, and temporary wallpaper. It's a really innovative way to decorate nurseries, kids' rooms, playrooms, and rooms for teens and adults. Once installed, WallCandy can be effortlessly rearranged or removed and used again without leaving any marks or damage on the walls.

Wallpapers come in a myriad of designs with child-friendly motifs and colors (some of the striped and patterned papers are suitable for grown-ups too). Each roll of wallpaper is 26 inches wide by 94 inches long (66 by 239 cm). A full kit includes four rolls of wallpaper; a half kit two rolls; a squeegee for applying the wallpaper and eliminating bubbles is included.

For people and families on the go, check out the

ELEPHANT CHALKBOARD

Discover these items at thecreativehome.com

CHILDREN

chalkboard, whiteboard, and Post-it panels. They adhere to walls just like the wallpapers and decals, but in their case you can actually write on them with chalk and markers. Great for lists, intrafamilial communiqués, and other missives. Consider using them in the office as well, where they can serve as communication tools for collaborative teams and group meetings, and jotting down those creative epiphanies before they are forever lost to synaptic discharges.

Materials for wallpapers, decals, and other adhesive WallCandy products are vinyl and are BPA- and phthalate-free. WallCandy is proudly made in America.

CHALKBOARD PANELS

FRENCH BULL CITY WALL

FRENCH BULL DOG BALLOONS

FRENCH BULL JUNGLE

GLOW-IN-THE-DARK NIGHTSCAPE

HAPPY FLOWERS

SMARTS

WHITEBOARD PANELS

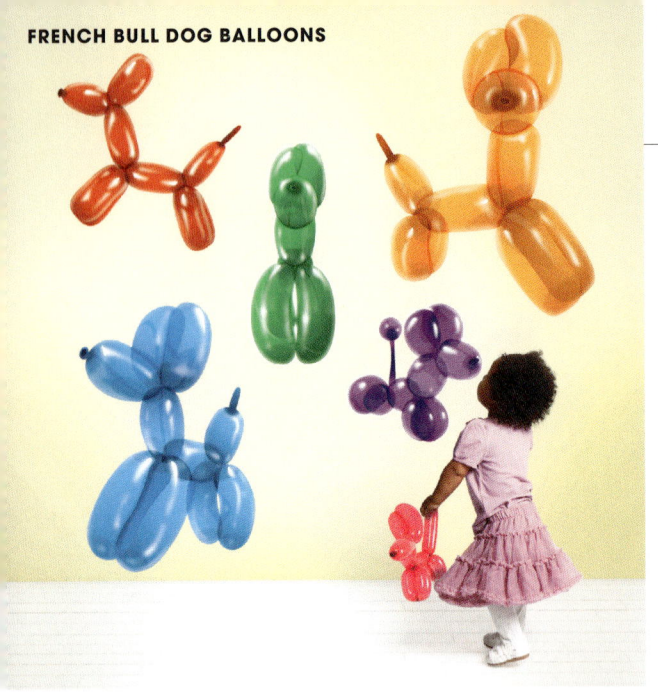

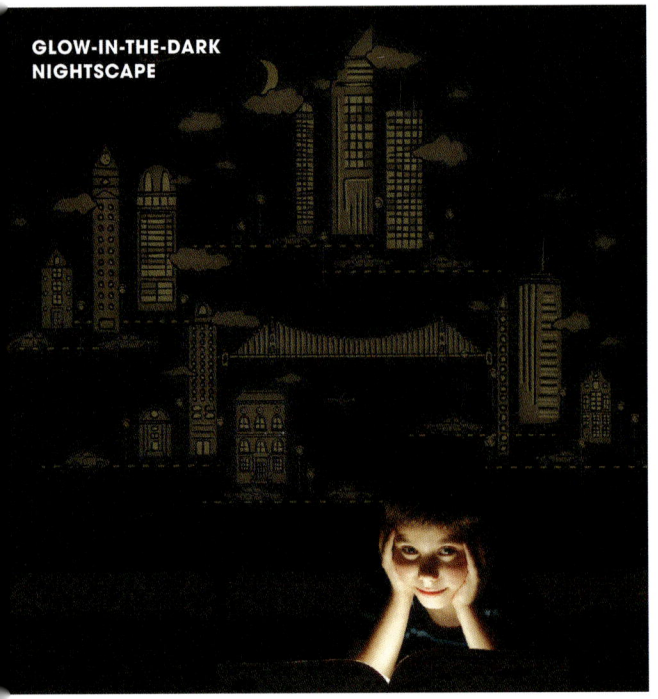

CHILDREN

WOOD BLOCKS BY UNCLE GOOSE

Uncle Goose is a throwback to a time in American history (1983-1998) when wood alphabet blocks were, well, made of wood. Hand-carved even, and often hand-painted. And did we mention that much of this craftsmanship took place in the American Midwest? Those days are back, at least when it comes to the stunning and truly funning wood blocks produced by this quirky and maverick Grand Rapids, Michigan—based company.

Let's start with their Classic ABC Blocks with pull wagon. What could be more classic? Beautifully adorned blocks with raised and colored lettering and adornment, all safely ensconced in a charming wood cart with pull string. Great for tots ready to break out with some serious spelling.

Then there's the Antics Ant Block set. This is where the quirky part comes in. Ant Blocks lets kids have fun with bugs without actually touching the yucky things. Illustrated with lines of marching ants on all six sides of the cubes, the blocks can be rotated to produce as many different ant colony configurations as there were ants at your last picnic. Besides the worker ants, the blocks also illustrate the queen ant with her eggs, and for a little drama, a spider—every ant's nemesis.

Uncle Goose blocks are 1¾ inches square (4.4 cm^2) and made in America from basswood.

WOODMOBIEL BY BEN FRITZ FOR OOTS!

DIY toys for kids who love to assemble things (almost as much as they like taking them apart and doing it again)! The Dutch-designed Woodmobiel gets young people away from the screen and engaged in hands-on activity building all sort of neat things they can actually use, like tricycles, planes, cranes, wheelbarrows, tables and chairs, wagons, scooters, and seesaws. Not to mention all the fantastic structures that come from a child's imagination.

Ben Fritz, a Dutch graphic designer, created Woodmobiel for his own grandchildren, so you know it was created from love, and will appeal across generations.

Woodmobiel is available in two kit sizes, Starter and Standard. The Starter Kit comes with instructions for building nine models out of twenty-five wood blocks, plastic panels, tools, and hardware, while the Standard Kit can make eleven models from forty-three blocks. Recommended for ages five and up.

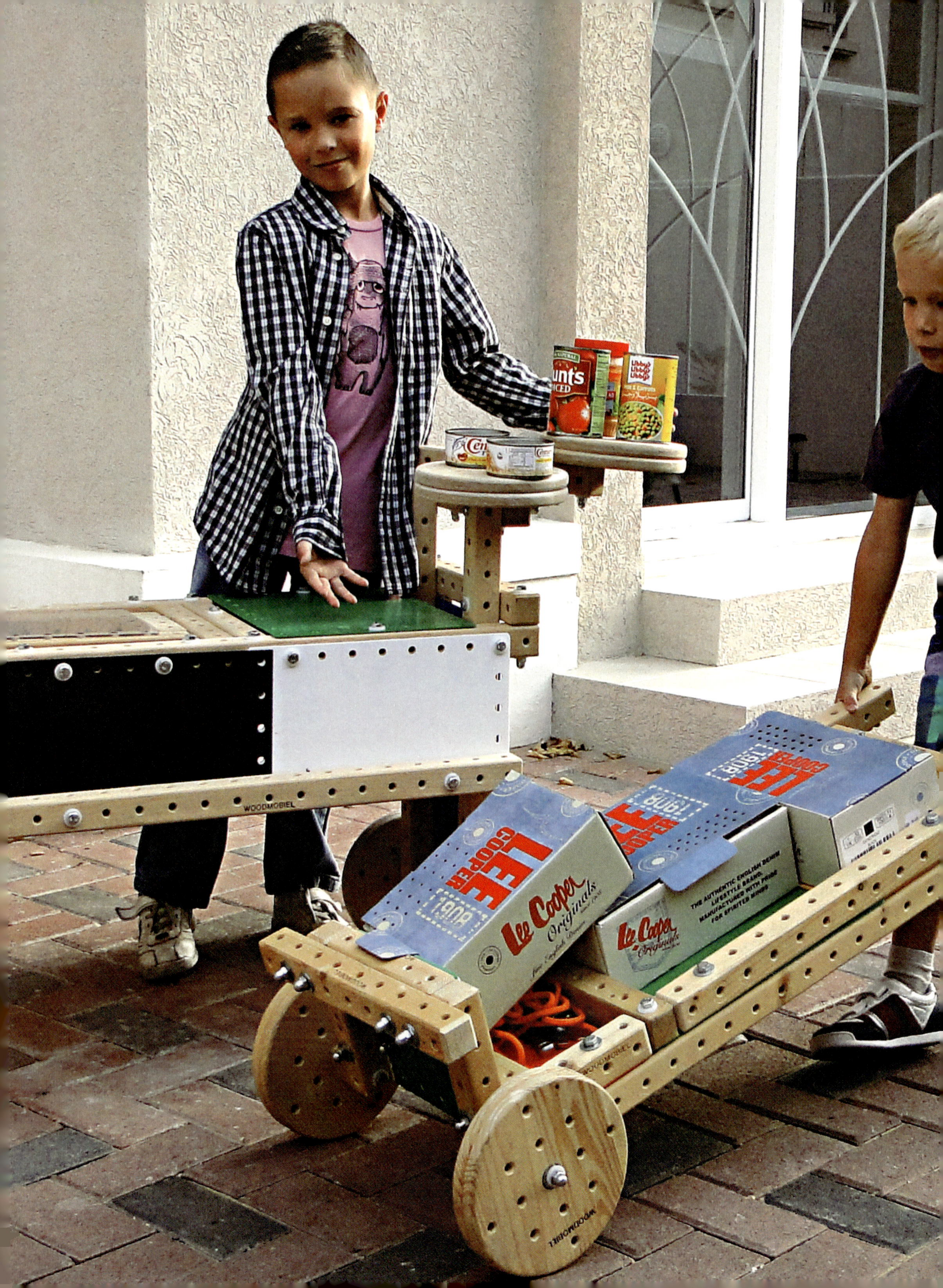
LEE COOPER
Lee Cooper
Originals
WOODMOBIEL

1x12 = 12
2x12 = 24
3x12 = 36
4x12 = 48
5x12 = 60
6x12 = 72
7x12 = 84

THE CREATIVITY CATALOG

WOODY CHALKBOARD TABLE AND CHAIR BY ERIC PFEIFFER FOR OFFI (1996)

A stylish, kid-sized chalkboard table for parents who love to combine form with function, and for kids who just love to draw. A metal bowl in the center neatly stores chalk and erasers. When the artwork is done, simply erase and start all over again. Hours of creative development means happy kids and a nice return on parental investment.

A great companion piece is the Offi Look-Me Chair. This chair is a playful expression in molded birch ply with a back that doubles as a handle for easy transport. Lightweight and yet extremely durable, the Look-Me Chair can handle normal child wear-and-tear and still look fresh after everyone's all grown up.

Table and chair are designed by Eric Pfeiffer for Offi. Order one or both in any quantities.

The table is 30 inches (76.2 cm) in diameter and 18 inches (45.7 cm) high. Made from birch ply and has a washable linoleum chalkboard surface. The chair measures 13 by 11 by 20 inches (33 by 27.9 by 50.8 cm), with a seat height of 11¼ inches (28.6 cm). Chair and table come fully assembled and ready for use.

144

XYZ ALPHABET BLOCKS BY CHRISTIAN NORTHEAST FOR FRED AND FRIENDS

Have your alphabet blocks been around the block? Like, A is for Apple, B is for Boring, Z is for Zzzzz . . .

The beautifully crafted wood XYZ Alphabet Blocks offer you and your kids a different perspective on the ABCs of modern life. They have all the traditional play and learning value you'd expect from blocks, but delivered with a whimsical humor and graphic punch that most block sets don't begin to convey.

Each set of XYZ Alphabet Blocks comes with twenty-six letters (wouldn't want to leave any out), fifty-two illustrated words, eleven numbers, and six moods (ah, something different!). Designed in the singular style of Christian Northeast.

For children three and up.

Discover these items at thecreativehome.com

ZOOB CONSTRUCTION TOY BY MICHAEL JOAQUIN GREY FOR INFINITOY (1993-1996)

ZOOB pieces snap, click, and pop together to form joints that rotate, limbs that extend, axles that spin, and lots more. Kids can create simple models in minutes, or get absorbed and spend hours at a time. There's no limit to what they can build: from animals to aliens, from dinosaurs to DNA.

ZOOB is a creative toy based on real-life systems, so its intrinsic educational value encourages kids to learn, explore, and create using the most important tool of all: their imaginations.

There are five parts that make up the ZOOB anatomy, each in their own color. Parts are interchangeable among sets, and there are over thirty sets to choose from. The toy is designed primarily for children age six and up, though there is a junior set for kids at least four-years-old.

Wondering about the name? It's an acronym for Zoology, Ontology (the branch of metaphysics that deals with the nature of being), Ontogeny (the development of an individual organism, usually from a simple form to a more complex form), and Botany. The company goes on to explain that the design of ZOOB is based on a living and natural system—the nucleotides found in DNA that are the building blocks of life—and that their mobility mirrors the natural movement of people, animals, and machines. This mobility also enhances ZOOB's instructional value, by allowing children to see an assembly as it moves and by demonstrating the movement of biological, anatomical, and mechanical parts. Whew.

ZOOB is in the permanent collection of MoMA, which is a pretty big deal for a toy.

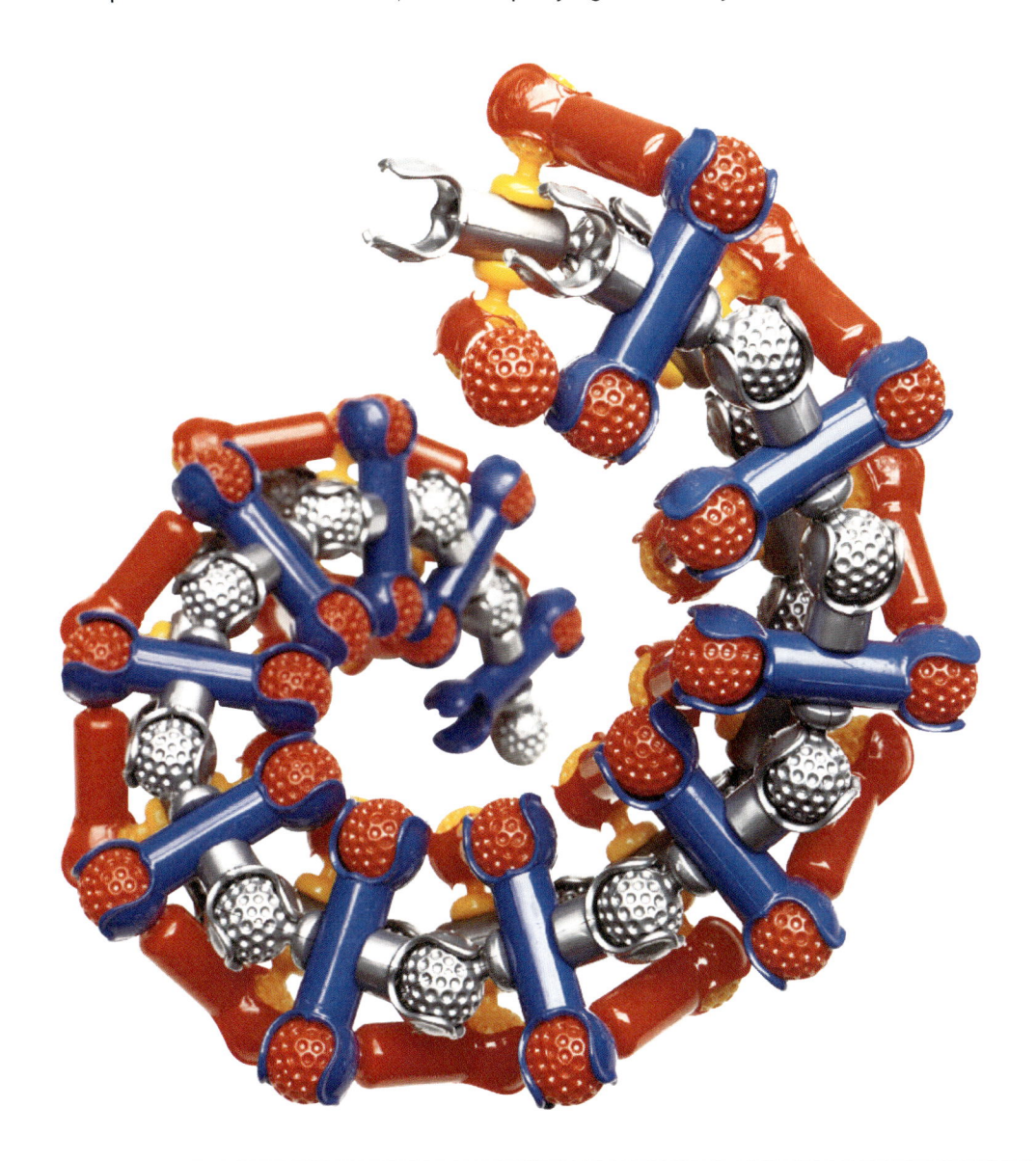

DESIGNERS AND BRANDS

Agayof Art & Judaica
Ron Arad
ArchitectMade
Areaware
Automoblox
Enrico Azzimonti
F. X. Balléry
Shigeru Ban
René Barba
Dror Benschetrit
Maxwell Bogue and Peter Dilworth
John Bennett and Gustavo Bonevardi
Black+Blum
Tord Boontje
Ronan and Erwan Bouroullec
Brave Space Design
Pil Bredahl
Brinca Dada
Robert Bronwasser
BuzziSpace
Cappellini
Peer Clahsen
Andrew Comfort
Laura Cowan
Cuboro
Gideon Dagan
Björn Dahlström
Jonas Damon
Dana Cannam Design
Decor Craft
Dante Donegani and Giovanni Lauda
Julia Dozsa
Charles and Ray Eames
Earnest Studio
eco-kids
Elenco
Enlisted Design
Fat Brain Toys
ferm LIVING
Anna Castelli Ferrieri and Kartell
Flensted
Fort Standard
Fractiles
Free Art & Technology (F.A.T.)
Ben Fritz
Matt Gagnon
Massimo Giacon
Ron Gilad
Stefano Giovannoni
Good Erdle
Grain
Michael Joaquin Grey
Grimm's Spiel und Holz Design
Jonas Grundell
Martí Guixé
Fritz Haller
Hape
HAY
Eija Helander
Scot Herbst
Heiko Hillig
Housefish
IdeaPaint
Patrick Jouin
Ludwig Hirschfeld-Mack
House Industries
Mirjam Hüttner
Incorporated
Italianissimo
Stephan Jaklitsch
Nauris Kalinauskas
Hila Rawet Karni
Peter Karpf
Frank Kerdil
Kathrin Kiener
Ed Kilduff
Pat Kim
KMN Home
Koziol
Dr. Lakra
Doron Lachisch
LEGO
Lerival
Bernd Liebert
Nel Linssen
Magis
Magna-Tiles
Makedo
Javier Mariscal
Patrick Martinez
Melissa & Doug
Metal ART
Metre Ideas and Design
Zoe Miller and David Goodman
MindWare
MIO
Mission Workshop
Modern-Twist
Lisa Monahan
Johannes Molin
Moorhead & Moorhead
MOS Architects
Muuto
Naef
Nendo
Jo Niemeyer
Christian Northeast
NuOp Design
Roger von Oech
Osko+Deichmann
Peleg Design
Brandon Perhacs
John Perry
Eric Pfeiffer
Liza Phillips Design
Pico Pao
Plus-Plus
Laura Polinoro
Giulio Polvara
Luis Pons
QisDesign
Quirky
Red Hen Books and Toys
Remember
ROOM Copenhagen
Roost
Royal Family Design Labor
Patrick Rylands
Ricardo Saint-Clair
Franco Sargiani
Selab
Héctor Serrano
SmallWorks
Julien De Smedt
Roxi Suger
Sy-Lab
Tamawa
Tegu
Tempaper
The Utility Collective
Carlo Trevisani
Tveit & Tornøe
Uncle Goose
Kristian Vedel
Vitra
WallCandy Arts
Wall Coaster
Marcel Wanders
Way Basics
David Weeks
Wexel Art
Yube
Yubo
Karl Zahn
Eva Zeisel
Clara von Zweigbergk

146

LEGO STORAGE BRICKS AND HEADS BY ROOM COPENHAGEN (2012)

THE CREATIVITY CATALOG

AGAYOF ART & JUDAICA
Menorahs (p. 43)
agayof.com

Avner and Aviah Agayof are a father-and-son team known for their finely crafted artistic Judaica. Avner is a trained silversmith and responsible for the design work, while Aviah manages the business operation. Avner founded Agayof Art & Judaica in 1970 and since then has become a leading figure in his craft, personally supervising the production of each design. From their Jerusalem-based studio the Agayofs produce a wide range of ritual objects, including mezuzahs, menorahs, candleholders, cups, and cutlery in an innovative contemporary idiom that nonetheless remains strikingly connected to its historical roots. Their work is characterized by a consistent adherence to the fundamental geometries of circle, square, and triangle, and the use of anodized aluminum cast in a distinctly metallic palette. Agayof designs can be found in major museums and shops all over the world.

RON ARAD
Infinity Wine Rack (p. 39) and Bookworm (p. 84) for Kartell
ronarad.co.uk

Born in Tel Aviv in 1951, educated at the Jerusalem Academy of Art and later at the Architectural Association in London, Ron Arad cofounded, with Caroline Thorman, the design and production studio One Off in 1981 and later, in 1989, Ron Arad Associates architecture and design practice. In 2008 Ron Arad Architects was established alongside Ron Arad Associates.

Ron was awarded the 2011 London Design Week Medal for design excellence and became a Royal Academician of the Royal Academy of Arts in 2013. He was Professor of Design Product at the Royal College of Art in London until 2009.

Along with his limited edition studio work, Ron's studio designs for many leading international companies, including Kartell, Vitra, Moroso, Fiam, Driade, Alessi, Cappellini, Cassina, WMF, and Magis. He has also created a number of public art pieces, most recently the Vortext in Seoul, Korea, and the Kesher Sculpture at Tel Aviv University, and has executed several architectural commissions. He was honored with a major retrospective at MoMA in 2009.

ARCHITECTMADE
BIRDs (p. 15) and Child's Chair (p. 108) by Kristian Vedel, Gemini Candle Holder by Peter Karpf (p. 32)
architectmade.com

Copenhagen-based ArchitectMade was founded in 2006 by Morten Jensen. The company offers a curated collection of unique architect-designed classics from the golden age of Danish Modern design. Among the creative talents represented in its catalog are Finn Juhl, Poul Kjærholm, Peter Karpf, Kristian Vedel, and Jørn Utzon. Following the tradition of Danish design, its products are made to high standards of quality and craftsmanship. They are sold in many leading design retailers and museum shops all over the world, including MoMA in New York, Skandium in London, and the Deutsche Guggenheim Museum in Berlin.

AREAWARE
Alphabet Blocks (p. 11) by Pat Kim, Cubebots (p. 22), Hanno the Gorilla (p. 33), and Ursa the Bear (p. 71) by David Weeks, Dovetail Wood Animals by Karl Zahn (p. 26), Infinite Tree by Johannes Molin (p. 39), Numbers Cube Clock by Jonas Damon (p. 53), Balancing Blocks by Fort Standard (p. 105)
areaware.com

Currently based in Williamsburg, Brooklyn, Areaware was founded by Noel Wiggins in 2003 and was originally known as Are Aware. Noel's goal in forming the business was to create useful products that would appeal to both imagination and intellect, with frequent doses of humor and wit. Since launching, Areaware has enlisted the talents of many emerging as well as world-class designers, including David Weeks, Pat Kim, Fort Standard, Rich Brilliant Willing, Karl Zahn, and Jonas Damon.

AUTOMOBLOX
Automoblox (p. 104)
automoblox.com

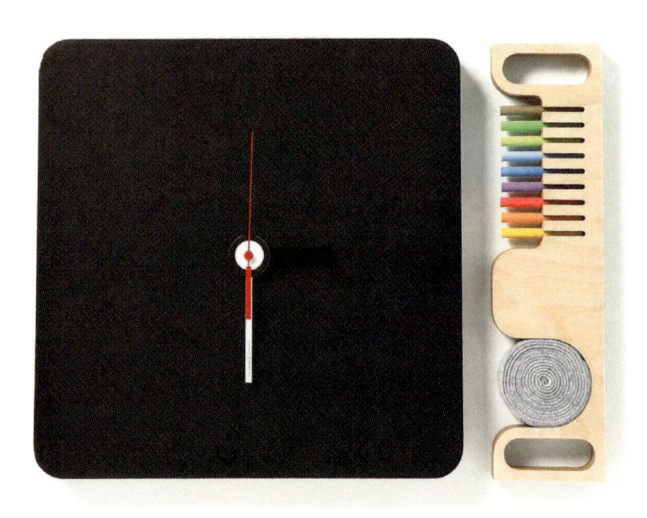

It was while studying industrial design at Carnegie Mellon University that student Patrick Calello was given an assignment to develop new concepts for the DIY wooden hobby industry. Being a car guy at heart, Patrick immediately began exploring a novel toy car concept involving interchangeable parts made out of wood. He believed that the key to a clever and innovative play vehicle was to merge modern automotive styling with traditional craftsmanship, and that this fusion would inspire creativity among children eager to devise and assemble cars of their own design. By the fall of 1992 Patrick had come up with the core design characteristics that would eventually evolve into Automoblox; five years of rigorous design and product development later, Automoblox arrived in the marketplace.

ENRICO AZZIMONTI
Chalkboard Clocks for Diamantini & Domeniconi (p. 19, pictured, opposite)
en.enricoazzimonti.it

Enrico Azzimonti studied at the Polytechnic of Milan, earning a degree in Architecture in 1993 and a Masters in Design and Management two years later. Prior to graduation he founded in his own architecture and industrial design studio. His firms' client list has counted BLM Group, Zava, TVS, Lavazza, Fratelli Guzzini, Coop, JVC, Diamantini & Domeniconi, Bilumen, Risolì, and Demolli.

Since 2006 Azzimonti has been teaching at the European Institute of Design in Milan and has run studios in several universities in Italy. His work has been published in multiple industry publications, and several of his pieces are in the permanent collection of the Museu de les Arts Decoratives in Barcelona.

F. X. BALLÉRY
Les Perles Candlesticks for Y'A PAS LE FEU AU LAC (p. 41)
www.fxballery.com

F. X. Balléry was born in 1977 in the French Jura. After initially pursuing studies in the sciences, he decided to go to the École Supérieure d'Art et de Design (ESAD) of Reims in 1996 to become a product designer instead.

A winning design for the Comité Colbert Young Talents Award for a Chanel bag led him to work on Issey Miyake's perfume line, and later to a stint at Ron Arad's studio in London. It was there that he discovered the Royal College of Art, from which he obtained a degree in 2000.

A second Comité Colbert Award—this time for a Hermès picnic set—spurred new clients and sponsors, among them BPI, Yves Saint Laurent Beauty, and Ricard.

Back in Paris, he founded his own studio and is currently pursuing projects in product, furniture, packaging, merchandising, and interior and industrial design.

SHIGERU BAN
10-Unit Modular Furniture System for Artek (p. 6)
www.shigerubanarchitects.com

Shigeru Ban (b. 1957 in Tokyo) is a Japanese architect widely known for his innovative designs to quickly and efficiently house disaster victims. In 2014, Ban was named the 37th recipient of the Pritzker Architecture Prize, the most prestigious prize in contemporary architecture. The Pritzker Jury cited Ban for his innovative use of materials and his dedication to humanitarian efforts around the world, calling him "a committed teacher who is not only a role model for younger generation, but also an inspiration."

Ban studied at the Tokyo University of the Arts, and then at the Southern California Institute of Architecture. Later he went to Cooper Union's School of Architecture in New York, where he studied under John Hejduk and was graduated in 1984.

Ban's portfolio now includes residential, cultural, commercial, and institutional building projects, as well as interior, industrial, and exhibition design. He has been widely published and was profiled by *Time* in their survey of 21st-century innovators in the fields of architecture and design.

RENÉ BARBA
Hanging Screens for Koziol (p. 33)
koziol.de/en/unternehmen/Designer/rene-barba-paris.php

Born in 1965 in Havana, Cuba, René Barba was educated at Miami Dade Community College and at the École National Supérieure des Arts Décoratifs (ENSAD) in Paris, where he received his diploma in Industrial Design.

René worked as a freelance designer in Paris for several years after school, and later for the Bombay Furniture Company in the U.S., for whom he won a Presidential Design Award for Best Product in 1997.

Returning to Paris he launched a private practice and began teaching at the Paris fashion school École Supérieure des Arts et Techniques de la Modérieure des Arts Décoratifs (ESMOD) International. Past clients include the Italian furnishings company BBB, Ligne Rosset, and Koziol.

DROR BENSCHETRIT
Quadror Blocks for DCI (p. 000), Try It Trivet for Alessi (p. 133)
studiodror.com

Founded by Tel Aviv–born and Eindhoven Academy–trained Dror Benshetrit, the eponymous New York firm Dror is a multidisciplinary practice encompassing product design, architecture, interior design, and art direction. His work is notable for exploring the nature of movement, transformation, and multifunctionality in the context of three-dimensional form.

Dror's client list includes Alessi, Bentley, Boffi, Bombay Sapphire, BBB Emmebonacina, Cappellini, Kiehl's, Levi's, Material ConneXion, Maya Romanoff, Marithe + Francois Girbaud, Rosenthal, Skins Footwear, Yigal Azrouël, Shvo, Swarovski, and Target.

Dror has lectured around the world and received numerous design awards, among them the GE Plastics Competition

(2001), iF Product Design Award (2006), the Good Design Award (2008, 2010), and the Red Dot Award (2012). He has gained international media exposure and has been widely exhibited. A number of the firm's design pieces are in the permanent collections of major museums in North America, Europe, and the Middle East.

MAXWELL BOGUE AND PETER DILWORTH
3Doodler Printing Pen (p. 100)
the3doodler.com

From film school student to computer scientist to toy inventor, Maxwell Bogue's past includes time working on the television show *She Spies*, as well as three years as an R&D Project Manager at WowWee. There he helped launch products such as Rovio, RS Media, and ChatterBots. Max cofounded 3Doodler manufacturer WobbleWorks in 2010.

Peter Dilworth is an alumnus of MIT's Leg Laboratory and the MIT Media Lab, where his work contributed to numerous innovations in the field of robotics. Peter previously worked as an inventor at WowWee, started WobbleWorks with Max in 2010, and is now the company's Chief Inventor and CTO.

JOHN BENNETT AND GUSTAVO BONEVARDI
Architect's Cubes for MoMA (p. 12)
west-side-industries.com

John Bennett received a Masters of Architecture from Columbia University in 1993, and Gustavo Bonevardi from Princeton University in 1986. The two are cofounders of the New York–based West Side Industries, an interdisciplinary firm engaged in architecture, digital filmmaking, and product and book design. Their videos have been included in the exhibitions *The Un-Private House* and *Mies in Berlin* (including the documentary *Mies and Exhibition Design 1926–1945*) at MoMA in New York. Bennett and Bonevardi were the principal designers of the highly acclaimed *Tribute in Light*, a rapidly formulated response to the devastation of September 11, 2001, for which they positioned high-powered lights pointed upward to recreate the image of the lost towers.

BLACK+BLUM
Flower Loop (p. 30), Loop Candleholder (p. 42)
black-blum.com

Black+Blum is an Anglo-Swiss partnership of Dan Black and and Martin Blum. Joining forces in 1998 and basing themselves in London, this design duo decided from the start to develop their own range of products as well as advise other companies on their creative ventures. Taking responsibility for both design and production has given them the means to fully explore and enjoy their personal vision of creative design, a decision which has been validated by numerous design awards and prominent display in select design and museum shops (not to mention domiciles) all over the word. The two met while taking the Design for Industry course at the University of Northumbria in Newcastle. Before starting their agency U.K.-born Dan worked at IDEO in London, Frog Design in California, and at Studio Brown in Bath. Martin, who was born and raised in Switzerland, spent his apprenticeship years as a commercial clerk with a product design company before receiving his design degree, as well as his love for all things British, at Newcastle.

TORD BOONTJE
Garland Light for Artecnica (p. 30)
tordboontje.com

Tord Boontje was born in The Netherlands in 1968. He was educated at the Eindhoven Design Academy, class of 1991, and the Royal College of Art London, graduating in 1994.

His studio has worked with a global array of clients, including Shiseido, Yamaha, Hewlett Packard, Bisazza, Target, Philips, Kvadrat, Alexander McQueen, Perrier-Jouët, Nanimarquina, Artecnica, Authentics, Meta, Swarovski, Moroso, and Habitat. Tord's portfolio counts lighting, graphics, textiles, ceramics, and furniture, with pieces in London's Victoria and Albert Museum, Design Museum, and Tate Modern, and MoMA and Cooper-Hewitt National Design Museum in New York. Tord has received awards from Red Dot, iF Product Design and Elle Decor, among many others.

Tord consolidated his studio, workshop, and a new retail outlet in Shoreditch in East London in 2012. From there he continues to launch new products as well as participate in educational and socially driven ventures around the world.

RONAN AND ERWAN BOUROULLEC
Algue (p. 9) and Corniches (p. 20) for Vitra, Cloud Modular Shelving for Cappellini (p. 84)
bouroullec.com

Ronan (b. 1971) and Erwan (b. 1976) Bouroullec were raised in Quimper, France, and studied at the École Nationale des Arts Décoratifs in Paris and at the École des Beaux-Arts in Cergy-Pontoise. In 1999 the two joined together as partners in their own design firm.

Their work ranges from small utilitarian objects to architectural projects. The bulk of their designs focus on domestic and office furniture, vases, porcelain dishware, jewelry, and various home accessories, as well as on the general organization of interior space.

The two credit designers from the past with giving them a solid foundation for their work. "To me, contemporary design stands atop two massive columns: one was created by the American designers like the Eameses, who were so innovative in the '40s and '50s and whose use of technology made such an incredible impact," says Erwan. "And the other column is made up of the Italian designers of the '70s and '80s, who created a whole new typology for modern living."

The Bouroullecs have collaborated with many top-tier international furniture and consumer product manufacturers, including Herman Miller, Vitra, Kvadrat, Kartell, Alessi, and Cappellini. Their designs can be found in numerous museum collections, among them the Centre Pompidou and the Musée des Arts Décoratifs in Paris, MoMA, The Art Institute of Chicago, and The Design Museum in London.

BRAVE SPACE DESIGN
Tetrad Shelving (p. 94)
bravespacedesign.com

Brave Space is a design-and-build furniture company that produces eco-friendly products and furnishings for home and office. Dedicated to providing quality furniture, the designers at Brave Space draw from a common set of influences to arrive at a style that is playful, modern, and environmentally conscious.

To achieve its social goals the company sources materials that are both durable and sustainable. It then optimizes these materials by minimizing the amount of waste and scrap generated, by carefully coordinating design and production, and through the use of advanced computer-aided-manufacturing technologies.

Brave Space was founded in Brooklyn and later relocated to Florida. Its custom and manufactured products are made exclusively in the U.S.

PIL BREDAHL
OTO 100 Storage System for Muuto (p. 92)
pilbredahldesign.dk

Pil Bredahl studied product and furniture design at the Denmark Design School and attended The International Centre for Creativity, Innovation, and Sustainability (ICIS) in 2006. As an award-winning Danish designer, Pil's work has been exhibited at leading international museums, and her OTO100 for Muuto is part of the permanent collection at the Danish Design Centre. She has run her own studio, Pil Bredahl Design, since 2005. Previous stints include design for Scandinavian Living A/S and Menu A/S.

BRINCA DADA
BiModal Blocks by Tim Boyle (p. 106)
brincadada.com

Doug Rollins founded Brinca Dada to bring together his love of design and toys. Prior to its launch Doug had a successful career as an entrepreneur, marketer, and toy buyer. He spent nine years at Toys"R"Us in Marketing, New Concept Development, and Buying. Before that, he helped successfully launch several different start-up companies.

Doug has a Bachelor of Arts in Humanities from Brigham Young University and a Master of Business Administration from Columbia University's Graduate School of Business.

ROBERT BRONWASSER
Grape Wine Rack for Goods (p. 32)
smool.nl

Son of an architect, Robert Bronwasser (b. 1968) was graduated from the Technical University of Delft in 1992 with a degree in Industrial Design. In 2002 he launched Smool Design to realize his vision of commercial product design. The agency works with large marketing-driven multinationals as well as smaller, design-oriented businesses.

The designer has received a number of prominent awards, including the iF Product Design Award, the Red Dot Award, GIO Awards, Interior Innovation Awards, a GIO Special Award for Design Excellence, and the Dutch Design Selection. His work has been exhibited at the Salone de Mobile in Milan, 100% Design Rotterdam, Via Milano, Orgatec, Interior Kortrijk, and the Dutch Design Week. Bronwasser's designs are widely published in industry and lifestyle magazines and online venues.

BUZZISPACE
KidzPuzzle Cushion (p. 122)
buzzispace.com

Antwerp-based company BuzziSpace is the creative subsidiary of Tecnospace, which specializes in partition walls for offices. BuzziSpace was an almost instant hit in the industry when it was launched in 2007, its very first products earning accolades for the company and its designer Sas Adriaenssens (b. 1971 in Antwerp, Belgium). Sas was graduated with a Masters in Graphic Arts and Illustration and eventually moved into the world of interior and product design before designing for Buzzi. Her work at Buzzi has garnered her several prestigious awards over the years, including an OVAM Ecodesign Award PRO in 2009 and the Henry van de Velde Award for most innovative company in 2011.

Staying true to its eco-conscious design principles, Buzzi has continually expanded its catalog to include wallpaper, acoustic panels and dividers, and other furnishings products suitable for home and office.

CAPPELLINI

Yuki Screen by Nendo (p. 74), Cloud Modular Shelving by Ronan and Erwan Bouroullec (p. 84)

cappellini.it/en

Cappellini was founded in 1946 in Arosio, Italy, as a workshop for handmade furniture. Its evolution to the global manufacturer of quality design products it is today can be traced to the day that Giulio Cappellini began working there in 1979. With a degree in architecture and studies in business management, Giulio was well positioned to take the company in an entirely new direction. By the 1980s his leadership had elevated Cappellini to global stature, fueled primarily by his strategy of enlisting top-tier designers to produce the striking and diverse portfolio for which it has become known. Among the many talents who have contributed to the company are Jasper Morrison, Ronan and Erwan Bouroullec, Marcel Wanders, Marc Newson, and Tom Dixon, as well as Konstantin Grcic, Alessandro Mendini, Alberto Meda, Ross Lovegrove, Ron Arad, Piero Lissoni, and Werner Aislinger.

PEER CLAHSEN

Cella (p. 17), Cubicus (p. 23), Diamant (p. 24)

peerclahsen.de

Peer Clahsen (b. 1938) is a freelance artist, art educator, and poet. He began studying art after an apprenticeship as a craftsman. Starting in 1967 Peer designed several reconfigurable play objects for premium Swiss toymaker Naef, all of which have since become classics. He lives and works in the Southern Black Forest in Germany.

ANDREW COMFORT

Q-BA-MAZE Marble Runs (p. 132)

q-ba-maze.com

Andrew Comfort had been bouncing in and out of formal architectural studies and practice for several years when he quit to start his own company for 3D computer renderings. To keep his hand in making physical things, he started work on designing a marble run loosely based on one he remembered his grandfather built during his (Andrew's) childhood. Inspired to make a run of it (pun fully intended), Comfort began rapid prototyping his modules while giving himself a crash course in business start-ups by reading seven years of back issues of *Entrepreneur* magazine. Finally pulling both his design and about $650,000 in seed money together, he launched his venture and has been running with it (yup) ever since.

LAURA COWAN

Menorahs (p. 45), Modular Magnetic Matzo Plate (p. 46)

lauracowan.com

Contemporary Judaica designer and artist Laura Cowan began her career in London after graduating in Silversmithing and Jewelry at London's Guildhall University. She now brings her ideas to the field of Judaica from her design studio and workshop in the artist's quarter of Neve Tsedek in Tel Aviv, Israel, where she moved in 1996.

Her work is sold and exhibited in design-quality shops, galleries, and museums around the world. One of her pieces even traveled to the International Space Station at the request of an American astronaut.

All Laura's products are original handcrafted pieces and signed by the artist.

CUBORO

Marble Track System (p. 125)

cuboro.ch

A young Matthias Etter laid the foundation for the Cuboro marble-run system in the 1970s while interning as a social education worker at a special education school in Switzerland. It all started with Matthias sculpting a few clay cubes to form a three-dimensional puzzle that he hoped would help children with impaired motor skills. Taken with his idea, Matthias found an ingenious joiner named Hans Nyfeler to help him figure out a way to carve wood blocks into the complex hollowed-out shapes called for by the design.

Blocks in hand, the unknown Matthias somehow managed to get hold of a booth at a fully booked trade fair in Bern in 1986, where he showed his new invention. Apparently the placement of the booth between the men's and women's toilets did not put a damper on the enthusiasm of the fair attendees, as several orders were placed for the marble runs by major European retailers. Today, Cuboro is sold in over thirty countries and is regarded as among the premium wood marble track systems in the world.

GIDEON DAGAN

Puzzle Wine Rack (p. 61)

dagandesign.com

Designer and inventor Gideon Dagan, born in Israel and based in Los Angeles, studied design at the Holon Institute of Technology and was graduated with a degree in Industrial Design from Tel Aviv University.

Best known for his innovative Perpetual Calendar and Timesphere Clock designed for MoMA, Dagan's work is noted for its streamlined minimalism and functional design. Dagan has designed numerous industrial and consumer products, including handheld computers, electronic instruments, and furniture. Several of his designs are patented, and have been featured in museums and design stores around the world.

BJÖRN DAHLSTRÖM
My Space Divider for Magis (p. 128)
www.dahlstromdesign.se

Born in Stockholm in 1957, Björn Dahlström launched his firm in 1982 with an intent to focus on graphic design. In time his portfolio shifted largely to product design, now accounting for more than three-quarters of his output.

Among his clients are Atlas Copco (building industry); Playsam (wooden toys); Krups (electrical appliances); Skeppshult (bicycles); Ittala (cookware); Magis, Lammhults, David Design (furniture); and Marimekko (printed textiles). In his spare time Björn designs exhibits for the Swedish Museum of Architecture.

He was awarded the Torsten and Wanja Söderberg Prize, one of the most prestigious Nordic design award programs, in 2001.

JONAS DAMON
Numbers Cube Clock for Areaware (p. 53)
jonasdamon.blogspot.com

Jonas Damon is a graduate of the Rhode Island School of Design. He began his career at Tom Dixon's Eurolounge in London before becoming a design manager for the European retail group Habitat UK. At Habitat, he took part in rebuilding the in-house design team that revived Habitat's reputation as the leading European retailer for home goods. Based in New York City since 2001, he has undertaken or overseen product design for companies and brands such as Areaware, AT&T, Chrysler, Harter, Malin+Goetz, The Home Depot, Tupperware, Vitra, and Wedgwood. He is currently a Creative Director at Frog Design.

DANA CANNAM DESIGN
All of a Piece Tableware (p. 10)
danacannamdesign.com

Dana Cannam (b. 1980 in Canada) received his Bachelors in Industrial Design at the University of Alberta (2007) and his Masters in Social Design at the Design Academy in Eindhoven (2010). Soon after graduation he established Dana Cannam Design in Rotterdam, The Netherlands, offering services in product development and design consultation.
Works have been exhibited during the Milan and the Dutch Design Weeks, the ICFF in New York, IDS in Toronto, and other international design exhibitions. Clients include Pablo Designs, Design House Stockholm, Municipality of Valkenburg, and the National Taiwan Craft Research and Development Institute.

DECOR CRAFT
Magnetic Vases by Peleg Design (p. 43), Building Block Menorah (p. 000) and QuaDror Building Blocks (p. 133) by Dror Benshetrit
shop.dcigift.com

Decor Craft Inc. (DCI) was launched as a small company in 1990, and has since become a leading gift manufacturer and distributor in multiple global markets. The company offers products in the categories of kitchen, bath, home, children, and general fun.

DCI distributes its products to numerous retailers, including Target, Bed Bath & Beyond, Sur La Table, Crate and Barrel, Organized Living, The Container Store, MoMA Design Store, and over 8,000 small retailers in North America and abroad.

The company maintains an open call to designers and inventors inviting them to submit ideas for bringing to market.

DANTE DONEGANI AND GIOVANNI LAUDA
Honey Lights for Rotaliana (p. 35)
www.domusacademy.com/site/home/alumni/success-stories/articolo4002582.html

Born in Pinzolo, Italy, in 1957, Dante Donegani earned a degree in architecture in Florence in 1983. From 1987 to 1991 he worked in the Olivetti Corporate Identity department. Since 1991 he has been the director of the Master Program in Design at the Domus Academy in Milan. In 1992 he opened the multidisciplinary D&L Studio with Giovanni Lauda.

Dante has designed art exhibitions, corporate identity projects, and products for such companies as Memphis, Stildomus, Isuz, Steel and Luceplan, Le Cose Nostre, Edra, Radice, and Viceversa. He has won important competitions in architecture, and his work has been displayed in numerous exhibitions.

Giovanni Lauda was born in 1956 in Naples, where he obtained a degree in architecture and was a member of the Morozzi & Partners studio from 1988 to 1991. In 1992 he cofounded the D&L Studio for architecture and interior and product design.

Giovanni has created housewares and furnishings for Sedie & Company, Uchino, Playline, Le Cose Nostre, Edra, Radice Lucepland, and Viceversa. He has taught at the Domus Academy in Milan since 1993.

JULIA DOZSA
Tetris Mirror for FIAM (p. 69)
dozsa-en-van-dalfsen.nl

Julia Dozsa was born in 1960 in The Netherlands. After studying architecture for two years at the Polytechnic School, she attended the Gerrit Rietveld Academy in Amsterdam, where she was graduated with a degree in industrial design.

In 1997 she founded the Dozsa & van Dalfsen design studio in Amsterdam for architectural, industrial, and interior design. Among the firm's product design clients are Calligaris, Driade, Fiam Italia, Glas Italia, IKEA, Studio Šípek, TAFT Shoes, and Tonelli. Architectural projects include apartments, offices, and retail spaces in Amsterdam and elsewhere in The Netherlands.

CHARLES AND RAY EAMES
House of Cards, reissued by Eames Office (p. 36), Eames House Blocks by House Industries for Uncle Goose (p. 111)
eamesoffice.com

Charles Ormond Eames, Jr. (1907–1978) and Bernice Alexandra "Ray" Eames (1912–1988) were American designers who made major contributions to industrial, exhibition, and graphic design, fine art, architecture, and film.

Charles Eames was born in 1907 in St. Louis, Missouri. Developing an interest in engineering and architecture, he attended Washington University until leaving to work in an architectural office. He started his own firm in 1930, but in time his interest grew beyond architecture, and in 1936 he received a fellowship to attend Cranbrook Academy of Art in Michigan, where he subsequently served as head of the Experimental Design Department from 1937 to 1940.

Ray Kaiser was born in Sacramento, California, and studied painting with Hans Hofmann in New York before moving on to Cranbrook Academy, where she met Charles. They were married in 1941, moved to California, and began producing furniture.

The Eameses' work had already garnered attention from their entries to the Organic Design in Home Furnishing competition held at MoMA in 1940. Charles, assisted by Ray and in collaboration with Eero Saarinen, won two prizes, the first for a molded plywood chair and another for modular design. In 1946 the Eameses produced their famous LCW (Lounge Chair Wood) molded plywood chair. This and other designs were shown at at MoMA that year, further cementing their reputation. A series of chairs and public seating followed from the late 1940s onwards, many using new materials such as glass-reinforced plastic, and proved equally influential.

The Eameses' modular work, first seen in the 1940 competition, reemerged in products like the ESU 421-C storage unit of 1949, which helped define the aesthetic of the postwar office environment. The Eameses' affinity for modular design was revealed yet again in the design of their home in Santa Monica (1947–49). Open-plan in layout, it was assembled largely from standardized, prefabricated parts.

Beginning in 1950, the Eameses produced several films and multimedia presentations. These included *Mathematica* (1961) for IBM, *Powers of Ten* (1968) for the Commission of the College of Physics, and commissions for the U.S. government.

Through their ceaseless experimentation in form, concept, materials, and media, the Eameses came to rank among the most influential designers of the 20th century.

EARNEST STUDIO
All of a Piece Tableware (p. 10, pictured)
earnestly.org

Earnest Studio is American designer Rachel Griffin. Her Rotterdam-based studio works on self-initiated projects and industry collaborations. She has exhibited in shows in Italy, Switzerland, Germany, Slovenia, and Taiwan. Her work has been recognized in several competitions and awards programs sponsored by the (D3) Design Talents Competition, AIGA, the Society for Environmental Graphic Design, and the Creative Industries Fund NL.

A partial list of media coverage includes *Abitare*, *Azure*, *Blend*, Bright TV, *Casamica*, *Casa Living*, Designboom, Dezeen, *Elle Decor Italia*, *Eigen Huis & Interieur*, *Frame*, It's Nice That, *L'Officiel*, MoCoLoco, Protein, Refinery29, *Thisispaper*, *TL Magazine*, *Viva Glam*, *Wallpaper**, and Yatzer.

ECO-KIDS
Eco-Dough (p. 112)
ecokidsusa.com

Meet Cammie, Kip, and their kids Jack, Maggie, and Gus. They are eco-kids — a family-run business that produces all natural art supplies. It began simply, as all good things do, with the molding-dough recipe Cammie's mom made for her as a child. After incorporating natural ingredients into the recipe, the dough was transformed into "eco-dough," rich in color, soft in texture, with a delicate aroma like no other. In 2008 Cammie and Kip began selling it at farmers markets. From there, eco-kids evolved.

This family business lives by their mantra—"creative play the natural way." Products are developed with this belief in mind. From using nontoxic, natural ingredients to the unique packaging, eco-kids works with environmentally friendly companies from around the U.S. to bring you fresh ideas in the world of art supplies.

ELENCO
Snap Circuits Electronic Toys (p. 134)
elenco.com

Gil Cecchin and Arthur Seymour established Elenco Electronics, Inc., in 1972. Gil began his career in electronics at Motorola's advanced development lab and worked as a designer there for over twenty-five years. He received more than twenty-five patents for his work in developing color television and integrated circuits. Arthur also worked at Motorola, and did consulting work for Zenith, IBM, and other large electronics firms.

The company name was derived from the first two letters of the words Electronic Engineering Corporation because both founders were electronic engineers. The first products produced by Elenco were convergence generators designed for television repairmen. Times being what they are, Elenco now supply products to the toy, education, telecommunication, and electrical engineering fields.

ENLISTED DESIGN
Urbio Modular Garden and Wall Organizer (p. 71)
enlisteddesign.com

Based in Oakland, California, Enlisted Design was founded by entrepreneurs Beau Oyler and Jared Aller. Staffed with product and graphic designers, the firm works on strategy, brand, and product development for clients like Williams-Sonoma, Ames Tools, Whole Earth Farms, Timbuk2, Intuit, Urbio, and Full Moon Treats.

FAT BRAIN TOYS
Dado Construction Toys (p. 109)
fatbraintoys.com

One day in 2002, ten-year-old Adam Carson received a magnetic building toy called Geomag for his birthday. Fascinated with the toy and looking to spend some additional birthday money, he went online to see if he could buy a larger set. Discovering how difficult it was to find online, he suggested to his father, a Web developer by trade, that they create their own online store to sell the specialty toy.

Shipping the toys out of the basement of their home in the small community of Elkhorn, Nebraska, this unlikely online toy store managed to challenge the likes of Toys"R"Us and Walmart to become one of the largest online retailers of Geomag in the world. Quickly outgrowing the basement, the family moved the entire operation several times before finally settling into an office, a warehouse, and two retail stores that they operate from today.

In 2006, the company began development of their own line of educational toys. Since that time, over sixty original products have been developed and are now sold around the world.

FERM LIVING
Molecule Building Set (p. 48)
www.fermliving.com

ferm LIVING started with a vision and a need. The vision belonged to Trine Anderson, a Danish graphic designer who started her own studio in 2005. One day Trine saw a bird on a branch, ready to take off, and took it as a sign about something in her life. The need? Looking to buy some wallpaper for her own use, Trine was disappointed to discover a lack of papers with the crisp graphics she wanted. Taking matters into her own hands, her first wallpaper collection was launched to great acclaim in 2006, and ferm LIVING became a reality. So the little bird took off after all.

ANNA CASTELLI FERRIERI AND KARTELL
Componibili Storage System (p. 85)
kartell.com

In 1943, Anna Castelli Ferrieri (1918–2006) became one of the first women to be graduated from the prestigious Milan Polytechnic Institute with an architecture degree. In 1949, she and her husband, Giulio Castelli, founded Kartell, which became a leading furniture company known for high quality designs in plastic. With the success of Kartell, the Castelli-Ferrieris helped fuel the rise of Italian modern design from the 1960s through the 1980s. They were joined by contemporaries Pier and Achille Castiglioni, Gae Aulenti, Ettore Sottsass, and Joe Colombo, each of whom looked to adopt new technologies and materials, including Kartell's signature medium of plastic, in their designs.

Emilio Ambasz's seminal 1972 MoMA exhibition *Italy: The New Domestic Landscape* displayed several pieces by Castelli Ferrieri, most notably her 1969 stackable Componobili storage units. At the time of the MoMA show, the Bloomingdale's department store constructed an entire New York skyline out of them in its home furnishings department.

FLENSTED
DIY 419 Mobile by Ryusaku Kawashima (p. 24)
flensted-mobiles.com

In 1953 Christian Flensted made his first mobile, to celebrate the christening of his daughter. He cut out three storks, mounted them on two straws, and the Stork Mobile was made. Thus was born Flensted Mobiles, which is run today by his son Ole out of a former schoolhouse in a quiet corner of the Danish island of Funen.

Around 80% of Flensted's designs are by Christian or Ole; other designers have included Sir Terry Frost (for a mobile for Tate Modern), Greenberg Kingsley, and Ryusaku Kawashima, the creator of the Flensted 419. The company also takes one-off commissions for unique pieces on behalf of companies like Microsoft and Michelin. All mobiles are handmade by locals working independently within a twenty-mile radius of the central facility.

Flensted currently sells in about thirty countries worldwide. The Stork Mobile is still in production.

FORT STANDARD
Balancing Blocks for Areaware (p. 105, pictured)
fortstandard.com

Fort Standard is a contemporary, multidisciplinary industrial design and fabrication studio founded by Gregory Buntain and Ian Collings in 2011. The two met while students at Brooklyn's Pratt Institute. Fort Standard boasts an impressive range of products and services, including home goods, toys, jewelry furniture, and branding.

The designers view their work is an ever evolving dialog between their individual perspectives and a shared approach to progressive design thinking. Working primarily in durable, natural materials, their design philosophy drives them to employ traditional production methods in innovative ways. Having developed a distinct form language rooted in simplicity and functionality, their attention to detail, connections, and materiality generate value through design in what they term a "warm-contemporary" aesthetic.

Their client list includes 1882, All-Clad, Areaware, Fjallraven, General Catalyst, Mociun, MoMA PS1, Roll & Hill, SCP, Thrive Capital, and Warby Parker.

FRACTILES
Fractiles Magnetic Tiling Toy (p. 113)
fractiles.com

Fractiles is a Colorado corporation formed in 1998 by Marc Pelletier and Beverly Johnson of Boulder, Colorado. A lifelong aficionado of geometry, Beverly currently serves as president of the company. Marc's passion for mathematical models began at age thirteen, when he began building paper constructions of his own invention. Since then he has conducted research, published findings, and collaborated with distinguished practitioners of applied geometry. Marc is also a creator of Zometool, a modular three-dimensional construction toy.

F.A.T. LAB
Free Universal Construction Kit for Adapterz LLC (p. 113)
fffff.at

By its own admission, the Free Art and Technology Lab (F.A.T.) is a New York organization dedicated to enriching the public domain through the research and development of creative technologies and media. The entire F.A.T. network of artists, engineers, scientists, lawyers, and musicians are committed to supporting open values and the public domain through the use of emerging open licenses, support for open entrepreneurship, and the admonishment of secrecy, copyright monopolies, and patents.

Its mantra is release early, often, and with rap music.

BEN FRITZ
Woodmobiel for OOTS! (p. 141)
madebyoots.com/woodmobiel.html

One day, Ben Fritz, a retired Dutch graphic designer, was asked by one of his grandchildren if he would help him build a house. A kid-sized house, that is. This sounded like fun to Ben, who began to look around for suitable parts and materials. But Ben couldn't find anything that satisfied him. So he took the bull by the horns and started developing his own DIY kit that would let him and his grandchildren build not just a house, but all sorts of wooden toys of their own invention. So successful was his eventual creation that he was inspired to bring it to others. Thus was launched Woodmobiel. The brand is currently distributed in the U.S. by OOTS!, an innovative product design and distribution company founded in 2004 by Arian Roefs and Godfried Konings, both from The Netherlands, in Santa Fe, New Mexico.

DESIGNERS AND BRANDS

MATT GAGNON
Joint Venture Shelving for RS Barcelona (p. 89)
mattstudio.com

Having studied architecture at Cornell University, Matt Gagnon established his eponymous studio in 2002 after stints with Frank Gehry and Gaetano Pesce. Gagnon's work has been published extensively in publications including *The New York Times*, *Metropolis*, *Surface*, *Interior Design*, and *Dwell*, and has been in numerous design exhibitions internationally. Clients have included W Resorts, Four Seasons Hotel, RS Barcelona, Ogilvy, and the Los Angeles Fire Department.

Matt has taught at Otis College of Art and the Parsons School of Constructed Environments and has been a visiting artist or critic at Savannah College of Art and Design, Woodbury School of Architecture, and City College of New York.

His studio is a full-service design firm providing concept development through project management in product, architecture, and installation design. It collaborates with artists, companies, real estate developers, home owners, hotels, city agencies, creative agencies, and manufacturers on projects around the world.

MASSIMO GIACON
Presepe Nativity Set for Alessi (p. 58)
massimogiacon.com

Massimo Giacon was born in Padua, Italy, in 1961. In 1979 he embarked on a multifaceted career trajectory, starting with publishing comics, then moving to indie music bands, next to performance art, and then to design, during which period he worked with major designers (Sottsass, Mendini, Thun) and just as major brands (Memphis, Swatch, Artemide, Alessi).

In the past decade he's designed carpets, laminate materials, illustrations for fashion magazines, Web sites, fabrics, virtual characters, TV theme songs, ceramics, and other products, and worked on graphic novels, various editorial projects, musical and commercial videos, art exhibitions, and music production with his band, Massimo Giacon and the Blass.

RON GILAD
CandlestickMaker (p. 17), VaseMaker (p. 72)
designfenzider.com

Born in Tel Aviv in 1972, Gilad was graduated with a degree in industrial design from the Bezalel Academy of Art and Design in Jerusalem. Gilad taught 3D Design at the Shenkar Academy of Engineering and Design from 1999 to 2001, during which time he developed one-of-a-kind objects that he later exhibited at shows. He moved to New York in 2001 and cofounded Designfenzider, where he designs, produces, and distributes his works around the world. He has since relocated his studio to Tel Aviv and expanded into limited edition fine art projects.

Gilad was chosen *Wallpaper** magazine's Designer of the Year in 2013. His work is notable for fusing elegant minimalism with strong doses of humor and wit, and for its continued exploration of the theme of home.

STEFANO GIOVANNONI
Boogie Woogie Shelving for Magis (p. 82)
stefanogiovannoni.it

Stefano Giovannoni was born in La Spezia, Italy, and was graduated with a degree in architecture in Florence in 1978. Since then he has taught at the Florence Faculty of Architecture, the Domus Academy in Milan, and the Università del Progetto in Reggio Emilia.

He currently works in architectural, interior, and industrial design in Milan. His clients include Alessi, Flos, Magis, Seiko, Pulsar, Cappellini, Kankyo, and Saab, among others. Giovannoni has received considerable recognition for his designs, their success earning him the moniker "The King Midas of Design."

GOOD ERDLE
Eliot Modular Planters (p. 27, pictured)
gooderdle.com

Good Erdle was started by Andrew Erdle in 2010 as a side project. By 2011 it was forced to become a little more real when Andrew was compelled to create a make-believe business in order to attend the New York International Gift Fair without paying. A year later he launched the business for real with his first real product at the very same fair.

Andrew's Dad, Richard Erdle, joined the company after it received its first purchase order. Richard's love of ceramics can be traced back to a briefe period studying at Alfred State, as well as the influence of his late brother, who had a great appreciation for art.

Since then Good Erdle has expanded its offerings in home accessories, all of which are manufactured domestically. The company is based in upstate New York.

GRAIN
Ty DIY Shower Curtain (p. 71)

graindesign.com

Grain, based in Washington State, is a practice dedicated to social and environmental responsibility. Its work seeks to unite current manufacturing technologies with time-honored craft techniques. Goods are produced in small batch runs at the firm's studio or through special collaborations with expert artisans in America and abroad.

As a full-service consultancy and studio, Grain offers expertise in research, strategy, and design for companies interested in uniting sustainability and business through design. Clients include Design Within Reach, Blu Homes, Trina Turk, and Anthropologie.

In 2008, Grain began work on a line of eco-friendly home products produced in the Pacific Northwest or in collaboration with artisan communities in Guatemala.

MICHAEL JOAQUIN GREY
ZOOB Construction Toy for Infinitoy (p. 145)

citroid.com

Born 1961 in Los Angeles, Michael Joaquin Grey is an American artist, inventor, educator, and toy designer based in New York City.

Grey holds a Bachelor of Arts degree in Art and a Bachelor of Science in Genetics from the University of California, Berkeley, 1984, and a MFA in Sculpture from Yale University, 1990.

Grey's work examines genetics, language, and the origins of form and has been published in such venues as *Artforum, Flash Art, The New York Times, The New Yorker, Leonardo, Artbyte, ID Magazine, Washington Post, Los Angeles Times, The San Francisco Chronicle, London Telegraph, Wired, Art & Auction,* and *The Wall Street Journal.*

He has shown at New York's MoMA, Whitney Museum of American Art, and The New Museum of Contemporary Art; the Museums of Contemporary Art in Miami, Chicago and San Diego; LACMA; Tel Aviv Museum of Art; Nordic Art Center, Helsinki; Norrtälje Konsthall, Sweden; Kunsthalle Loppem, Belgium; and at several international art galleries.

GRIMM'S SPIEL UND HOLZ DESIGN
Creative Toys (p. 115)

grimms.eu

Grimm's Spiel und Holz Design is a toy manufacturer founded in 1978 and located in Hochdorf, Southern Germany. The company produces wooden toys including puzzles, building blocks, baby rattles and stackers, dollhouses, stacking rainbows, mobiles, decorative items, roll-along animals and vehicles, and magnetic play sets.

Their product line is inspired by Waldorf (in Europe, referred to as Steiner) education principles. Sustainability is an equally important company goal to educational value; all Grimm's woods are sourced from sustainably managed forests in Europe and finished with certified nontoxic, water-based colors.

All products are designed in-house.

JONAS GRUNDELL
Nordic Light Candleholder for Design House Stockholm (p. 53)

designhousestockholm.com/designers/jonas_grundell.html

Jonas Grundell was born in 1963 and was graduated from the Carl Malmsten School in Stockholm in 1986. In addition to work for the brand Design House Stockholm he has undertaken furniture and interior design projects for private residences.

MARTÍ GUIXÉ
Blank Wall Clock for Alessi (p. 16)

www.guixe.com

Marti Guixé (b. 1964) is an award-winning Spanish designer living in Barcelona and Berlin. He was graduated in interior design from ELISAVA in Barcelona in 1985 and enrolled in an industrial design study program in Scuola Politecnica di Design di Milano in 1986. Though Guixé has spoken out against the widespread view of the designer as a stylist and has even presented himself as an "ex-designer," he has undertaken work for numerous high profile brands, including Alessi, Authentics, B-sign, Camper, Corraini, Danese, Dentsu, Desigual, Drill, Droog Design, Imaginarium, Isee2, Mediamatic, Magis, Saporiti Italia, Trico, Very Lustre and Vitra. His designs, installations and performances have been presented in fine art contexts such as MoMA, Centre Georges Pompidou, and the Design Museum London. Ever the polymath, Mr. Guixé has even written a cookbook.

DESIGNERS AND BRANDS

FRITZ HALLER
USM Modular Furniture (p. 95, pictured)
smow.com/designers/fritz-haller

Fritz Haller (1924–2012) worked with several Swiss architects before traveling to Rotterdam to help work on postwar rebuilding projects. In 1949 he returned to his native Swiss town of Solothurn, where he began working in his father Bruno's architecture firm, before eventually founding his own.

His early works, such as the Kantonsschule, Baden, from 1960 or the 1957 Weststadtschulhaus in Solothurn, established a systematic approach to design derived from principles of steel frame construction. It was his expertise in this type of construction that led to an invitation in 1963 from a local manufacturer of metal products, Ulrich Schärer Münsingen, to design a suite of office furniture that would eventually become the USM Haller modular furniture line.

HAPE
Organeco Building Blocks (p. 128)
hapetoys.com

Hape's story begins with Peter Handstein, who grew up in a rural town in central Germany. Peter began his career as a salesman for an educational toy company servicing German kindergartens. In 1986, Peter formed Hape Kindergarten Supply with his sister and a close friend.

The company expanded rapidly into international markets in the 1990s, and today sells in over fifty countries. In 2005 it launched its first full line of toys made of bamboo, committing itself to sustainable design. Today Hape is one of the world's largest producers of creative playthings made from eco-friendly materials. From the beginning of the design process, through production and delivery, to the final unwrapping of the consumer packaging, Hape toys embody the fusion of global thinking and responsible ecology.

HAY
Kaleido Trays by Clara von Zweigbergk (p. 42, pictured)
hay.dk

Founded in 2002, HAY launched its inaugural collection at IMM Cologne in 2003. HAY's mission is to encourage a return to the golden age of Danish design within a contemporary context. It strives to make good design accessible to a broad market by offering trademarked furniture and products at affordable prices. Its pieces are designed by young, emerging talent as well as by internationally established designers.

HAY sells its products through branded stores in Denmark, Norway, Germany, Belgium, and The Netherlands, as well as through a global network of dealers, high-end design shops, and, for contract work, through architects and interior designers.

EIJA HELANDER
Programma 8 Tableware for Alessi (p. 58)
alessi.com/en/1/155/eija-helander

Eija Helander was born in Lathi, Finland, in 1944. Following school, Helander embarked on a lengthy collaboration with Marimekko, eventually managing the firm's visual merchandising and its corporate identity in the Scandinavian market. She has directed advertising shoots and short films, and has served as a consultant on many interior design magazines. In 1969 she moved to Italy to work in industrial design, creating projects for companies such as Fivep, Inda, and Alessi, where she worked closely with Franco Sargiani on forming the brand's identity as well as on the Programma 8 product suite.

SCOT HERBST
Rhombins Desktop Storage and Play for AMAC (p. 61)
www.herbstprodukt.com

Scot Herbst is a second-generation partner at Herbst Product, a landmark design firm in the San Francisco Bay Area. Formed by Walter Herbst in 1962, HLB has grown to be the largest independently owned product design firm in the U.S.

159

Scot has created products for Fortune 100 brands and small to mid-size entrepreneurial start-ups. His own products, issued under the KAIKU label, have been selected for MoMA's curated retail collection, and one received their Product of the Year distinction in 2010.

In addition to his work at Herbst, Scot is Creative Director at SLICE, a Director of Design at global brand experience firm Liquid Agency, and an advisor for the life science start-up CUE.

HEIKO HILLIG
Ikamo (p. 38) and Imago (p. 38) for Naef
form-ost.de/designer-heiko-hillig.php

Heiko Hillig was born in 1971 in Marienberg, Germany, and studied at the University of Art and Design Burg Giebichenstein in Halle from 1990 to 1995. After graduation he worked as a product designer for three years with the German craft manufacturer Ulbricht. Since 1997, Heiko has served as chief designer and product manager for the Swiss toymaker Naef.

HOUSEFISH
Key Modular Storage (p. 90)
housefish.com

Housefish was founded by Scott Bennett. Driven by a childhood love of Formula 1 racing, Scott earned an automotive engineering degree from Loughborough University in England. He went on to be part of design teams for cars that have won the Indy 500, IndyCar championship, and Baja off-road races. He also helped set up new American-based Indycar and Formula 1 constructors, and branched out along the way to work on aircraft, industrial equipment, and consumer products. A changing landscape in racing led to a permanent shift to furniture design, and the formation of Housefish in 2008.

IDEAPAINT
IdeaPaint Erasable Surface Covering (p. 36)
ideapaint.com

IdeaPaint Inc. was founded in 2008 to help people and businesses collaborate more effectively, be more creative, and accelerate innovation. Widely recognized as an originator of high-performance dry-erase paint, it has been covered in *The Wall Street Journal*, *Mashable*, *Fast Company*, and CNBC. To date IdeaPaint has been used in more than 75,000 offices, schools, and homes around the world, that number increasing every day.

IdeaPaint is an environmentally responsible product, being LEED and CalGreen compliant, and UL GREENGUARD Gold Certified for indoor air quality. It's available in over fifty countries around the world.

PATRICK JOUIN
Optic Storage Cubes for Kartell (p. 92)
www.patrickjouin.com

Born in 1967, Patrick Jouin earned a bachelor's degree in 1986 and a degree in Design from the École Nationale Supérieure de Création Industrielle (ENSCI) in Paris in 1992. After graduation he began working for Thomson Multimedia before going to work for Philippe Starck the following year. In 1998, he founded his own firm for product design and interior architecture. Among his design clients are Ligne Roset, Cassina, Fermob, Kartell, and Alessi. His architectural projects include restaurants, hotels, and retail and urban design across Europe.

LUDWIG HIRSCHFELD-MACK
Bauhaus Optical Top (p. 106)
bauhaus-online.de/en/atlas/personen/
ludwig-hirschfeld-mack

A founding member of the Weimar Bauhaus, and recognized as both an artist and art teacher, Ludwig Hirschfeld Mack was born in Germany in 1893, moved to England in 1936, and died in 1963 in Australia, where he had been deported by the British as an "alien" at the start of the War. There he had introduced Bauhaus methods into the country's art education while producing a substantial body of his own work over several decades.

Hirschfeld Mack was an inventive and experimental artist. His Bauhaus training established the importance of a deep understanding of materials and their properties. As an art teacher, he avidly promoted that experimentation with materials was the foundation of an art education. His inventive approach extended beyond traditional fine art media, such as the design and construction of highly original musical instruments and a patented device that he envisaged could be used in illuminated advertising.

DESIGNERS AND BRANDS

HOUSE INDUSTRIES
Alexander Girard Alphabet Blocks (p. 9), Alphabet Factory Blocks (p. 102, pictured, opposite), and Eames House Blocks (p. 111) for Uncle Goose
houseind.com

Widely known as a prolific type foundry, House Industries has designed fonts for billboards, greeting cards, consumer products and logos, clothing, and mainstream media. It has also collaborated with manufacturers to produce design products under their and its own brand names. The company is based in Yorklyn, Delaware.

MIRJAM HÜTTNER
Colorem Chalk Cubes for Naef (p. 109)
huettners.com

Mirjam Hüttner is an industrial designer working in partnership with her husband, Claude Muller, on lighting, accessories, furniture, and children's products. They do business with several European brands and have been featured in a number of design magazines and media venues. Their studio is located in Ettlingen, Germany.

INCORPORATED
Hex Table (p. 34) and PolyHex (p. 57) for Lerival
incorporatedny.com

Incorporated is a New York–based multidisciplinary architecture and design studio with experience in a wide range of project types. Its architectural portfolio includes commissions for hotels, residences, restaurants, galleries, and retail environments. Incorporated has also designed exhibitions for institutions such as the Jewish Museum and the Museum of Arts and Design in New York.

Several of its design products have been issued by Lerival, including a suite of hexagonal furniture. Its products are notable for their explorations of modularity and serial design.

Published work has appeared in *Elle Decor*, *House Beautiful*, *Surface*, *Spaces*, *Interior Design*, and *Metropolitan Home*.

ITALIANISSIMO
Sportivo Linkable Jewelry (p. 78)
www.italianissimoinc.com

The Italianissimo brand was founded in 1986 by Diane and Mauro Gennaretti (an Americana from Boston and an Italiano from Rome), with the intent of introducing the U.S, market to a unique collection of contemporary design products with Italian quality, style, and craftsmanship. Their catalog now ranges from modern Murano glass vases and designer kitchenware to photo frames and avant-garde clocks.

Then, in 2012, Diane and Mauro decided to capitalize on their many years of professional expertise by designing and launching their own brand of unique fashion jewelry, called Tubino, which is the Italian word for the iconic little black dress, and translates literally to "little tube." Made in Italy, of course.

STEPHAN JAKLITSCH
Terrain Vase for MoMA (p. 68)
jaklitschgardner.com

Jaklitsch / Gardner Architects (J/GA) is an award-winning New York City–based studio with an expertise in designing high-end commercial and residential buildings and interiors, furnishings, and objects. Over the firm's fifteen year history, J/GA has built several hundred projects throughout North and South America, Europe, Asia, and the Middle East, giving the firm an international perspective on design and project management. J/GA has collaborated with fashion brands including Marc Jacobs International, Shelly Steffee, Moscot Eyewear, and Shinsegae International. J/GA's work has been exhibited widely and featured in numerous publications, including *Architectural Digest*, *Elle Decor*, *The New York Times*, *Time*, *The Wall Street Journal*, *Azure*, *Hinge*, *Surface*, and *Wallpaper**.

Stephan Jaklitsch received his Bachelor of Science in Architecture from the Georgia Institute of Technology and a Master of Architecture from Princeton University. He is actively involved in numerous New York architectural and nonprofit organizations.

KALEIDOGRAPH DESIGN
Kaleidograph Pattern Design Toy (p. 120)
kaleidographtoy.com

Kaleidograph Design was established in 2011 by Norman Brosterman and Scott Bultman to develop products that inspire creative play. Norman is the author of *Inventing Kindergarten* (1997), a history of the original kindergarten system and its influence on the development of 20th-century abstract art and modern architecture. Architect, woodcarver, and a dealer-collector of historical toys, Japanese Ikebana baskets and kimonos, and architectural drawings, Norman resides in East Hampton, New York.

Scott Bultman is the owner of Red Hen Books & Toys (p. 172).

NAURIS KALINAUSKAS
Stitch Interlocking Rug (p. 66)
contraforma.com/en/designers

Nauris Kalinauskas (b. 1972 in Lithuania) started his career in advertising but soon turned to furniture and product design. Having studied architecture and received degrees from Vilnius Technical University and Vilnius Academy of Arts in 1996, Nauris was well positioned to launch the design studio Contraforma in Vilnius in 2000 in partnership with several colleagues. He currently serves as its art director. The company operates principally as a design consultancy for furniture, interior, and product design, with over thirty pieces currently in its catalog. Its designs are fabricated in collaboration with local manufacturers and sold all over the world.

Contraforma has received numerous design awards and has been published in trade and general interest media.

HILA RAWET KARNI
Kishut Modular Jewelry (p. 76)
industrial-jewellery.com

Hila Rawet Karni is the driving force behind Industrial Jewelry designs. As the granddaughter of a woodworker and daughter of an industrial designer, Hila has been surrounded by art and design since childhood. Inspired by her roots, Hila often utilizes the early designs of her grandfather, who created modern geometric jewelry in a small town in Israel over seventy years ago. The geometric patterns stemming from her rich family history are incorporated in numerous pieces throughout her collections.

Hila's jewelry collections are designed and handcrafted in her London studio and promoted worldwide through exhibitions and boutique stores. Her passion for innovation continues to push the boundaries of industrial materials with each new season.

PETER KARPF
Gemini Candleholder (p. 32)
dwr.com/category/designers/h-l/peter-karpf.do

Peter Karpf was born in Copenhagen, Denmark, in 1940, trained as a cabinetmaker under Fritz Hansen, and qualified as a furniture designer from the Copenhagen School of Arts & Crafts. During his career, Peter Karpf has, among other things, worked with furniture design for Grethe Jalk, interior design with Arne Jacobsen, and industrial design with Erik Herløw.

Early on in his career, Karpf experimented with adjustable chairs that could be ganged to form multiple seating arrangements and stacked once the upholstery was removed. He continued to ponder flexible, simple seating solutions incorporating ganging, stacking, and folding into the 1980s and 90s when developing his NXT, Oto, and Tri plywood chairs. Karpf developed his first prototype for NXT in 1962, although the design was not patented until 1986. Over the years, Iform, Fritz Hansen, and Dansk have manufactured Karpf's designs.

Karpf collaborated with architect Fini Bolbroe on Spectaculume, a versatile consumer-assembled lamp for Dansk in which the kit-of-parts could be configured 119 different ways. While some early controversial Karpf creations—such as the multispoked lounge chair and the string chair—were valuable experiments, other designs have endured. His candlesticks, monolithic molded plywood chairs, and light fixtures have become Modern Danish classics.

FRANK KERDIL
Mondri 3-in-1 Vase (p. 49)
frankkerdil.com

Frank Kerdil was born in 1946 in Odense, Denmark. He was trained as a graphic designer and was the co-owner of an advertising agency from 1984 to 1998, when he launched his own design firm to develop design ideas for products.

Kerdil founded the PO: brand of home accessories to bring creatively designed products to a global audience. The company name was inspired by the concept of "po" devised by Edward de Bono, who introduced the idea of lateral thinking as a creative problem-solving method in 1967. The goal of lateral thinking is to help people approach problems in a novel and unconventional way. It seeks to break down barriers, awaken imagination, and invite surprise.

Kerdil's motto is "When more of the same is not enough!"—another way of saying that there should be a compelling and creative rationale for making a new product.

KATHRIN KIENER
Mosaik for Naef (p. 50)
kienertoys.ch

Kathrin Kiener practically grew up helping out at her uncle's timber yard and in the process forming a bond with all things wood—so much so that in 1981 she founded a toy company that makes toys out of wood. Today, the Swiss company makes delightful and well-constructed playthings by hand, from mobiles to starter books, each designed in-house. Along the way she also found time to design some nice things for her fellow countrymen at Naef, an iconic Swiss brand that knows something about wood as well.

ED KILDUFF
Houdini Wine Rack for Metrokane (p. 35)
pollendesign.com

Ed Kilduff cofounded Pollen Design in New York in 1997. The award-winning firm specializes in innovative and aspirational product designs. Before co-founding Pollen Design in 1997, Ed designed for Smart Design, Nike, Reebok, Fisher-Price, and Starbucks, creating hundreds of products and packages over the course of many years. This output has garnered Ed over fifty patents, many international design awards, and representation in the MoMA permanent collection.

Ed earned a Design Department Student Merit Award and was graduated with honors from Carnegie Mellon University with a Bachelor of Fine Arts in Industrial Design.

PAT KIM
Alphabet Blocks for Areaware (p. 11)
patkimdesign.com

Pat Kim is a designer and maker born in Virginia. He was graduated with a degree in Industrial Design from Brooklyn's Pratt Institute in 2009. After completing an internship with Fisher-Price and working for a high-end furniture designer and fabricator, he set up his own studio in Red Hook, Brooklyn. There he focuses on toys and furniture, while also designing home accessories and jewelry.

KMN HOME
DrawerDecor Liner System (p. 88)
kmnhome.com

KMN Home started in spirit in 2005 when Keith M. Nielson and Kevin M. Vann—friends since the fourth grade—began getting together late on a Thursday night after the kids and wives were asleep to rebuild a 1941 Chevy truck. Despite all the fun they had on "Truck Night," their nocturnal gatherings eventually turned into a serious pursuit of innovation, product development, and start-ups.

KMN's product debut of the DrawerDecor system in 2010 was a significant achievement in its efforts to succeed in the consumer product market. The product's innovative design and manufacturing quality helped establish KMN as a rising consumer brand. KMN Home is based in Traverse City, Michigan.

KOZIOL
Hanging Screens by René Barba and Werksdesign (p. 35, pictured)
koziol.de/en-usa

A brush is a brush is a brush, unless it's a brush made by German housewares manufacturer Koziol. In that case it's a very cheery and colorful brush, one that many of us can afford to have. In operation since 1927, the company is currently run by Stephan Koziol, who just so happens to be a sculptor with a proven business acumen sufficient to make an MBA jealous.

Design-driven, Koziol collaborates with some of the world's top designers (Matteo Thun and Alessandro Mendini, for starters) to create some of its iconic products. For others it draws on the talents of Werksdesign, its in-house design team.

To ensure that its designs achieve a consistent aesthetic and production quality, every single Koziol item is manufactured at just one plant in Germany, where it follows stringent German regulations concerning environmental safety and sustainability.

DR. LAKRA
Dr. Lakra's Mutant Laboratory for General Monsters (p. 111)
www.katemacgarry.com/artists/dr-lakra

Dr. Lakra is the pseudonym of Jerónimo López Ramírez, born in 1972 in Mexico. The Doctor is an artist and tattooist based in Oaxaca, Mexico. Much of his work involves the embellishment of found images and objects with macabre or tattoo-style designs.

He has participated in a number of gallery shows, among them Stolen Bike at the Andrew Kreps Gallery in New York, Los Dos Amigos at MACO in Mexico, Pin Up at Tate Modern, the Yokohama Museum of Art, and Pierced Hearts and True Love at The Drawing Center in New York. In 2007, he co-produced the book *Los Dos Amigos* with artist Abraham Cruzvillegas.

His works are held in the collections of MoMA, the Hammer Museum, and the Walker Art Center. Dr. Lakra is represented by kurimanzutto, Mexico City and Kate MacGarry, London.

DORON LACHISCH
Cubit and Cubitec Shelving for DLP Plastics (p. 86)
dlp-design.com

Born in Tel Aviv in 1948, Doron Lachisch was virtually steeped in plastics, having grown up in a family-run business that was just beginning to take advantage of mid-20th-century advances in flexible polymers. All aspects of plastics technologies—machinery, materials, molds—became familiar sights and smells to Lachisch, and served as the foundation for his subsequent career in the industry. And the world has taken notice, with press coverage in *Fast Company*, *Wired*, *Good Design*, and other media outlets,

After graduating from the Hebrew University of Jerusalem with a degree in economics, Lachisch became designer and general manager of his own plastics business in 1979. Launched in 1998, his Cubitec modular shelving system was awarded first prize for Contemporary Design at the Israel Furniture Trade Show and went on to become a fixture of design showrooms, galleries, store displays, offices, trade show displays, and homes around the world.

LEGO
playart.de/designer.html

The company that would eventually grow into a toy colossus started as a small shop in Billund, Denmark. Established in 1932 by master carpenter Ole Kirk Christiansen and assisted by his twelve-year-old son Godtfred Kirk Christiansen, the company initially made wood toys, stepladders, and ironing boards. Yet it was not until 1947 when the business bought a plastic injection-molding machine that it began to evolve into the global brand it is today. Within two years this machine was producing about 200 different kinds of plastic toys, including a fish, a sailor and a product called Automatic Binding Bricks.

The bricks were inspired by an earlier construction toy called Kiddicraft Self-Locking Bricks, which was patented in the U.K. in 1939 and first sold in 1947. LEGO recast the design (and soon the product name) to suit their production method, and by 1958 had perfected manufacturing to the point where bricks produced today will precisely fit bricks made in the original batch.

The company name is a contraction of the Danish phrase "play well" (*LEgt GOdt*). And "long," it could be added: any six standard-sized LEGO blocks can be put together in 102,981,500 combinations.

LEGO was deemed the "Toy of the Century" by both *Fortune* magazine and the British Association of Toy Retailers in 2000. Today the privately-owned company is the fourth largest toy manufacturer in the world, and its products are sold in 130 countries.

LERIVAL
Hex Table (p. 34) and PolyHex (p. 57) by Incorporated, Modular Screen by Moorhead & Moorhead (p. 43), Table Table (p. 67) and Ivy Modular Coatrack (p. 88) by MOS Architects
lerival.com

A design house bridging contemporary furniture and architecture, Lerival was founded by Dominique Gonfard and James Coombes in 2008. Their goal was to push the boundaries of design and promote untapped talent by inviting architects from around the world to create furniture pieces that used innovative or unconventional materials and were flexible or modular in design. Since then the company has worked with such firms as MOS Architects, Moorhead and Moorhead, Incorporated, Anthony Froger, and Della Valle Bernheimer.

BERND LIEBERT
PlayableArt Creative Toys (p. 130, pictured)
playart.de/designer.html

Bernd Liebert has been working as an independent toy designer and craftsman in Germany since 1978, and is an important figure in the PlayArt movement. Like his father, he started out as a painter, but then went on to study visual communication in Hamburg. It was during his studies there that he was given an assignment to produce a toy for children with disabilities, a project which sparked his interest in design for play. Since then he has developed many interactive toy products and is currently licensed for worldwide distribution with a U.S. company.

His work is sold in major museum and design shops around the world, including the Guggenheim Museum and MoMA in New York. He is especially popular in Asia, where his work is hung as art in offices and public spaces.

NEL LINSSEN
TableTalk Trivet for Goods (p. 67)
nellinssen.nl

Nel Linssen (b. 1935) was graduated from the Academy of Fine Arts in Arnhem, The Netherlands, in 1956 and has since become renowned as a designer of paper jewelry. Her work appears in the permanent collections of museums all over

Europe and in the U.S.; she has been exhibiting in galleries in solo and group shows across these same regions since 1995. Nel's designs for wearable art have received several awards and have been published in a monograph of her work.

MAGIS
Flare Table (p. 28), Boogie Woogie Shelving (p. 82), Ladrillos Shelving (p. 122), My Space Divider (p. 128), Little Flare Customizable Table (p. 123)
www.magisdesign.com

Magis SpA is a made-in-Italy design company founded by Eugenio Perazza in 1976 in Motta di Livenza, a town near Venice. The company offers a diverse collection of accessories and furnishings created by a global roster of designers, including Konstantin Grcic, Jasper Morrison, Björn Dahlström, Stefano Giovannoni, Marc Newson, Marcel Wanders, Javier Mariscal, and Karim Rashid. In 2004 it launched Me Too, a collection of furnishings designed exclusively for children. The initiative was launched after Eugenio found it nearly impossible to source a properly flexible desk for a grandchild who liked to draw.

Magis products are distributed in the U.S. by Herman Miller.

MAGNA-TILES
Magna-Tiles Construction Toys (p. 124)
magnatiles.com

Founded in 1997, Valtech LLC, the makers of Magna-Tiles, offers innovative tiles designed to hold a child's interest and attention, build critical developmental skills, and promote imaginative play and creativity. The company has received numerous awards for its creative product; a short list includes Parents' Choice Gold and Silver Honors Award Winner, Teachers' Choice Award, Astra Best Toys for Kids Winner, National Parenting Publications Award, Parents' Choice Recommended Award, and Parenting Magazine Toy of the Year. It's been featured in *The New York Times*, *The Wall Street Journal*, *The Chicago Tribune*, and many other media outlets.

MAKEDO
Connector Kits (p. 124)
mymakedo.com

Not long ago, Australian Paul Justin had been running a client-based industrial design practice and was feeling the urge to create something of his own. He and his wife had just had had their third child, a life change which motivated him to think about the toys that inspired him as a child to eventually become a creative professional, a builder and designer. With limited means at his disposal, and a time-honored laboratory in the form of his home's garage beckoning, Paul was clearly going to have to keep things to a manageable scale if he was to pull off his dream.

The concept he arrived at was dead-on in its simplicity and attainability: a reusable connector system that enables kids and grown-ups to freely create and construct things with found or reclaimed materials. Calling his product Makedo, Paul went on to build not only the product but a company to distribute it, first in Australia and now in the U.S. and countries worldwide. And the world has taken notice, with press coverage in *Fast Company*, *Wired*, *Good Design*, and other media outlets.

JAVIER MARISCAL
Flare Table (p. 28) and Ladrillos Shelving (p. 122) for Magis
mariscal.com/en/home

Sometimes dubbed the Peter Pan of Spanish design, Javier Mariscal defies easy professional categorization. Born in Valencia in 1950, he went to Barcelona in 1971 to study graphic design at Escuela Superior de Diseño e Ingeniería de Barcelona (ELISAVA) . There he came into contact with comic book writers and illustrators of the day, with whom he began to collaborate on the production of underground comics. In the 1980s, his portfolio expanded to embrace interior and product design projects, for which he quickly won national and international recognition. He continued his multidisciplinary pursuits over the years, sometimes working solo, other times collaboratively, and since 1989 as principal of the Barcelona-based Estudio Mariscal.

His credits are ever more far ranging, from the creation of the corporate image for the Barcelona Zoo, TV and Internet animations, textiles for Nani Marquina, furniture for the Memphis group, comic characters such as El Señor del Caballito and Twipsy, to published illustrations and stories, retrospective exhibitions, an Olympic mascot, the Acuarinto playground at a Nagasaki theme park, installations, theatrical productions, and he directed the animated film *Chico & Rita* (2010), nominated for an Oscar and winning several other film festival prizes.

PATRICK MARTINEZ
Jix Straw Connectors (p. 118)
www.blankbubble.com

Patrick Martinez is a visual artist born and raised in France. He studied at the Institut Supérieur des Beaux-Arts in Besançon, L'école Supérieure d'Art in Grenoble, and at the École Nationale Supérieure des Arts Décoratifs in Paris. In 1997, he received a grant to work in Tokyo, where he stayed for several years before relocating to New York.

Since then he has been working in a variety of media,

including video, drawing, sculpture, installation, and sound art. His award-winning product design Jix was successfully funded through Kickstarter and has been presented in several galleries, museums and trade shows, including NY NOW, where it received the Blogger's Choice Award, Wanted Design 2013 and the Children's Museum of the Arts in New York, Parker's Box Gallery in Brooklyn and Centre Clark in Montreal.

Patrick's artistic work has been exhibited in France, Germany, Spain, England, Switzerland, and Brazil, as well as in Japan and the U.S. He is represented in New York by Parker's Box Gallery.

MELISSA & DOUG
Architectural Standard Unit Building Blocks (p. 103), Suspend (p. 136)
melissaanddoug.com

Toy designer and manufacturer Melissa & Doug is a classic American success story. It even started in a garage, in Westport, Connecticut, in 1988. Not just any garage, mind you, but the one belonging to Doug's parents. Their first toy was brought to market in 1991 (it takes time to make good stuff). Fast forward years later, and the company has grown beyond all expectations. By the way, Melissa married Doug somewhere on the way, even though he proposed starting a business together with her before he proposed marrying her.

METAL ART
Playable Metal (p. 129)
www.metalart.com.tw

Playable Metal was created by Taken Fun and Art Co., a designer and manufacturer of metal toy products in Taiwan. Founded in 2009, it is a subsidiary of a large Taiwanese cutting tool manufacturer and a supplier of woodworking machinery. Its founder was inspired to create an interchangeable metal block construction toy for his son, with the goal of helping him develop his personal creativity. It now distributes its metal toy products all over the world.

METRE IDEAS AND DESIGN
Toobalink (p. 138)
metreideasanddesign.com

The initial idea for Toobalink came to its creator Will Sakran from fellow designer Sara Ebert. Sara had taken a class at Brooklyn's Pratt Institute focusing on classic play. Will had recently left his job as an engineer in the toy industry to start his own product design business, and was very excited by the prospect of a construction toy made in the U.S. and utilizing repurposed materials. He and Sara teamed up on the development, with Will handling final design and manufacturing under the aegis of the Brooklyn-based product design company Metre Ideas and Design. The product came to market in 2012 after fourteen months and numerous drawings, revisions, and mock-ups.

ZOE MILLER AND DAVID GOODMAN
Wood Toys (p. 126)
www.millergoodman.com

Zoe Miller and David Goodman are designers who live and work in Brighton, on the south coast of England. In addition to their wooden toys, the two have written, illustrated, and produced several children's books for the Tate Gallery in London. Titles include *A Is for Artist* (2004), *Colour* (2006), *Shape* (2008), and *Faces* (2011). In 2008 they launched the Miller Goodman brand, and now produce wood toys from their own designs. In their spare time Zoe and David run the consultancy firm Silence, which helps creatives explore their ideas through still and moving image references.

MINDWARE
Imaginets (p. 118), Q-BA-MAZE Marble Runs (p. 132)
mindware.com

MindWare is a creator, manufacturer, and distributor of educational products for people of all ages. Its wide-ranging line includes games, puzzles, brainteasers, arts and crafts activities, mysteries, mazes, and more. Over the years, MindWare games have won many prestigious awards, including Mensa Select, Parents' Choice, and the Spiel des Jahres in Germany.

Founder Jeanne Voigt started MindWare in 1990 with a small retail store in Minneapolis. Since then, the company has evolved into one of the largest catalogers in its segment, mailing to consumers and educators throughout the U.S. It has also become a Web retailer and distributor, selling its MindWare line to 2,000 retailers in the U.S. and to distributors in over twenty countries worldwide.

MIO
Nomad Modular Screens (p. 52), PaperForms Wall Paneling (p. 56, pictured, opposite), Trask Lamp (p. 69)
mioculture.com

Jaime Salm was born in Medellin, Colombia, in 1978. From an early age he showed an interest in the arts, especially sculpture. He studied at several art academies with independent artists and local architects, and eventually received a Bachelor of Science in Industrial Design in 2001 from The University of the Arts in Philadelphia.

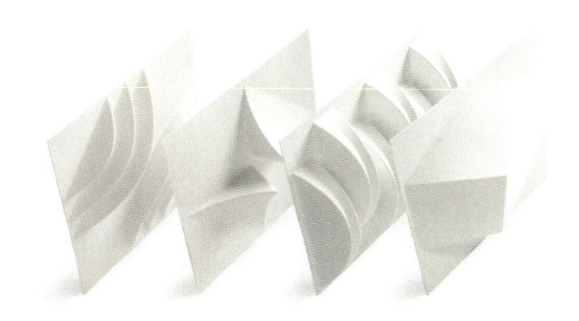

Following graduation, he cofounded MIO with his brother Isaac. His first collection was exhibited at the 2003 International Contemporary Furniture Fair. Since then, products from the MIO catalog have been showcased by Material ConneXion, Felissimo Design House, The Ontario Science Center, The National Building Museum in Washington, and The Museum of Scotland in Edinburgh, among others.

Jaime's work has been widely published in periodicals and newspapers including *Metropolis*, *I.D. Magazine*, *Metropolitan Home*, *Interior Design*, *The New York Times*, *Newsweek*, *Contract Magazine*, and *Azure*.

Jaime was presented with the People's Choice Award in 2002 for the Need International Design Competition sponsored by Core 77. In 2005, his designs were recognized with the Best Collection Award at the New York International Gift Fair. His work is part of the Cooper-Hewitt National Design Museum's permanent collection.

MISSION WORKSHOP
Arkiv Modular Knapsack (p. 13)
missionworkshop.com

A couple of guys started Chrome, a messenger bag company in San Francisco. Then they sold it, hung out for a while, and went on to launch a new bag and apparel company called Mission Workshop, in 2009. Now they make lots of bags and apparel products, all in the U.S.

MODERN-TWIST
Kidz Paintable Placemats (p. 121)
modern-twist.com

Modern-Twist is a San Francisco Bay Area–based company that has pioneered the use of pure food-grade, hand-silk-screened silicone. In 2005, it became the first business to produce hand-silk-screened products for the home using this material, which is durable, organic, and flexible.

Kat Nouri conceived of the idea for the company from her conviction that what we eat on should be as wholesome as what we eat. Kat's vision was driven by her respect for organic farming and nutrition, her experience as a U.S. manufacturer with a background in marketing and sales, and her personal sense for design.

LISA MONAHAN
Switch Gear Interchangeable Jewelry (p. 79)
lisamonahan.com

Lisa Monahan is an architect as well as metalsmith designing jewelry and sculptural metal works. She studied art and architecture in Boston, Arizona, and London, and practiced architecture in Boston until 2003. She received training in metalsmithing at Metalwerx, the DeCordova Museum School in Massachusetts, and in various workshops.

Lisa's work has been published in the *Boston Globe*, *Los Angeles Times*, *Lucky*, and the Huffington Post, among others, and exhibited at various galleries and shops. She lives with her family in Newton, Massachusetts.

JOHANNES MOLIN
Infinite Tree for Areaware (p. 39)
areaware.com/collections/johannes-molin

Johannes Molin is a Swedish-born designer and mathematician. He became enamored with the beauty of wood having spent his youth in the forested countryside of his native country. After being graduated from the University of Gothenburg with a degree in mathematics and science, Johannes went on to a career in teaching, furniture making, and interior design.

Johannes finds inspiration in classic Scandinavian design and the grace and proportions of mathematical expressions. He believes that beauty can be imagined through the purity of algorithms in combination with the idiosyncrasies of wood. The designer applied his philosophy to the construction of his own house, where he built a beautifully twisted staircase out of a ash tree he used to climb as a child.

MOORHEAD & MOORHEAD
Modular Screen for Lerival (p. 46)
moorheadandmoorhead.com

Moorhead & Moorhead is the New York–based studio of brothers Granger and Robert Moorhead. Trained as an architect and industrial designer, respectively, the two collaborate on projects ranging in scale from furniture to buildings.

Their diverse body of work is united by a common theme: the inventive use of everyday materials to solve issues of function and form in simple, unexpected ways. Their successful interpretation of this theme has been recognized by the Cooper-Hewitt National Design Museum in New York (2007), The Architectural League of New York (2008), New York Foundation for the Arts (2010), MoMA (2013), and the

New York City Department of Design + Construction (2013).

Clients include The Architectural League of New York, Center for Architecture, Cosentino SA, Cooper-Hewitt National Design Museum, Dacra Development, Design Miami, Lerival, MatterMade, Metropolis, Public Art Fund of the Times Square Alliance, Standard Socket, Van Alen Institute, and Warby Parker Eyewear, as well as numerous private commissions.

Moorhead & Moorhead is represented in the permanent collection of MoMA.

MOS ARCHITECTS
Table Table (p. 67) and Ivy Modular Coatrack (p. 88) for Lerival
mos-office.net

Michael Meredith and Hilary Sample founded MOS, an interdisciplinary architecture and design practice based in New Haven, Connecticut. Projects designed in their office have been showcased in numerous publications, including *Architectural Record*, *Architect*, *A+U*, *Wallpaper**, *Surface*, *Space Korea*, *Mark*, *AV Proyectos*, and *The New York Times*, and exhibited at the Venice Biennale, SMOCA (Scottsdale, AZ), MoMA, and the Arts Institute in Chicago.

Their portfolio includes a villa in Ordos, Inner Mongolia, a public art installation at PS1/MoMA in Long Island City, an inflatable factory in Newfoundland, and a teen center in Lowell, Massachusetts.

Michael is an Associate Professor at the Harvard Graduate School of Design, and Hilary is an Assistant Professor at Yale's School of Architecture. Both received their Bachelor of Architecture from Syracuse.

MUUTO
OTO 100 Storage System (p. 92), Stacked Shelving System (p. 93)), The Dots Coat Hooks (p. 26)
muuto.com

The name of the Danish design company Muuto derives from the Finnish word *muutos,* meaning "new perspective." And for good reason: the company was founded in 2006 to restore the great tradition of Scandinavian product design while simultaneously taking it in fresh directions. Its roster of designers reads like a directory of the region's finest talents: Harri Koskinen, Ole Jensen, Matti Klenell, Thomas Bernstrand, Claesson Koivisto Rune, Ilkka Suppane, Julien De Smedtj, and Tveit & Tørnøe to name just a few.

The company is based in Copenhagen, Denmark.

NAEF
Cella (p. 17), Cubicus (p. 23), and Diamant (p. 24) by Peer Clahsen, Ikamo (p. 38) and Imago (p. 38) by Heiko Hillig, Modulon (p. 48) and Tectus (p. 68) by Jo Niemeyer, Mosaik (p. 50) by Kathrin Kiener, Bauhaus Optical Top (p. 106) by Ludwig Hirschfeld-Mack, Colorem Chalk Cubes (p. 109) by Mirjam Hüttner, Spiel Building Blocks (p. 115) by Kurt Naef
naefspiele.ch

Kurt Naef (1926–2006) was a woodworker and the founder of Naef Spiele AG. Born in Switzerland, he grew up in Eptingen and apprenticed as a carpenter in Olten. In the 1950s he studied interior architecture in Basle and Amsterdam before starting a woodworking and interior design business in the Swiss city.

Customer requests for high quality toys prompted him to begin designing and making them himself. His first products were the Kauring teething ring and the building toy Naef Spiel. By 1967 demand had grown enough to warrant opening a factory in Zeiningen for producing handcrafted wood toys created by Kurt and other well-known designers.

In 1988 Kurt sold the company and went into retirement in France. By 2003, however, Naef was on the verge of bankruptcy, leading Kurt and his stepson Hans-Peter Engeler to buy the company back and eventually restore it to health. Today the company operates out of Kurt's hometown of Zofingen, Switzerland with production facilities in Southern Germany.

NENDO
Yuki Screen for Cappellini (p. 74)
nendo.jp

Founder of Japanese design studio Nendo, Oki Sato (b. 1977 in Toronto) was graduated with a Masters in Architecture from Waseda University in Tokyo. He formed the firm in 2002 after an inspiring graduation trip to the Milan Design Furniture Fair, and since then has turned it into one of the most prolific design firms in the world.

In Japanese *nendo* means free-form clay, a soft, fluid substance similar to children's Play-Doh. The reference suits a studio that wants to evolve and flex to produce design solutions for the wide range of clients that knock on its doors, including Established & Sons, PUMA, Starbucks, Cappellini, Moroso, DePadova, Maruni, and Foscarini.

Nendo has been the subject of high praise. *Newsweek* named Oki one of the world's 100 Most Respected Japanese People in 2006 and honored the firm in 2008 as one of the Top 200 Small Japanese Companies. In a double score, Oki has earned the title of Designer of the Year by both *Wallpaper** and *Elle Decor* magazines in the same year. Nendo is represented in many museum collections and has exhibited in venues around the world.

JO NIEMEYER
Modulon (p. 48) and Tectus (p. 68) for Naef
partanen.de

Jo Niemeyer (b. 1946 in Germany) is a painter, photographer, sculptor, and designer. His work is based on the observation of the nature through the prism of mathematics, with an emphasis on the Golden Section.

From 1962 to 1965 he studied graphic arts and photography before going to the Helsinki Institute to pursue industrial design in 1967. He began working as an independent artist in 1970 and had his first show in 1974. In 1989 he made the first drafts of his most well-known piece, *20 Steps*, a global land-art installation eventually realized in 1997.

Jo's work has been featured in solo and group shows in museums and galleries in Scandinavia, Italy, Switzerland, Israel, England, Japan, Argentina, Finland, and the U.S. He currently works and lives in Germany, France. and Finland.

CHRISTIAN NORTHEAST
XYZ Alphabet Blocks for Fred and Friends (p. 144)
www.christiannortheast.com

The illustrator and graphic designer Christian Northeast has worked with *The New Yorker*, *Nickelodeon*, *GQ*, *Time*, *McSweeney's*, and *The New York Times*, to name just a few. He has created a book for *Drawn and Quarterly*, illustrated blocks for Fred and Friends, and produced animation art for Nick Jr. His work has appeared on posters, book covers, billboards, and liquor bottles.

Christian's work has been recognized by *American Illustration*, *Communication Arts*, SPD, *Graphis*, and AIGA to name just a few more.

When not doing great work, he can be found hanging around with his wife, two daughters, and a dog in Ontario, Canada.

NUOP DESIGN
Strawz Connectible Drinking Straws (p. 135)
nuopinc.com

NuOp Design was started in 2005 by Frank Frisari and John McCoy. Based in New York, the company's mission is to serve up levity for the masses in the form of doodads and doohickeys for home and office.

ROGER VON OECH
Ball of Whacks for Creative Whack Company (p. 105)
creativethink.com

Roger von Oech is an author, inventor, and educational speaker whose seminars and products have reached millions of people around the world. He is the author of several books on creativity, namely: *A Whack on the Side of the Head*, *A Kick in the Seat of the Pants*, and *Expect the Unexpected*.

Roger earned his Ph.D. from Stanford University, is the married father of two grown children, and lives in Woodside, California.

OSKO+DEICHMANN
Abyss Reconfigurable Table Lamp for Kundalini (p. 8)
oskodeichmann.com

In the 1990s Blasius Osko and Oliver Deichmann found themselves in the formerly divided city of Berlin, together with many other creatives who had been moving there en masse. After finishing their studies at the Berlin University of the Arts, they cofounded a design studio and called it Die Wunschforscher, meaning "researchers of desire." In this period they created pieces at the intersection of design, invention, and art, as well as concepts for fashion and music events. In 2005, they renamed their studio Osko+Deichmann and decided to focus on developing products.

The firm's work has been exhibited at major institutions and museums, including the Louvre, Vitra Design Museum, Cube Gallery in Manchester, MoMA Berlin, Guggenheim Museum Berlin, VIA Gallery Paris, Holon Museum, and at the Design Biennial in Saint-Étienne, France.

PELEG DESIGN
Magnetic Vases for Decor Craft (p. 43)
peleg-design.com

Tel Aviv-based Peleg Design was founded in 2004 by Shahar Peleg, who holds a Bachelor in Design and Interior Architecture from Israel's Holon Institute of Technology. Shahar designs, develops, and produces accessory products sold in design stores in Israel and other countries worldwide. His work revels in optical illusions that humorously stretch limits and break conventions, prompting the user to take a closer, fresh look at everyday products.

BRANDON PERHACS
Adaptation Vase (p. 8), Stix+Stones Necklace (p. 78, pictured next page)
perhacs-studio.com

Brandon Perhacs was born in 1979 in Port Townsend, Washington, and ran a metal fabrication and machine shop in Seattle for several years before going to study environmental design at Art Center College of Design in Pasadena in 2001. Upon returning to the Pacific Northwest, he designed and built the concrete, steel, and glass home, studio, and gallery in Seattle where Perhacs Studio is now based.

Perhacs has worked in industrial design, lighting,

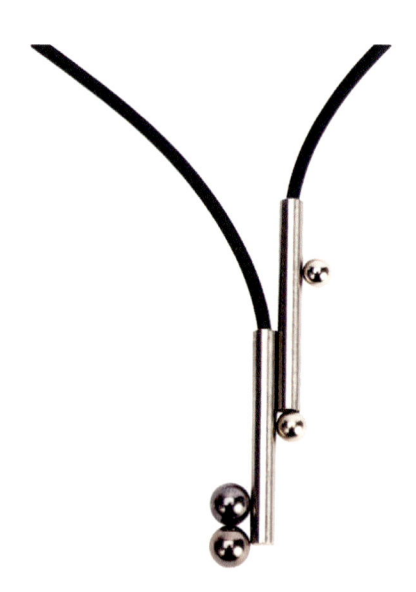

sculpture, jewelry, packaging design, furniture, architecture, interior design, and disciplines in between. His designs are found in stores and museums around the world.

JOHN PERRY
Equilique Acrobats (p. 28)

johnperrystudio.com

Born in Bath, England, at the outbreak of World War II, as a baby John Perry narrowly escaped death when his home was destroyed by a German bomb. Growing up in Plymouth, Norwich, and London, he attended Nottingham University (whose only famous scion of note was D. H. Lawrence), where he obtained a degree in geology. Changing direction immediately, he moved to studying business administration at the London Polytechnic, and then briefly went into management. Changing direction again, he rode the British wave to California in 1967 and within a year found himself making a living, albeit modest, as a sculptor. He had developed his artistic skills while bedridden as a child, but had no formal training. He's been sculpting ever since, with many successful ventures along the way.

ERIC PFEIFFER
Rhombins Desktop Storage and Play for AMAC (p. 61), STACT Wine Wall (p. 63), Woody Chalkboard Table and Chair for Offi (p. 144)

pfeifferlab.com

Eric Pfeiffer is the founder of Pfeiffer Lab, whose products have attained worldwide distribution and currently sell in more than 350 stores in the U.S., Europe, and Japan, including Design Within Reach, MoMA Design Store, Room & Board, HHstyle, The Conran Shop, and Illums Bolighus. Gap Inc., Levi's, Burton Snowboards, The North Face, Paul Frank Industries, and Williams-Sonoma are among his corporate clients.

Prior to setting up the Lab, Pfeiffer had developed product concepts for Design Within Reach, Target, Crate and Barrel, MoMA, Room & Board, OXO, and CB2. In 2000 he merged his firm with the company Offi, where he served as VP of Design overseeing all product design and development for several years.

Pfeiffer is the author of numerous articles and publications, and cowrote *Bent Ply: The Art of Plywood Furniture*, the definitive book on the history and manufacturing of bent ply furniture.

LIZA PHILLIPS DESIGN
Alto Modular Stair Carpets (p. 11)

www.lizaphillipsdesign.com

Liza Phillips's lifelong involvement with art and design can be traced to a childhood spent in an environment filled with modern art and design. Her grandfather was Duncan Phillips, the art collector and founder of The Phillips Collection, and her grandmother was painter Marjorie Phillips. After earning her undergraduate degree in art history and philosophy at Vassar College, Liza worked at The Phillips in Washington, D.C. and later in set design, architectural illustration, magazine production, and graphic design in New York City. She received a Master of Fine Arts in painting from Chelsea College of Art and Design in London and continues to exhibit her artwork.

Liza launched her rug company in 2004, three years after she designed her first rug for her own house.

PICO PAO
The Chairs Game (p. 18) and The Ladders Game (p. 41) for MoMA

picopao.com/en

Pico Pao is a workshop that began in a house in a small Spanish village on the border of Portugal in the late 1970s. It takes its name from the much loved local woodpecker known as Pico Pao, which translates as "stick-beak."

Its original association with the manufacturing of toys and games resulted from the impoverished life led by the home's early inhabitants. The six children who grew up in the house could not afford to buy the playthings most children get, so they made their own games from things they could find. As time went on the makeshift workshop grew and with it the demand for its handcrafted games.

Today Pico Pao is bringing in younger members of the next generation and focusing its activity on developing two game collections. The first, Juegos de la Antigüedad, is based on old-fashioned toys and games the workshop has resurrected from oblivion; the second, Ludus Ludi, looks to newer games and is notable in the products' lack of defined rules and their encouragement of creative experimentation through direct contact with artistic objects.

PLUS-PLUS
Plus-Plus Building Toy (p. 132)
plus-plus.dk/UK

From the land of LEGO comes the newest permutation on the plastic building block concept: Plus-Plus. In just a short time it has already won awards from the Canadian Toy Testing Council, EDExpo trade show in Atlanta, and Kid's Biz Fair in Warsaw.

The company manufacturers its interlocking bricks near Copenhagen, Denmark. It now enjoys international distribution.

LAURA POLINORO
Presepe Nativity Set for Alessi (p. 58)
laurapolinoro.tumblr.com

Laura Polinoro was graduated with a degree in Art and Communication from DAMS in Bologna. Laura has been the head of the Alessi Study Centre since 1990, acting as a designer and art director for products, advertising, and publication. In her role at Alessi she's worked with designers Guido Venturini, Stefano Giovannoni, Massimo Giacon, and Marc Newson, among others. In 2004 she set up a business that organizes business briefing workshops for designers from around the world.

GIULIO POLVARA
Modular Bookshelf System and Bins for Kartell (p. 91)
kartell.com

Giulio Polvara is an Italian designer noted principally for his design of a modular bookshelf and bin system for Kartell in 1974. He hasn't been heard much from since.

LUIS PONS
UNO Magnetic Jewelry (p. 80)
luispons.com

Luis Pons is an award-winning designer whose work has been featured in leading publications including *Vogue*, *Elle Décor*, and *Architectural Digest*. His furniture and lighting collections were shown at the International Furniture Fair in Milan in 2005, his Floating Inflatable Villa was shown at Art Basel also in 2005, and most recently his Pre-Fab Chapel was shown in Art Basel 2011. Luis Pons Design Lab's projects include private residences, hotels, and commercial properties.

UNO Magnetic was founded by Pons in 2011. It produces original wearable and interactive magnetic objects in the form of jewelry (necklaces, bracelets, rings, and earrings) and accessories (belts, buckles, and charms) for both men and women.

The company, which strives to engage in the creation of socially and environmentally responsible products, currently distributes its products in Europe, Asia, and the U.S. UNO Magnetic is a member of the Fair Labor Association and works to ensure all levels of manufacturing are free from abusive labor practices and pays all workers living wages. To further its social goals, UNO Magnetic has partnered with important nonprofit organizations, including Breast Health International in Italy and MTV's Ashoka Partnership in the U.S.

QISDESIGN
Crystal LED Light (p. 21)
qisdesignusa.com

Launching in 2009, QisDesign is part of the BenQ Group, a multibillion dollar conglomerate comprising over a dozen Taiwan-based independent companies active in diverse industries. The Group controls a value chain sufficient to deliver critical expertise and production in all significant areas of design: industrial design, graphic design, market research, user interface, mechanical design, computer-aided design, and prototype production.

The Group's design capabilities have won it numerous accolades, including Germany's iF Product Design Award, Red Dot Design Award, and Japan's G-Mark Award.

QUIRKY
Loopits Stretch and Store (p. 90)
quirky.com

Ben Kaufman was still a teenager in high school when he invented Mophie, a mobile charging device. Convincing his parents to mortgage their Long Island home, he was able to manufacture and market the product with sufficient success to sell the business several years later. In 2009 he turned his experience as an inventor and entrepreneur into Quirky, a platform for community-based product development and distribution. Based in New York City, the company has developed almost 400 products to date and has a growing user base of nearly a million people. It has recently entered into a joint venture with GE to develop smart home accessories, an initiative which earned it a place on Fast Company's 2014 list of the World's Top 10 Most Innovative Companies in the Internet of Things.

RED HEN BOOKS AND TOYS
Froebel Gifts (p. 114)

redhentoys.com

Red Hen Books & Toys provides specialized, hard-to-find educational materials, toys, and books to parents and educators worldwide. The online store was established in 2006 by Scott Bultman, a former co-owner of Uncle Goose Toys, his family's toy manufacturing business, and a father of three children raised in Montessori and nature education programs. With over thirty years in the toy business as a manufacturer, retailer, and award-winning toy designer, Scott is knowledgeable in the field of playthings and has the industry experience to locate unique, quality items. He is a toy collector and active in early childhood and K-12 design education initiatives through his work with Froebel USA.

REMEMBER
Paolo Creative Toy (p. 129)

remember.de

Founded in 1996, Remember is a design and product development company based in Krefeld, Germany. Its colorful designs can be found in fine museum shops and retailer outlets all over the world. It is the recipient of numerous awards, including Red Dot Design Award, the Chicago Museum's Good Design Award, an iF Product Design Award, and several International Calendar Show awards.

ROOM COPENHAGEN
Pantone Food Trays (p. 55), LEGO Storage Bricks and Heads (p. 123)

roomcopenhagen.com

ROOM Copenhagen was founded in 2010 in Copenhagen, Denmark, with the goal of creating aesthetically driven, functional design that makes the world more beautiful and pleasurable. The company realizes its goal by interpreting and developing the designs of internationally renowned brands into modern design classics for the home. It currently collaborates with LEGO, Pantone Universe, Ole Jensen, and Paul Frank.

ROOM Copenhagen is a spin-off from the Danish-owned Plast Team Group, a company renowned for designing and producing high quality, functional houseware products since 1986.

ROOST
Numero Clock (p. 54)

roostco.com

Roost is a California-based wholesale line of modern home furnishings and accessories that emphasizes accessible and livable design. Their line includes furniture as well as lighting, unique mouth-blown glass vessels, metal vases and candleholders, home textiles, baskets, stone, wood, wax, and botanicals. The majority of its products are designed by a small group of in-house design associates, and the finished pieces are typically handmade, small craft productions. Roost products are exclusively manufactured in workshops and factories where the company has had long-standing relationships.

ROYAL FAMILY DESIGN LABOR
Nolastar Modular Screen (p. 51)

www.royalfamily-designlabor.de

Royal Family Royal Family Design labor was founded 1993 by Ana Motjér and Oliver Schneider. Based in Köln, Germany, the firm works in the fields of furniture, product, set and communication design.

PATRICK RYLANDS
PlayPlax (p. 131)

tinyurl.com/patrick-rylands-interview

Patrick Rylands was still a student studying ceramics at the Royal College of Art in London in 1966 when he invented a construction toy called PlayPlax, which would go on to sell over a million units. Just four years later he was awarded the prestigious Duke of Edinburgh's Prize for Elegant Design (now known as The Prince Philip Designers Prize) and thus began a lengthy career in toy design. For several years after graduation he worked as a freelance designer with such important toy companies as Creative Playthings and Naef. In 1976 he became the in-house designer for Ambi Toys, a historic Dutch company of games for young children, and remained with the company until 2002. During that period he was awarded the title of Royal Designer for Industry.

Several of Rylands's creations are entered in the permanent collection of London's Victoria and Albert Museum of Childhood.

RICARDO SAINT-CLAIR
Chalkboard Vase for MoMA (p. 20)

dialogodesign.net

Brazilian designer Ricardo Saint-Clair earned a Masters of Arts in Communication Design in 2003 at Central Saint Martins College of Art and Design in London. He also spent a year at The Art Institute of Chicago, where he took courses in design and typography, and saw Michael Jordan play. In 2007 he opened the design studio Dialogo and made the leap into product design after several years of working in art direction and graphic design. Rio de Janeiro–based

Saint-Clair currently divides his time between teaching, designing for corporate clients, developing personal projects, diving, and surfing.

FRANCO SARGIANI
Programma 8 Tableware for Alessi (p. 58)
www.francosargiani.it

Architect Franco Sargiani was born in Modena in 1940 and was graduated from the Faculty of Architecture at Milan Polytechnic. His work is multidisciplinary, embracing civil, commercial and interior architecture, industrial design, and corporate identity. Alessi, Fantini, Filasp, Fidenza Vetraria, Inda, Emicar, and Sipea count among his many clients. His award-winning designs have been widely published and presented in numerous museums, including the Beaubourg in Paris, the Metropolitan Museum and MoMA in New York, the Tel Aviv Art Museum, Rio de Janeiro's Museum of Modern Art, Helsinki's Museum of Applied Art, and several others. Sargiani's work is in the permanent collections of the Milan Triennial, the Museo de Arte de São Paolo in Brazil, the Kunstgewerbemuseum in Berlin, and the Kunstmuseum in Düsseldorf.

SELAB
Assemblage Modular Storage (p. 14), Morpheo Crystal Candlestick (p. 000), My Bricks (p. 49), My House of Cards (p. 51), Opaline Glass Modular Vase (p. 54)
seletti.it

The Seletti brand was founded in Mantova, Italy, in 1964 by Romano Seletti. Today Seletti continues to operate as a family business, now run by Stefano and Miria Seletti. Selab (Se(letti) + lab), which Stefano established as Seletti's in-house creative lab in 1988, has been creating innovative and whimsical products for the parent company ever since. It frequently collaborates with designers Alessandro Zambelli, Vittorio Boni, and the Badini CreaTeam Studio, as well as other creatives to produce the innovative and whimsical products Seletti is known for.

Seletti products flaunt a refined and fun quality that brings any setting to life. A unique use of color combinations, sly artistic references, and minute attention to detail remain Seletti hallmarks.

HÉCTOR SERRANO
Desktructure Desktop Organizer for Seletti (p. 23)
hectorserrano.com

Héctor Serrano (b. 1974) studied industrial design in Valencia, Spain, before moving to London for his Masters in Product Design at The Royal College of Art. He founded his design studio in London in 2000. The firm has produced work for such clients as FontanaArte, Gandia Blasco, Roca, Seletti, Lexon, Muji, Moooi, ICEX (Spanish Ministry of Industry, Tourism, and Trade), Droog, Metalarte, La Casa Encendida, and the Valencia City Council.

Among its awards are the Peugeot Design Award, the Premio Nacional de Diseño No Aburridos, and the Designer of the Year for 2009 by *AD* magazine.

Its designs have been exhibited at the Victoria & Albert in London and the Cooper-Hewitt National Design Museum in New York, and have been widely published.

SMALLWORKS
BrickCase for iPhone 5 (p. 16)
smallworks.com

SmallWorks is the brainchild of a twelve-year-old LEGO fan who thought it would be fantastic to add bricks to his hand-me-down iPhone. Always ready to support clever children with great ideas, the brains behind the company worked out how to make an iPhone case with LEGO-compatible studs. Apparently this is harder than it looks.

The company is located in Austin, Texas, where it manufactures its iPhone cases and packaging.

JULIEN DE SMEDT
Stacked Shelving System for Muuto (p. 93)
jdsa.eu, mwa.eu

Julien De Smedt (b. 1975 in Brussels) is the founder and director of JDS Architects, which has offices in Brussels, Copenhagen, Belo Horizonte (Brazil), and Shanghai. He received a diploma with commendation from the Bartlett School of Architecture in London in 2000.

Prior to founding JDS Architects, Julien worked with OMA/Rem Koolhaas and cofounded with Bjarke Ingels the architecture firm PLOT in Copenhagen. Among other awards and recognitions, Julien has received the Henning Larsen Prize, an Eckersberg medal, several Architizer A+ Awards, and the Maaskant Prize for Architecture. He has lectured and exhibited around the world. JDS Architects has published two monographs, *PIXL to XL* and *Agenda*.

In addition to his work for the homewares company Muuto, Julien designs products for Makers With Agendas, a Copenhagen-based company which he cofounded with William Ravn and Wouter Dons.

ROXI SUGER
Thewrap for Angelrox (p. 79)
angelrox.com

Roxi Suger designs, markets, manufactures, and distributes her contemporary women's apparel line Angelrox. Her designs have been featured in *InStyle*, *Lucky*, *The New York Times*, *Delta Sky*, *New York Magazine*, *WWD*, *Sportswear International*, *Cosmopolitan*, and *Russian Eva*. Her designs have been worn by Bette Midler, Bebe Neuwirth, Suchin Pak of MTV, and Cara Buono, lately of *The Sopranos*, and have been featured on *Sex in the City*, MTV's *Made*, The Learning Channel, and on BBC Productions.

Prior to launching her own brand, Roxi designed for Vivienne Tam, Urban Outfitters, and Le Chateau Stores of Canada. She has taught fashion at Parsons The New School for Design.

SY-LAB
Free Universal Construction Kit for Adapterz LLC (p. 113)
sy-lab.net

Synaptic Lab (Sy-Lab) is home to the work of Shawn Sims and collaborators. Shawn is an artist and designer who works across various disciplines, including interactive and industrial design, architecture, robotics, and fabrication. He received a Bachelor of Architecture from Brooklyn's Pratt Institute and a Master of Tangible Interaction Design from Carnegie Mellon University's Computational Design Lab. In 2012 he received a Prix Ars Electronica Award for the Free Universal Construction Kit. His work has been exhibited internationally and featured in numerous print and web publications.

Shawn is currently Director of NOTlabs at NOTCOT (www.notcot.com), where he leads cross-platform, multidisciplinary projects.

TAMAWA
Tamawa Interchangeable Earrings and Watches (p. 40, pictured)
tamawa.be

Hubert Verstraeten received his training in Pforzheim, Germany, and opened a workshop in Brussels in 1999. He fuses traditional jewelry craftsmanship with serial production methods (3D, electro-erosion, injection molding), and contemporary plastics such as Aramith and polycarbonate.

Established in 2008, Tamawa grew out of a meeting between Hubert and Belgian snooker ball manufacturer Saluc SA. Taken by the beauty, flexibility, and durability of the Bakelite material used to manufacture the balls, Hubert entered into an agreement with the company to supply him with the materials for a new line of jewelry he would design. Tamawa, meaning "ball on steel ring" in Japanese, was launched with two interchangeable watches, and has since grown to include several jewelry pieces and home accessories.

TEGU
Magnetic Blocks (p. 136)
tegu.com

Chris Haughey was graduated from Stanford in 2002 with a degree in mechanical engineering and had been traveling extensively through Latin America in his job as a management consultant. Returning from a trip to Honduras in 2006 during which he reconnected with some missionary friends met on previous trips, he asked himself a question: "Could a for-profit company based in Honduras be created that would foster a positive social impact through its business?"

He was later joined by his brother Will, a graduate of Indiana University's Kelley School of Business in 2004 and a Goldman Sachs alum. The two have answered that question by creating a thriving toy business called Tegu, after the Honduran city of Tegucigalpa, where they opened a factory to product magnetic wood blocks using sustainably harvested local woods. True to its founding principles, the company pays its workers a living wage and remains committed to their long-term career growth, as well as to the future of their community.

Tegu products are designed by Nate Lau.

TEMPAPER
DIY Art Wallpaper (p. 25)
tempaperdesigns.com

A group of set decorators in New York found themselves increasingly stymied by not having a source for an appealing temporary and repositionable wallpaper to use in their work. Tempaper was launched in 2008 as their solution to this market gap, and as a fun alternative for consumers looking to decorate their homes and workplaces easily and attractively.

DESIGNERS AND BRANDS

THE UTILITY COLLECTIVE
Mix Boxes (p. 91)
theutilitycollective.com

The Utility Collective is a joint venture of designer Eric Pfeiffer from Pfeiffer Lab (see page 00) and Steve Piccus. The stated goal of The Utility Collective is to create everyday objects that address the needs of both the home and office through solutions that are minimal in form but optimal in function, beauty, and utility. It views the everyday objects we use as things that help define our daily routine and enable us to interact with the world. Designed and responsibly manufactured in the U.S., Collective products are intended to last a lifetime.

CARLO TREVISANI
Appo Cork Tray for Seletti (p. 12)
carlotrevisani.com

Carlo Trevisani was born in 1975 in Verona, Italy. After being graduated from Istituto Superiore per le Industrie Artistiche (ISIA) in Faenza in 2000, he collaborated with the designers Paolo Zani, Stefano Gallizioli, and Matteo Thun in their Milan design studios. Continuing to live and work in Milan since 2008, he currently works as an independent designer in the production of furniture, lighting, tableware, kitchenware, and other home goods.

TVEIT & TORNØE
The Dots Coat Hooks for Muuto (p. 26)
larstornoe.com, cargocollective.com

Tveit & Tornøe was a design studio established in 2006 and based in Bergen, Norway. The firm was a collaboration of Atle Tveit and Lars Tornøe, both with Masters in Furniture and Spatial Design from the Bergen National Academy of the Arts. The partners focused primarily on furniture and product design in their practice, while also developing concepts for interiors, exhibitions, and other environmental projects.

The firm operated for four years, which resulted in many products for Scandinavian furniture manufacturers, as well as awards, among them the Award for Design Excellence and the Young Talent Award from The Norwegian Design Council.

The partners now operate independent design studios in Norway.

UNCLE GOOSE
Classic ABC Blocks and Antics Ant Blocks (p. 141)
unclegoose.com

Uncle Goose was founded in 1983 and is based in Grand Rapids, Michigan. It's grown to become a premier manufacturer of wooden blocks in the alphabet, special needs, foreign language, and specialty categories. Most remarkably, its products are all handcrafted in America. Why anyone would so completely row against the global economic tides is beyond us, but we're very glad they are. The only explanation we can offer to unravel this mystery is that they are artists, who often don't know any better.

KRISTIAN VEDEL
BIRDs (p. 15) and Child's Chair (p. 108, pictured)
kristianvedel.dk/cvbio_uk.shtml

Kristian Vedel (1923–2003) was a Danish industrial designer and an important figure in the Scandinavian Design movement. In 1946, he was graduated from the Furniture Design Department of the School of Arts, Crafts, and Design, where he lectured from 1953 to 1956. Kristian was instrumental in establishing the Industrial Designers of Denmark and served as its first chairman from 1966 to 1968.

Influenced by Kaare Klint and the Bauhaus, his classically modern designs are characterized by a creative use of materials, especially plastics and wood, and a deep respect for ergonomic and functional requirements. His children's furniture, which was designed to adapt to a growing child's needs rather than simply miniaturize adult furniture, epitomizes the strong underpinnings of his designs in physiological practicalities.

Among many other awards, Kristian received the silver medal at La Triennale di Milano for children's furniture (1957), a gold medal at La Triennale di Milano for his line of stackable melamine dishes and containers, and the Lunning Prize (1962).

The Trapholt Museum in Denmark mounted a retrospective exhibition of his major works in 2007, which was accompanied by the publication of a monograph by Arkitektens Forlag.

175

VITRA

Algue (p. 9) and Corniches (p. 20) by Ronan and Erwan Bouroullec

vitra.com

Vitra was founded by Willi and Erika Fehlbaum in 1957. Initially it focused on selling furniture licensed from the Herman Miller Collection in the European market, the majority of the early designs being those of Charles and Ray Eames, and George Nelson. By 1967 the company was launching its own designs, most notably the Panton Chair by Verner Panton, which was the first cantilevered chair made from plastic. Since then the company has expanded into office, public, and home markets, combining classic pieces from the early Herman Miller collection, Alexander Girard, and Jean Prouvé, with newly commissioned works from Antonio Citterio, Jasper Morrison, Alberto Meda, Maarten van Severen, Ronan and Erwan Bouroullec, Hella Jongerius, and BarberOsgerby.

Vitra operates a renowned privately owned museum for design in Weil am Rhein, Germany, regarded both for its collection of modern design and the roster of top-tier architects who have designed buildings for its campus.

WALLCANDY ARTS

Wallpapers and Stickers (p. 138)

wallcandyarts.com

Allison Krongard's first WallCandy client was a three-year-old named Max. Her career at Knoll International had given her a keen eye for design, so friends (including Max's mom) often sought her decor advice. It turned out that Max was one tough customer. Just as soon as Allison had pulled together the inspiration, swatches, and paint chips to suit his dinosaur obsession, he politely informed her that he had moved on to spaceships. This gave Allison a big idea: if kids' imaginations grow as fast as their bodies, why not create a decor element that's easy to change and easy to apply? With this insight, WallCandy Arts was born in 2002.

WALL COASTER

Extreme Stunt Kit (p. 112)

wallcoaster.com

The idea for Wall Coaster started with a twelve-year-old boy playing with marbles in his basement. The problem he wanted to solve was straightforward: how to make a marble roll down the wall? After weeks of experimenting with different materials and concepts, Wall Coaster was born. Another year of product development, and it was on the market.

MARCEL WANDERS

Flare Table (p. 28) and Little Flare Customizable Table (p. 123) for Magis

marcelwanders.com

Marcel Wanders (b. 1963 in The Netherlands) was graduated cum laude from the Hogeschool voor de Kunsten in Arnhem in 1988 after being expelled from Eindhoven Design Academy. In 1995 he opened his studio in Amsterdam, quickly coming to worldwide attention in 1996 for his iconic Knotted Chair, which paired high tech materials with low tech production methods.

Today Marcel's powerhouse studio numbers around fifty international design specialists, and he is a prolific product and interior designer and art director, nearly ubiquitous, with over 1700 projects to his name for private clients and premium brands such as Alessi, Bisazza, KLM, Flos, Swarovski, and Puma, among scores of others.

Regarded by many as an anomaly in the design world, Marcel looks to bring the human touch back to design, ushering in what he calls design's "new age," in which designer, craftsperson, and user are reunited.

In 2001 Marcel cofounded the successful design label Moooi, of which he is also art director. Conceived as a platform for design talent from around the world, today the company has a presence in seventy-nine countries and is renowned for its quirky, eccentric, but altogether inspired take on the objects around us.

WAY BASICS

Storage Cubes (p. 98)

waybasics.com

Based in California, Way Basics was founded in 2008 by Jimmy Chang. The company grew out of a thought Jimmy had one day to create a recycling bin made from recycled paper, this being one of the most commonly recycled materials. In Jimmy's mind the bin would come flat and then pop open like a paper grocery bag, though with a little more design pizzazz than the typical supermarket version. The concept was that people could toss their recyclables in it each day, and then, when full, put the entire bin and its contents in a container for recycling. Pop another bin open and start again. Simple. Elegant. And the beginnings of the eco-friendly Way Basics brand.

DAVID WEEKS
Cubebots (p. 22), Hanno the Gorilla (p. 33), and Ursa the Bear (p. 71) for Areaware
davidweeksstudio.com

David Weeks (b. 1968) is an American designer and principal of the David Weeks Studio in New York. His work encompasses lighting, home accessories, mobiles, lounge seating, and custom retail, commercial, and residential projects. David's designs have been used by Barneys New York, Kate Spade, Saks Fifth Avenue, Bliss Spa, Brasserie NYC, and The W Hotels.

Originally from Athens, Georgia, Weeks studied painting and sculpture at the Rhode Island School of Design, where he earned a BFA. Weeks went on to work in the Manhattan studio of Ted Muehling before founding his own firm in 1996. His work has been widely published and recognized by numerous awards.

Weeks currently lives in Brooklyn with his wife, Georgianna Stout, a partner in design studio 2×4, and family.

WEXEL ART
Wall Frames (p. 73)
wexelart.com

Natasha McRee (an entrepreneurial mom of two) and Morgan Kimble (a custom framer and muralist) had collaborated on several design projects when they came together to solve a practical problem. Natasha was struggling with the challenge of framing children's artwork in an attractive and thoughtful way that would also be easy to change out as new work came into being. Their elegantly simple solution was to float a sheet of acrylic off the wall by means of handsome stand-off hardware, and to use strong magnets to hold the display pieces in place. Their discovery led to the founding of Wexel Art in 2010, and a steadily growing collection of standard and custom-built frames for users of all ages. The company is based in Austin, Texas.

YUBE
Yube Cube Modular Storage (p. 99)
yubecube.com

Creativity with a conscience—that's how the Yube story begins. Before Yube, most modular cube systems available were either nice to look at but expensive, or economical but flimsy and not nice to look at. Seeing a market opportunity for a modular, creative product that would be sturdy, affordable, eco-friendly, and attractive all at the same time, cofounders Errol Drew and Jeff Greenstein set out to create a better system.

To develop their concept the founders assembled a team of innovators led by industrial designer Phil Karl, who worked in association with German designers. Yube was successfully launched in 2010.

YUBO
Changeable Lunchboxes by Whipsaw (p. 107)
getyubo.com

In 2007, after another day of making lunch for their daughters, Cyndi and Dan Pedrazzi found themselves unhappy with the realization that they were continually consuming vast amounts of environmentally unfriendly plastic bags with each meal. Turning to conventional lunch boxes as a remedy, they were soon thwarted by the challenge of cleaning and keeping the boxes fresh. Equally problematic, once the novelty of these boxes wore off, their kids were not particularly inspired by the products to get enthusiastic about taking their lunches. That was the start of their journey to reinvent the lunchbox.

Realizing the scope of their ambition, the Pedrazzis turned to Whipsaw Inc., a highly acclaimed industrial design firm in Silicon Valley. Dan Harden, Whipsaw's president and chief designer (and also a parent of lunchbox kids), was excited by the opportunity to reconceptualize the conventional product, and joined forces with the Pedrazzis.

The result was Yubo, and a lot more happy parents and kids.

KARL ZAHN
Dovetail Wood Animals for Areaware (p. 26)
karlzahn.com

Karl Zahn is a freelance product and furniture designer in Greenpoint, Brooklyn. Born and raised in rural Vermont in 1981, his attraction to wood and other natural materials grew out of the time spent playing in forests and his father's woodshop during childhood. After earning a degree in product design from the Rhode Island School of Design in 2003, he traveled to San Francisco, where he immersed himself in the area's thriving metalworking culture. He then moved to New York to begin working independently in 2007.

Clients include Artecnica, Areaware, Teroforma, Lindsey Adelman Studio, and Roll & Hill. Zahn also collaborates on projects with emerging designers.

EVA ZEISEL
Wall Frames by Wexel Art (p. 73, pictured next page)
evazeisel.org

Zeisel was born Eva Striker in Budapest in 1906. Her father ran a textile factory and her mother was among the first women to earn a doctorate at the University of Budapest. It was at her mother's urging that Zeisel turned to ceramics at the Budapest Royal Academy of Fine Arts. She then joined a

CLARA VON ZWEIGBERGK
Kaleido Trays for HAY (p. 41)
claravonzweigbergk.com

Born in Stockholm, Clara von Zweigbergk studied graphic design and illustration at Beckmans School of Design there, and later at the Art Center College of Design in Pasadena, California. She has worked as a graphic designer with advertising agencies and designers in Stockholm, Los Angeles, and Milan.

In 1997 she cofounded Rivieran Design Studio, a multidisciplinary agency spawning many successful collaborations within fashion, illustration, architecture, furniture, product, and graphic design.

porcelain factory as an apprentice, an unusual path for an educated woman at that time. Zeisel persisted, graduated to journeyman status, and became the first woman admitted to the local pottery guild. It was during this time that her work took on the sensuous, flowing, and biomorphic forms that would continue throughout her career.

In 1932, Zeisel moved to Russia out of "curiosity," as she later explained. She took work for the Communist government as artistic director of the glass and ceramics industries. In May 1936 she was accused of plotting to assassinate Stalin and sent to prison for sixteen months, most of which were in solitary confinement, before being unexpectedly released.

Zeisel married and moved to Vienna, where she lived until the rise of Hitler prompted her to emigrate to America, arriving in October 1938. The next day she went to the magazine *China and Glass* and immediately received a commission for ceramic work. She was also hired at Pratt Institute in Brooklyn, where she became the first person to teach ceramics as industrial design for mass production, rather than handicraft. Her growing reputation reached new levels in 1946 when her all-white modern dinner service—a first by an American designer—was honored with an exhibition at MoMA. Today her work is in the permanent collections of museums worldwide. In 2005, she was awarded the National Design Award for Lifetime Achievement by the Cooper-Hewitt National Design Museum in New York. She died in 2011.

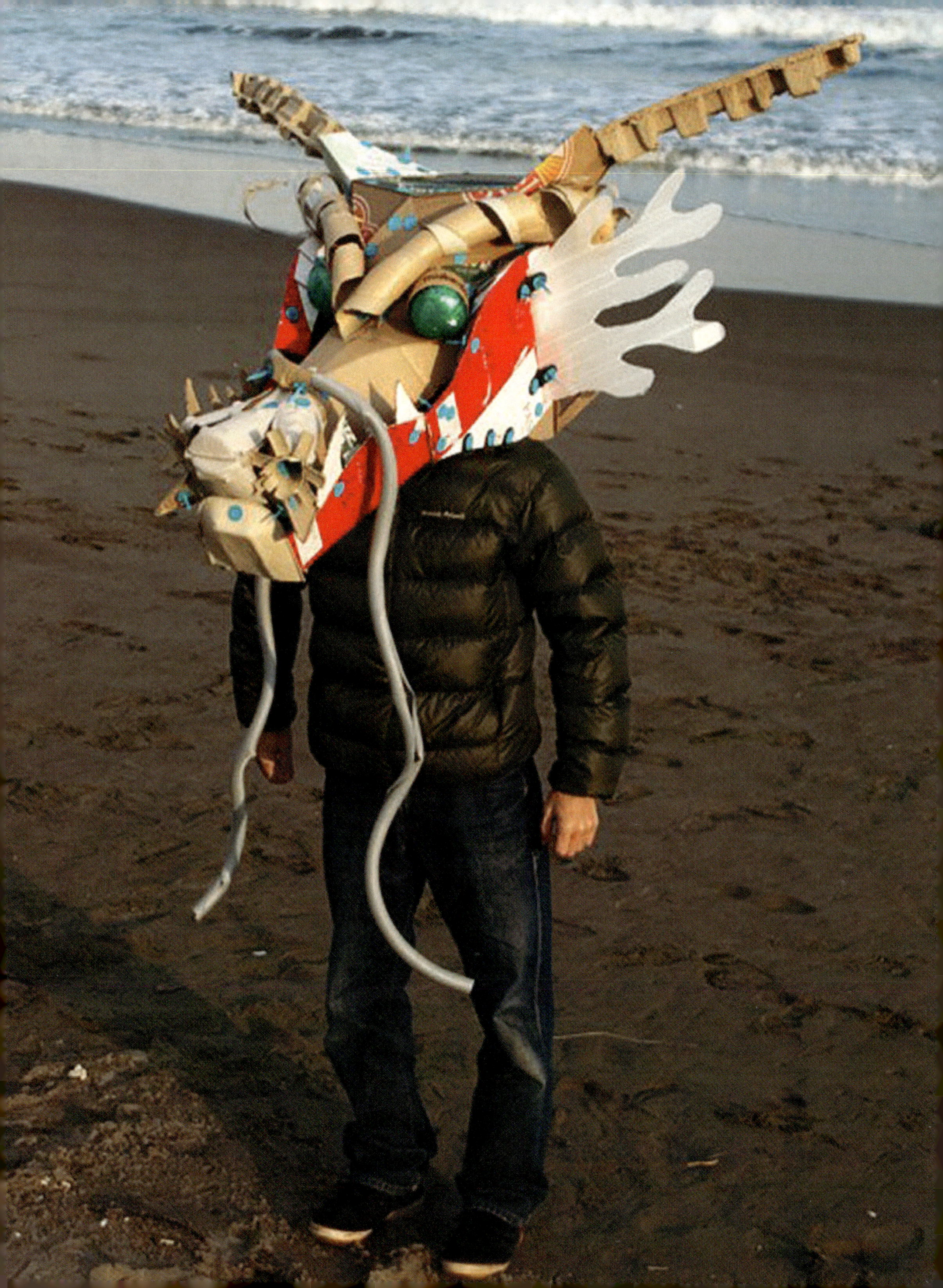

BIBLIOGRAPHY AND SUGGESTIONS FOR FURTHER READING

Brosterman, Norman. *Inventing Kindergarten.* New York: Harry N. Abrams, 1997.

Brown, M. D., Stuart and Christopher Vaughan. *Play: How it Shapes the Brain, Opens the Imagination, and Invigorates the Soul.* New York: Avery, 2009.

Burkus, David. *The Myths of Creativity: The Truth about How Innovative Companies and People Generate Great Ideas.* San Francisco: Jossey-Bass, 2014.

Csikszentmihalyi, Mihaly. *Creativity: Flow and the Psychology of Discovery and Invention.* New York et al: HarperCollins, 2007.

———. *Flow.* New York et al.: HarperCollins, 1990.

Dubner, Stephen J., narrator). "Think Like a Child" (podcast transcript). http://freakonomics.com/2014/05/22/think-like-a-child-full-transcript.

Gray, Dave, James Macanufo, and Sunni Brown. *Gamestorming: A Playbook for Innovators, Rulebreakers, and Changemakers.* Sebastopol, CA: O'Reilly Media, 2010.

Howard-Jones, P. A., J. Taylor, and L. Sutton,. "The Effects of Play on the Creativity of Young Children" in *Early Child Development and Care* 172 no. 4 (2002).

Iyengar, Sheena. *The Art of Choosing.* New York: Twelve Books, 2010.

Kelley, Tom and David Kelley. *Creative Confidence: Unleashing the Creative Potential Within Us All.* New York: Crown Business, 2013.

Kleon, Austin. *Steal Like An Artist: 10 Things Nobody Told You About Being Creative.* New York: Workman, 2012.

Kinchin, Juliet and Aidan O'Connor. *Century of the Child: Growing by Design 1900–2000.* New York: The Museum of Modern Art, 2012.

Marcus, Clare Cooper. *House as a Mirror of Self: Exploring the Deeper Meaning of Home.* Lake Worth, FL: Nicolas-Hays, 1995.

McGrath, Molly and Norman. *Children's Spaces: 50 Architects & Designers Create Environments for the Young.* New York: William Morrow and Company, 1978.

Meadows, Donella H. *Thinking in Systems: A Primer.* White River Junction, VT: Chelsea Green Publishing, 2008.

Michalko, Michael. *Thinkertoys: A Handbook of Creative-Thinking Techniques.* Berkeley: Ten Speed Press, 2006.

Norton, Michael, Dan Ariely, and Daniel Mochon. "The 'IKEA Effect': When Labor Leads to Love." *Journal of Consumer Psychology* 22 (2012).

Ogata, Amy F. *Designing the Creative Child: Playthings and Places in Midcentury America.* Minneapolis: University of Minnesota Press, 2013.

O'Reilly, Doorley and Scott Witthoft. *Make Space: How to Set the Stage for Creative Collaboration.* Hoboken, NJ: John Wiley & Sons, 2012.

Roam, Dan. *The Back of the Napkin: Solving Problems and Selling Ideas with Pictures.* New York et al.: Penguin Books, 2009.

Robinson, Ken. *Out of Our Minds: Learning to be Creative.* Chichester, UK: Capstone Publishing, 2011.

Sawyer, Keith. *Explaining Creativity: The Science of Human Innovation.* New York et al.: Oxford University Press, 2006.

———. *Zig Zag: The Surprising Path to Greater Creativity.* San Francisco: Jossey-Bass, 2013.

Seelig, Tina. *InGenius: A Crash Course on Creativity.* New York: HarperOne, 2012.

Simonton, Dean Keith. *Origins of Genius: Darwinian Perspectives on Creativity.* New York et al.: Oxford University Press, 1999.

Sutton-Smith, Brian. *The Ambiguity of Play.* Cambridge, MA, et al.: Harvard University Press, 2001.

Tharp, Twyla. *The Creative Habit: Learn It and Use It For Life.* New York: Simon & Schuster, 2003.

Wilson, Frank R. *The Hand: How Its Use Shapes the Brain, Language, and Human Culture.* New York: Vintage Books, 1999.

URAL HOME
of light
IKEA the book
NEW YORK 2000
STERN
FISHMAN
TILOVE
Scandinavian Design
100 SUNS
Dieter Rams:
As Little Design as Possible
Sophie Lovell
bill
DAN GRAHAM
THE PHILIP JOHNSON TAPES
Spiral Jetty
OPTIC NERVE
INSIDE THE BMW FACTORIES
LIFTING THE YOKE
The DASH Diet Action Plan
IMMERSION
Varnelis

RESOURCES

HELP YOURSELF

99U
   99u.com

Creative Thinking
   creativethinking.net

Design Thinking for Educators
   designthinkingforeducators.com

Human-Centered Design Toolkit
   hcdconnect.org

The Napkin Academy: Drawing for Dummies
   napkinacademy.com

The National Institute for Play
   nifplay.org

Post-It Culture
   post-it.com

SOCIAL

LinkedIn
   linkedin.com

BLOGS

Austin Kleon
   austinkleon.com

Brain Pickings
   brainpickings.org/index.php/tag/creativity

PsychCentral: The Creative Mind
   blogs.psychcentral.com/creative-mind

Creativity and Learning Insights
   scoop.it/t/creativity-and-learning-insights

The Creativity Post
   thecreativitypost.com

David Burkus
   davidburkus.com

Keith Sawyer's Creativity & Innovation
   keithsawyer.wordpress.com

Psychology Today: Creativity
   psychologytoday.com/topics/creativity

ACADEMIC PROGRAMS

Drexel University, Torrance Center for Creativity and Innovation
   drexel.edu/soe/academics/graduate/creativity-and-innovation/torrance-center

Hasso Plattner Institute of Design at Stanford
   dschool.stanford.edu

Saybrook University, Creativity Studies Specialization
   saybrook.edu/academic-affairs/areas/pii/cs

University of Georgia, Torrance Center
   www.coe.uga.edu/torrance

University of New York at Buffalo, International Center for Studies in Creativity
   creativity.buffalostate.edu

IMAGE CREDITS AND ACKNOWLEDGMENTS

Most of the photographs in this book have been provided by the designer or brand responsible for creating or distributing the illustrated product. Some photographs were commissioned by the author from NYC Product Photography (nycproductphotography.com). The photograph on the bottom of page XIX is courtesy of The New York Public Library, Miriam and Ira D. Wallach Division of Art, Prints and Photographs. The photographs at the top of pages XVIII and XIX are courtesy of Norman Brosterman (brosterman.com), and originally appeared in his 1997 book *Inventing Kindergarten*, which we enthusiastically recommend to all who are intellectually curious about creativity, modern art, and the education of the child. (It has been reissued in 2014, thanks in part to Kickstarter funding.) I am indebted to Norman and his wonderful book for teaching me a great deal about all these subjects, as well as about Friedrich Froebel and the value of thinking with things.

Cover: Ty DIY Shower Curtain by Grain (2008). Photograph by Ben Blood and courtesy of Grain.

The Creative Catalog was designed by Alan Hebel and Ian Koviak, cofounders and creative brain trust behind *the*BookDesigners (bookdesigners.com). Their work impressed me from the start for its deft aesthetic touch, and it has been a pleasure collaborating with them for the production of *The Creativity Catalog* in its printed and electronic formats. Mark Burstein (markmywords.ws) expertly copyedited the text while providing invaluable guidance and encouragement throughout the process.

Thanks to my mathematician cousin Ross Goluboff for guiding me through some of the intricate calculations required to determine the number of potential permutations afforded by several products in this book.

I owe special debts of gratitude to my wife, Gaby, for supporting this project and everything that has led up to it, and our son, Remy, for affording both of us a view into a truly creative mind.

183

ABOUT THE AUTHOR

DONALD RATTNER (modularscholar.com) received a B.A. in art history cum laude from Columbia in 1979 and an M.Arch. from Princeton in 1985. Three years later he joined Ferguson Murray Architects as an intern, and eventually rose to partnership there before founding Studio for Civil Architecture with Andrew Friedman in 2002. The firm now operates as Studio for A.R.T. and Architecture. Rattner's architectural portfolio has garnered over a dozen awards for design excellence in the course of his career and has been widely published.

Studio s practice comprises a range of services and building types. For private clients the firm has designed custom single-family residences and refurbished existing homes in urban, rural, and suburban settings. For resort developers it has designed amenity buildings, planned neighborhoods, produced residential prototypes, created architectural pattern books, formulated design guidelines, and generated renderings and authored printed materials for marketing purposes. The firm has also forayed into fine art, having exhibited work in several gallery environments and won a competition award in the 2010 Philagrafika art festival.

In addition to advancing his practice, Rattner has sought to share his knowledge and experience with the profession and public through teaching, writing, and speaking at such venues as New York University, New York Academy of Art, University of Illinois at Chicago, and Parsons School of Design. Published writings have appeared in *Architectural Record*, *The International Dictionary of Architects and Architecture*, *Design Professionals and the Built Environment*, and *Residential Architect*.

His professional and academic activities have been featured on CNN and in *The New York Times*, *Town & Country*, *House & Garden*, *Robb Report*, *Residential Architect*, *Builder*, *Progressive Architecture*, and numerous blogs and online channels.

In 2010 Rattner launched MODULE R, a retail design store offering customizable, interactive, reconfigurable, and modular products by contemporary designers and brands from around the world. This eventually morphed into THE CREATIVE HOME (thecreativehome.com), a forum for people to learn about personal and professional creativity, find techniques and things to nurture creativity at home, and share examples of what people are doing to make themselves, their families, and their homes more creative places.

COPYRIGHT

Copyright © 2014 by THE CREATIVE HOME. All rights reserved. No part of this book may be transmitted or reproduced in any form by any means without permission in writing from the publisher (thecreativehome.com).

ISBN 978-0-9907787-0-7
ISBN ebook 978-0-9907787-1-4
ISBN ebook 978-0-9907787-2-1